Let My People Know

Let My People Know

AMERICAN INDIAN
JOURNALISM, 1828–1978

By James E. Murphy and Sharon M. Murphy

FOREWORD BY JEANNETTE HENRY

Norman   *University of Oklahoma Press*

To our parents

Published with the aid of a grant from
the George Lynn Cross Publication Fund

Library of Congress Cataloging in Publication Data

Murphy, James Emmett, 1940–
  Let my people know.

  Bibliography: p.
  Includes index.
  1. Indian newspapers—United States—History.
  2. Indian periodicals—United States—History.
  3. Indians of North America—Mass media—History.
  I. Murphy, Sharon. II. Title.
  PN4883.M8   071'.3'08997   80-5941
  ISBN 0-8061-1623-4   AACR2

Foreword

A complex system of native communications covered most of
North America before white contact. It was a unique network of
trails and footpaths that crisscrossed the continent, passing through
dense forests, over rivers and streams, across mountains and mead-
ows. Traversing these trails were Indian runners, known as tribal
messengers, who were officially recognized by governing systems
such as those of the Iroquois in the East, the Cherokees in the South
and Southeast, the Yuroks in the Northwest, and the Eskimos in
present-day Alaska. Other tribes, having less complex tribal governing structures, named and trained young men, and sometimes young
women, to act as messenger communicators carrying news from tribe
to tribe. Their extraordinary strength and endurance, their fleetness
of foot, and their intimate knowledge of the land amazed early European immigrants.

A *system* of communications existed among the native tribes as a
traditional, historical, and necessary part of their society. However,
evidence like this, of a complex native civilization, is usually ignored.
It is not seen as part of a social structure in a natural (as distinguished
from a "primitive") society.

News moved more slowly following white expansion, despite
the availability of modern technology. The world of we natives nar-
rowed even more when, soon after the European population began to
grow and its land hunger increased, a reservation system was established. The reservation system made it unlawful for the Indian to
leave the confines of his concentration camp. For Indians who did not
live on reservations, fear of the government's sometimes genocidal
policies toward them was sufficient to preclude travel for any distance.
Communications declined even more with the destruction of tribal
government and society, a crime committed by both federal and state
governments. Still another difficulty, after travel strictures were elim-
inated, was the cost of travel and communication. One Eskimo
scholar observed recently, "We had better communications with Sibe-

ria and Greenland before the Europeans came, with their high technology, than we have today."

Native systems of communications, in the form of journalism and publishing, began in 1828 with the *Cherokee Phoenix* and have continued to this day. Newspapers have come and gone. The life they enjoyed varied from a brief year to as long as thirty years. Often they were confined to a mere mimeographed sheet, and they varied in professional technique and content from excellent to very poor. But always there was a string of print media either living or being born. The natives took to their hearts the system of writing, the process of publishing, and the techniques of serving their people through the written word.

There has been no serious study of American Indian journalism, however. The fascinating, profoundly moving nature of such a study has been generally overlooked. Indeed, few if any scholars have dared to venture into the troubled waters of Indian history, culture, and politics that such a study entails. Thus it is with particular satisfaction that this book on Indian journalism is greeted. Indian journalists who give their energies and intelligence to the development of a media that is still foreign to many natives will find *Let My People Know* an important tool in their labors, and an inspiration for producing newspapers of high quality. Scholars who teach journalism courses now have a source of information and a means of creating an understanding of Indian people and Indian issues.

This book is badly needed and long overdue. We owe a debt of gratitude to the authors for producing it: an enormous amount of painstaking research has gone into it, bringing to light many previously unplumbed sources. What has emerged is a good book, an important addition to scholarship, and an exciting inducement—to Indian scholars particularly—to continue the study of Indian culture, historical as well as modern, through various systems of communications, both printed and broadcast.

The authors have done a remarkable job of gathering a mass of information, refining the data, and placing the most important material between the covers of a relatively small book. They have read and understood hundreds upon hundreds of Indian newspapers, a task formidable in itself. Too, they have professionally and wisely chosen the most significant information. The writing of such a book is fraught with certain dangers, however. Indian history can be said to have at least one distinguishing feature: the element of constant change. Newspapers and magazines have known even more change than other areas of native history. Thus, some of the information may be outdated; some of the newspapers mentioned in the glossary may no longer exist; and many new communications media may have been born in the short time since this book went to press.

Nonetheless, it is important to study the information, to learn what happened in the past and what exists today. This book amply fulfills its purpose and can be studied and read with profit and pleasure for many years to come.

There are some significant conclusions to be drawn from Indian journalism, conclusions that are a matter of concern for all of society. One example of the need to draw certain conclusions from known facts is the matter of the Sequoyah syllabary, created by a Cherokee and described and lauded by many authors, including the authors of this book. All agree that this was an achievement unique in its time, a grand testament to the creativity of man. But the ideological and historical meaning of such an extraordinary advance in the civilization of the Cherokee Nation is not often understood and is only seldom mentioned.

In a matter of months, through the use of the Sequoyah system of writing, the Cherokee Nation had wiped out illiteracy, and this at a time when most of the world's peoples could not read or write. Indeed, even in Europe, home of the first printing press, writing and reading still were monopolized by the church hierarchy and the upper classes. With the development of modern print journalism, Indian scholars and writers eagerly embraced the media, producing magazines and newspapers that delineate the modern history of the American Indian often far better and more accurately than anthropological studies. Historians must perforce make a special effort to examine these historic documents if they are to understand Indian history.

Today the Indian is lost in the general population, an invisible race. Although once comprising the majority of the inhabitants of this continent, the Indian population now has been replaced by people of European and Eastern ancestry. Moreover, the natives who remain are likely to be of mixed blood. Unless they wear braids and are festooned with Indian jewelry, Indians walk the land unrecognized as the First Americans.

But there is no mistaking Indian newspapers. They are Indian to the core. One finds news items of interest to the American Indian alone. This is true to a fault. Almost no international news is covered, and the only national issues they report upon are those directly affecting Indian interests. Two national Indian newspapers, *Akwesasne Notes* and *Wassaja*, do carry national and international news, but each in its own way and according to its own interests.

Book reviews, as a regular news feature, are carried only in *Wassaja*. Before the *Indian Historian* was merged with *Wassaja* (as *Wassaja/The Indian Historian*), the quarterly *Historian* carried book reviews as a regular feature. All newspapers are "heavy" on sports news, indicating the enormous interest of the native people in such sports as basketball, baseball, swimming, footracing, and golf. Ice hockey is of great interest to people on the northern reservations.

A critical review of current journalism is badly needed. We do not expect non-Indian scholars to perform this chore for us, although professional criticism is very welcome. (It shows we are not ignored.) Usually, non-Indian scholars are sympathetic to Indian efforts; they would do nothing to impair the effectiveness of an Indian endeavor. But we Indians are not under such constraints, and the time will come when an objective, critical survey can be made of the current communications industry among the native people. Such a study would be most helpful in setting beginning journalists and editors upon the right path and in helping professionals improve their products.

The authors describe the bilingualism of various Indian newspapers in the past, and note that this is a diminishing feature of the native print media. (Not so the broadcast media, in which radio stations on or near reservations use both the native tongue and English.) Most Indian journalists feel, however, that content is of greater importance at this time than utilization of the native language. With the continued use and the improved teaching of native languages, it is thought that the use of the Indian language will increase.

Examining the many native organs in the print media, one is

struck by how, except for issues that deal specifically with Indian interests, the newspapers generally are only fair copies of establishment, small-town papers. Originality in content appears to be lacking. One newspaper, however, is unique. In its standard-size format it carries articles reflecting the tribal life as does no other paper among the two or three hundred now being published in the Indian world.

This is *Qua Toqtii*, an independent Hopi newspaper published by Hopi individuals. *Qua Toqtii* even has a column devoted to family affairs and problems, including advice to the "lovelorn." In choice of subjects, use of language, and wry humor, this newspaper is truly original, a pleasure to read even when one may not agree with the policies expressed in its choice of and emphasis on certain issues. Most Indian newspaper people would do well to study *Qua Toqtii* and uncover for themselves, in their own tribes, the profound human forces shaping their lives, their governments, and their future.

Until a few years ago, one was struck by the general lack of humor in Indian newspapers. Because of this, the stereotype of the stoic, solemn, unfeeling Indian has continued. Beginning in the early 1970s, however, humor began to steal into the pages, particularly in the Canadian Indian papers, and more particularly in the work of the Indian cartoonists. Nobody loves a joke more than the native, and few people have a larger repertoire of stories that evoke laughter, as well as tears, than the native people.

The need for experienced editorial personnel, however, overshadows all other matters, whether of content, format, or stability. The shortage of trained personnel is critical, perhaps desperate. Editorial personnel must have not only an excellent education in the humanities and in the English language, a knowledge of the principles of journalism, and business experience, but they also must have a profound knowledge of Indian history, culture, and current affairs. Many non-Indians have given valuable assistance in starting and continuing Indian newspapers, but Indians themselves are the best editors and the best writers—in fact, the best personnel for every part of the paper's production. It may be superfluous to explain why this is so. But a "feel" for Indian issues, for Indian affairs and history, and a knowledge of the people, can be held only by the Indian journalist, or by those very close, in a deep personal sense, to the American Indian.

Many programs in journalism apprenticeship have been funded by foundations or by the federal government. Most often, however, the money has been poorly spent, and the time of busy professional instructors wasted. That is probably because Indian newspapers, paying so little, can not compete with better financial opportunities "out there" in government and private industry. The American Indian Historical Society conducted a foundation-supported program in journalism apprenticeship for two years. Fifteen Indian would-be journalists attended. Ten did not complete the training, and none of the other five remained in journalism. Considering the difference in salary, between $18,500 a year for a "consultant's" job and $12,000 a year maximum for working on an Indian newspaper, who can blame them? Only too late, all the students in the program realized that journalism is a tough, difficult, relentless, and time-consuming job and that the rewards are generally within the individual, not in the money.

Can the Indian press continue? Can it acquire experienced, professional journalists and broadcasters? Where will the funds come from to produce the print media, the broadcast equipment, the films and documentaries so badly needed? An unreality seems to permeate the new, burgeoning, enthusiastic adventurers as they go forth to conquer the newspaper and broadcast worlds. Some blithe spirits venture into the project of producing a film or a newspaper without considering the ultimate needs of such an effort. How much money will be needed? (One film group sent out a call for funds to produce a well-described documentary, setting as its goal the sum of $250,000. The experienced broadcast technician would have known that at least eight million dollars would be needed for the project they envisioned, and probably closer to ten million to do it well.) Where will personnel come from? Will newsprint be available? Indians should be prepared to tap their own excellent resources. (Some few years ago, for example, *Wassaja* could not be published regularly because there was a shortage of newsprint. Knowing that tribes with timber on their land sell it to paper companies for the production of newsprint, we felt chagrined that we had not thought of preparing for our needs by taking an inventory of such reservations and of the paper mills they supply, and then by demanding special consideration for Indian newspapers.)

Newspapers and magazines are born in the dominant society every week. They too either live awhile and fade away or simply die in short order. Those that continue are generally funded by corporate people with considerable amounts of money, entrepreneurs who have large staffs of editorial, technical, and sales-distribution people, as well as advertising and promotion personnel. As for the Indian papers, the only ones capable of continuing and growing today are those being published by the more well-to-do tribes, and these must be subsidized fully for at least five years. The *Navajo Times* is such a newspaper. Each year, however, this paper is troubled by tribal budgetary cuts as well as by the pressures of political factions demanding representation in the *Times*. This newspaper, as well as an estimated five others, have their own word-processing and printing equipment. They could not possibly survive if they had to have their type set and their printing done by contract with outside firms. It would be too expensive.

Economically, the tribal newspapers have so far proved more successful than urban-based papers. It is to their tribal papers that the people look for news of their government, for an understanding of the issues they face, and for information about more personal matters (such as the tribe's sports activities, often their only form of entertainment). But only a national newspaper can deliver hard political news, exert pressure in opening up channels of information, and create a system of uniform information delivery that has a chance of effecting needed changes. Indeed, only a national newspaper has the clout to "let the *other* people know" what the Indian needs, demands, and expects—namely, his rights as a First American.

Such a newspaper must be totally independent, cannot accept federal or any tax-derived funds, and must be able to compete professionally with the mass media. Enormous difficulties face those who would establish such a medium of news coverage, and some of these difficulties have been mentioned.

For tribal newspapers freedom of the press is an ongoing controversy. This controversy has existed since the first Indian newspaper was founded. Probably it will continue. Tribal officials state that the newspaper, as an organ of tribal government, is subsidized by the tribe and should reflect its policies. They add, "Would you expect

Exxon Corporation to publish a newspaper that criticizes the company?" That is why, in reading many tribal papers, one searches in vain for the variety of ideas and opposing political stances that characterize tribal members. Some editors are now content to publish the exact words from the minutes of the tribal council, the motions it passed, the amount of money it expended for such incidentals as travel, entertainment, and salaries. We noted in an issue of one newspaper that the staff had painstakingly and accurately listed the amounts of money spent by tribal officials on travel: who had traveled where and at what cost, and how many travel requests had been approved by the tribal council. The feature was greeted with glee and great interest by the readers, but after appearing approximately twice in that paper, it disappeared. Was it an embarrassment to the tribal officials? It would seem so.

Tribal governments are more sophisticated today in controlling the content of their newspapers. The controversy this creates arises again and again. How will the issues of grave concern to the people be handled by the tribe's newspaper? There is indeed a question of freedom of the press, but as one can see, it is not so easily solved when publication funds are delivered as a subsidy from any governmental entity, including the tribal government. Could an Indian newspaper be funded independently by an individual or a group of individuals? In our view, this is the best and perhaps the only way to produce a free press for the Indian people, whether local, tribal, or national. But there are too few Indians who have the funds to contribute to such a cause. The time will come, however, when various Indian people will agree to contribute.

An American Indian establishment has become a fact of life for the people today. This establishment is usually entrenched in tribal government, in government agencies, and in programs with plenty of money. The newspapers are thus subject to establishment policy, establishment goals, and establishment factional interests. It is recognized that the media can and usually do influence thought among the people, and that information can be slanted to accord with one or another policy. This effort to tilt the information goes on in the Indian—as well as the national—media more than ever before. Another point that shows the interrelationship of all the problems mentioned here is the argument made by many tribal officials that the editors of their newspapers are "not competent" to grasp the issues, or to "place them in a context" that would best benefit tribal interests. An effort by the editors of *Wassaja* to train top-flight Indian scholars and officers in editorial positions was met with scorn by the three tribes thus approached. "When a feller is earning $24,000 a year, he'd be nuts to go for $12,000," was the response.

One can not talk about a homogeneous Indian press, speaking as "with one voice" for all the people. It just isn't there. Indians, like all other people the world over, differ in their opinions, their policies, and their solutions to situations affecting the life and death of a tribe and its people. The struggle for Indian water rights, for example, has lasted many years, but there are still Indians in the media who can not or will not understand the issues and, by doing so, take up positions harmful to the tribe.

An editor of one tribal paper lauded the secretary of the Department of the Interior for his "friendship toward the Indian people" when in fact that official had stood in the way of Indian water rights, had espoused a policy that would give the five Arizona "dry" tribes reclaimed water instead of their own water, and had been attempting to force construction of the Orme Dam, which would destroy the land of the Fort McDowell Yavapai Indians.

The time is coming when tribal controversies will be discussed in a manner reasonable enough to produce real understanding. Today, however, fear of impairing the often tenuous tribal interrelationships remains an obstacle to candor.

On the other hand, there was a difference of opinion among the Indian people and the native newspapers on the issue of the book *Hanta Yo*. Most papers criticized the book as inaccurate, demeaning, and unfair to the Oglala Sioux. Others—equally outspoken, although far less numerous—rushed to the defense of the author and the book. One expects differences of opinion, and one must be prepared to deal with such differences in an objective manner, providing a fair hearing for both sides of an issue. That is in the Indian tradition, and, indeed, in the best tradition of democracy.

The authors of the book in hand may not have touched on these issues and problems, but they have opened the door to further exploration of the Indian press. There will be other books on this subject. But the credit for pioneering an area filled with so many difficulties belongs to these two authors.

There are other areas of study that might be examined, and in this statement I allow myself the privilege of pointing them out. These ideas come to me as an actual participant in the Indian world of journalism, one who has toiled in that marketplace and that institution of educational effort and who, having fallen quite often, has perhaps also gained a little foothold now and then.

Generally unknown to most outsiders is a relatively new phenomenon, the Indian underground press. Papers have appeared quite often, usually in an effort to change tribal policy, to expose the misdeeds of tribal officials, or to demand changes in the economic conditions of tribal members. These papers usually are printed in mimeographed form, are written by unnamed individuals, and are distributed quickly and silently by other people who also prefer to remain unknown. One such underground paper was the *Cherokee Wildfire*, published for five or six months several years ago and, for all we know, even now alive. A group of tribal members, both young and old, failed to achieve changes in the tribal government that they considered critical. They charged that the cultural life of the tribe was being monopolized by an institution that was not Cherokee, not Indian, and they wanted the situation changed. All public efforts unavailing, they published *Cherokee Wildfire* and distributed some thousands of copies of it in the dead of night, from door to door, at the Cherokee colonies on the reservation. The underground writers looked on innocently as tribal leaders, using the official Cherokee tribal newspaper, lashed out at the secret paper. The *Cherokee Wildfire* dissidents earlier had been subjected to censorship when they had attempted to make their views known through this official newspaper.

Other, not so secretive, newspapers now coming upon the media scene operate in defiance of tribal officials and in opposition to tribal policy. Two newspapers are of this stripe, one on the Oglala Sioux reservation in South Dakota, the other on the Colville reservation in the state of Washington. The Oglala paper is published by an individual Oglala who wants the tribal government to be more responsive to the needs of the people and who attempts to expose mismanagement and alleged misappropriation of funds. Charges such as these are sometimes substantiated. Quite often they are not. The Colville paper's concern is the mining of molybdenum on the reservation, which will result in the destruction of a mountain. Both papers are widely read, but they offer no solutions, no recourse to remedies for the situations they describe, and so the readers remain frustrated and gradually tire of what is perceived as an irritant.

For those of us who labor in the field of Indian affairs, particularly in the profession of journalism, there is no more fascinating study, no more intriguing activity, than what is to be found in the creation and production of an Indian newspaper, an Indian broadcast program, or an Indian film.

Since the overriding need of the native people is communication, it is often suggested that more Indian journalists are needed in the mass media. Training courses have been offered by mass-media newspapers, for example in Albuquerque, New Mexico. At this time, there are no more than two or three Indian reporters working on non-Indian newspapers, and usually they are employed by small-town papers. None are to be found on the great mass-media papers. When Indians do obtain employment with a mass-media, establishment newspaper, they are soon frustrated, disappointed, and disgusted. After all, who wants to cover the city and county news items about visits, divorces, obituaries, and other local social events that make up the regular features of a newspaper with a large circulation?

Those of us who have gone through this apprenticeship know that it is tiresome, unfruitful, and time-consuming. But that is the nature of the business. No newspaper would allow a cub reporter to march into the city room and immediately receive a feature-story assignment or news-coverage assignments strictly about Indian issues. You take your turn; substantive and prominent stories are coveted by most news people. They will fight to the teeth to be allowed the privilege of doing a story filled with human interest, one usually carrying a byline. Too, they will parade their seniority before the young reporter, their years of star coverage of stories all over the country or the world. Thus, a career in mass-media newspaper work requires youth, patience, great talent, and a taste for drivel.

What lies in the future for Indian journalism? One dares not predict. But we at *Wassaja*, whose masthead proclaims "Let the People Know," truly believe that before this century has ended the Indian people will have created their own system of communications, in both print and broadcast media, bringing together the best of their two worlds. We still believe what the *Cherokee Phoenix* so proudly announced, that the Phoenix will rise again from the ashes of a social conflagration set by the European invaders. Then we can let the people know.

In this ultimate goal, we feel sure that the authors of this book will have had a share.

JEANNETTE HENRY

Contents

Preface

The American Indian press celebrated 150 years of publishing in 1978. Nonetheless, virtually no thoroughly researched account of Indian journalism has yet been published. Only rarely do scholars and historians of American media allude to a century and a half of Indian press accomplishments, to the struggles that accompanied them, or to the powerful and unique needs that spawned and nurtured the journalistic efforts of America's native peoples.

This book offers a survey of that neglected history and includes an overview of the thriving contemporary Indian media. It provides a wider perspective than was hitherto available from which to judge the performance of the nation's press as a whole. When one is allowed to look at the history of American journalism only from the majority— or white establishment—viewpoint, a myopic or otherwise distorted view of that history necessarily results.

The picture of the establishment press that emerges in this book is not an altogether pleasant one. Study of historical sources indicates that, when Indian news was presented at all, it often contained wholesale misinformation about American Indians. Moreover, white editors contributed their part to the denigration of Indian cultures and the despoliation of Indian homelands. Chapter 1 deals with this treatment of American Indians by the nation's mass media.

Chapters 2 to 4 focus on the development of Indian journalism itself, beginning in 1828 and continuing—through periods of relative strength and of bare survival—to the present day. Chapters 5 to 9 look at the American Indian press of the 1970s, when it emerged as stronger and more active than at any other period in its history. By the late 1970s widespread communications activity was beginning to spill over from print into electronic media. Radio and telecommunications form the material of Chapter 10. Finally, Chapter 11 surveys the consolidation of effort that was going on in Indian country during the 1970s, in the form of media associations and consortia that were starting to give Indians a stronger, more unified voice.

Like Indian society generally, the Indian communication picture is far from static. It refuses to hold still long enough to be captured in print and portrayed as it is. That was never more true than it is now, with the needs of Indians changing as quickly as communications technology and expertise develop. Although every effort has been made to keep the book accurate and complete through 1979, the very fluidity of the American Indian press makes complete accuracy all but impossible. Thus the parts of this book dealing with the contemporary scene are in real danger of being dated before they appear in print; one notable example of this is the 1980 merger of *Wassaja*, the monthly newspaper, and *Indian Historian*, the quarterly publication of the American Indian Historical Society. (The new *Wassaja/Indian Historian* is a news magazine that combines investigative journalism and in-depth reports of the issues behind the news.) We have tried to minimize that problem by staying within the framework of the 150 years from 1828 to 1978, but with all that is emerging in Indian media, and since broadcasting was just getting started in earnest in the late 1970s, such a device is at best only partly successful.

Whatever the problems and the risks, the story of Indian communications must be told now. The struggles of 150 years have flowered into an era of widespread activity both on reservations and in urban Indian communities. By the 150th year of Indian journalism, the number of newspapers, newsletters, and periodicals of every sort had grown to nearly four hundred. Regularly scheduled Indian-managed or Indian-oriented programming was being carried by about one hundred radio stations and a handful of television stations. Half a dozen Indian-owned radio stations were on the air, and at least three tribes were planning to start television stations. Satellite telecommunications projects were moving beyond the proposal stage.

Most of the research for this book has of necessity been with primary sources—Indian newspapers and newspaper accounts and interviews with scores of American Indian scholars, newspaper editors, and broadcasters. The work has taken us to all parts of the country and given us a chance to glimpse the wide range of Indian communication activities. Although librarians, curators, and archivists in many states have cooperated in our research, special acknowledgment must be made of the staffs of the following institutions: Research Library,

Thomas Gilcrease Institute of American History and Art, Tulsa, Oklahoma; the Rare Books Collection, Princeton University Library, Princeton, N.J.; the Newberry Library in Chicago, the Interlibrary Loan Services of the University of Wisconsin Library at Milwaukee; the Five Civilized Tribes Museum in Muskogee, Okla.; the Cherokee Room at Northeastern Oklahoma University in Tahlequah, Okla.; the Newspaper Archives Division of the Oklahoma State History Museum in Oklahoma City; and the Wyoming State History Department in Cheyenne.

We wish to acknowledge with admiration and deep gratitude the many individuals who took time from their work to share with us their experiences and their dreams. Their courageous efforts reaffirm the power of the media of communication in uniting and supporting communities. To these journalists, to their staffs, and to the many others we contacted in person and through correspondence or by telephone, our thanks and best wishes for long and increasingly effective life in Indian communications. Whatever good this book contains is, ultimately, their doing. The book's shortcomings we acknowledge as our own.

Thanks is offered to the Graduate School of the University of Wisconsin—Milwaukee, for partial funding in support of the research. Our thanks also to the directors of the American Indian Historical Society; Rupert Costo, editor of *Wassaja*; and Jeannette Henry, editor of *Indian Historian*, for help with the manuscript and for permission to use in its title the slogan from *Wassaja*: "Let My People Know." Our research assistant, Neva Lehde-White, provided many valuable services, including completion of the first edition of the media directory, here updated as an appendix. Mary LeMire and Angela LaMaster, research assistant, expertly typed the manuscript, and Shannon Murphy helped in its preparation.

JAMES E. MURPHY AND SHARON M. MURPHY

Carbondale, Illinois

Let My People Know

CHAPTER ONE

American Indians and the Media: Neglect and Stereotype

The mass media of the United States have historically followed a policy of not-so-benign neglect of this country's native peoples. Media coverage is also marked by a fair amount of cynicism about Indians, a prime manifestation of which has been the portrayal of Indians as stereotypes. This chapter traces nearly two centuries of such neglect and stereotyping.

When one thinks of such mistreatment, images of the Indian in Hollywood westerns come immediately to mind. Yet portrayals of the savage Indian of the Old West are limited neither to film nor to the twentieth century. Long before television and films, printed accounts did their part to foster inaccurate images of Indians. In fact, much news reporting about Indians was done in such a fashion that it encouraged or at least condoned savage treatment of Indians. One scholar, Elmo Scott Watson, wrote:

> Depending mainly on volunteer correspondents more gifted in imagination than in accurate reporting, [eastern newspapers] spread before their readers the kind of highly-colored accounts of Indian raids and "massacres" that the most sensational yellow journalism of a later period would have envied.[1]

Watson saw in the press performance of the 1860s a reflection of the strong, sometimes violent anti-Indian sentiment of the frontier. What the frontier readership wanted, the newspaper supplied, including hair-raising accounts of alleged Indian "uprisings."

According to historian William Blankenburg, before the Camp Grant (Arizona) massacre of 1871, for example, the three English-language newspapers in Tucson made every effort to arouse the white settlers, and the rest of the country, against the Indians of the region. Referring to the Apaches, the *Weekly Arizonan* recommended, as an appropriate Indian policy, "to receive them when they apply for peace, and have them grouped together and slaughtered as though they were as many nests of rattlesnakes."[2]

The papers continued to encourage white settlers to kill Apaches who raided livestock and who sometimes killed white persons in retaliation against white slaughter of Indians. They actively supported recruitment of volunteer whites and mercenary Papago Indians for the purpose of raiding the tiny Apache settlement at Camp Grant. The *Arizonan* urged: "Would it not be well for the citizens of Tucson to give the Camp Grant wards a slight entertainment to the music of about a hundred double-barrelled shotguns. We are positive that such a course would produce the best results."[3]

A week later, just before dawn, a hundred Apaches, mostly women and children, were slain in their wickiups.[4] Although the massacre might have occurred without encouragement from the press, it is hard to ignore the effect of unremittingly negative images of Indians. One would probably be justified in expecting something better of the journalists. Blankenburg, however, concludes his study with a commentary that is descriptive of much media treatment of Indians even today: "It's probably wishful thinking to suppose that those editors might have risked iconoclasm in those agonizing times."[5]

In 1876, as the United States prepared to celebrate its Centennial, the Oglala Sioux and the Northern Cheyennes successfully defended their women and children and old people against Colonel George A. Custer and his cavalry. The Sioux and Cheyennes fought with little advance warning and without the superior weapons available to the cavalry. But accounts in the eastern press called the Custer debacle at the Little Bighorn a slaughter of brave soldiers by the red devils. The *Bismark* (Dakota Territory) *Tribune* printed an extra edition on July 6, 1876, with such headlines as "Massacred," "General Custer and 261 Men the Victims," "Squaws Mutilate and Rob the Dead," and "Victims Captured Alive Tortured in a Most Fiendish Manner."

The report, pierced together from various accounts, spoke of the death of one soldier, Lieutenant McIntosh, who "though a half-breed, was a gentleman of culture and esteemed by all who knew him." McIntosh, the account reads, was

4

pulled from his horse, tortured and finally murdered at the pleasure of the red devils. It was here that Fred Girard (another soldier) was separated from the command and lay all night with the screeching fiends dealing death and destruction to his comrades within a few feet of him, and, but time will not permit us to relate the story, through some means succeeded in saving his fine black stallion in which he took so much pride.[6]

Throughout the account, the Indians were pictured as marauding savages who were inhumanly cruel to the "gallant defendants" of the embankments thrown up by the cavalry. No acknowledgment was made that Custer's attack, unprovoked by the Indians, was part of a government campaign to steal the territory from its original inhabitants. Neither was there mention of the brilliant strategies employed by Crazy Horse and Sitting Bull at the Little Bighorn, leaders of its rightful defenders. Instead, the day was lost for Custer, and "of those brave men who followed Custer, all perished; no one lives to tell the story of the battle." The writer adds, however, that "we said of those who went into battle with Custer none are living. One Crow scout hid himself in the field and witnessed and survived the battle. His story is plausible, and is accepted, but we have not the room for it now."[7] It is curious that the journalist had no room for the only eyewitness account of the battle.

The tale of brave Custer and his band of heroes was carried in papers from east to west. It strengthened the whites' fears of the Indians. It also fed its readers' curiosity and sold newspapers.

Less than fifteen years later, fears were again fanned by reports of the dangers posed by the growth of the Ghost Dance Religion, a messianic, pan-Indian religion of hope and peace. Its doctrine of nonviolence and brotherly love called only for dancing and singing. The Messiah, who had the appearance of an Indian, would bring about the resurrection of the land and of the many Indians slain by white soldiers. Newspaper coverage of the Ghost Dance movement and subsequent hostilities in 1890 and 1891 was inaccurate, sensational, and inflammatory. As one writer put it, the accounts "foreshadowed the 'yellow journalism' that was soon to stampede the nation into a real war. But that was not to happen until the seeds of journalistic jingoism, sowed on the bleak prairies of South Dakota, had borne their first bitter fruit in an 'Indian massacre' in which red men, instead of white, were the victims."[8]

One reason for this comparison to "yellow journalism" was the outright lying by reporters who were "space writers," free-lancers who sold gore by the column inch. They faked "reliable sources" and "eyewitness accounts" and wrote propaganda disguised as news that sent waves of alarm, preceded by vicious rumor, across Nebraska, the Dakotas, and Iowa. The stories, although repudiated by a few serious journalists near the scene, convinced the frontiersmen that Red Cloud's Oglala Sioux were preparing to go on the warpath. They also convinced the federal government that more troops must be sent to the South Dakota towns that were eager for the business that troops would bring to their merchants.

As soldiers began arriving, the Indians fled. The press interpreted and trumpeted their flight as an outbreak of hostilities. Big-city papers began preparing to cover the new Indian "war."[9] Correspondents on the scene were under pressure to send exciting stories. When Chief Big Foot's band was massacred at Wounded Knee as the Indians were being disarmed by the cavalry, the media again ignored the story of the Indians, outnumbered five to one and fighting for their existence. The story was rather one of the protection of innocent white settlers by soldiers who were finally putting an end to Indian treachery.

Only rarely did coverage of the Ghost Dance religion and the Wounded Knee massacre reflect a more accurate picture. One such better-informed account was that of reporter Teresa Howard Dean, who was sent by the *Chicago Herald* to Pine Ridge, South Dakota, in 1871. Before this assignment she had covered weddings, church and social events, and Indian affairs. Douglas C. Jones wrote: "Like a great many other writers who had never been near a Plains Indian, she wrote a number of items deploring the state of Sioux existence, brought on, she indicated, primarily through a native laziness and indolence."[10] She carried a gun and heeded a warning that reporters who were too friendly risked being asked to leave. She filed such tidbits as, "The only incentive to life is this fear of being scalped by red men."[11]

Yet because Teresa Dean boarded at the Indian school while she was in Pine Ridge, she got to know some young Indian students, and she soon became aware of the conditions under which the government forced them to live. Her copy soon reflected her impressions: hunger caused by lack of provisions, education far inferior to that offered by the nearby Catholic mission school for white children, the nonarable lands assigned by the government, and the inability of the local Indian agent to deal with the Ghost Dance religion in any way other than to send for the army, which he had done (his response would be echoed in more contemporary reactions to "Indian problems").

Teresa Dean also met and talked with Indian adults (and brought what she called a "scalping knife," failing to note in her copy that such knives were used by Indians for skinning game and preparing food).[12] Other examples of her work show how even she, like her fellow reporters, failed to see Indians as people. One of her dispatches contained the statement that "the greatest crime for which the government must answer is sending the educated Indian girl back to her tribe where virtue is unknown." Again, after watching a Sioux policeman identify the bodies of his sister and her three children slain near the Wounded Knee battle site, she wrote: "He looked at me with an expression that was unmistakable agony and his lips quivered. For the first time, I realized that the soul of a Sioux might possibly in its primitive state have started out on the same road as did the soul of a white man."[13] The product of white schools and books and a reader of white newspapers written by reporters like herself, Teresa Dean's statements mirror the attitudes and viewpoints in the media of the time, as well as those of a political system that permitted and propagated the atrocities she was witnessing.

From the early years of the twentieth century through the 1960s, during that long period of Indian anguish and tribulation, little coverage of Indian affairs or events was provided by white newspapers.

Then in the 1970s a series of events in Indian country touched off the widespread media coverage that left some wondering if perhaps the earlier policy of media neglect of Indians was not somehow preferable. For the coverage was crisis-activated and did little to further the ongoing story of Indian life and needs in this country. The media gave heavy coverage to the 1973 occupation of Wounded Knee,

South Dakota, by the American Indian Movement. One on-the-scene reporter at Pine Ridge said that correspondents "wrote good cowboy and Indian stories because they thought it was what the public wanted. . . . the truth is buried in too many centuries of lies like fossils embedded in layers of shale." [14] The Associated Press, United Press International, *Newsweek*, *Time*, the *Washington Post* and the *New York Times* were there, as were the three major networks and many foreign press correspondents. The pattern this time was different, however, because the American Indian Movement was in control and was orchestrating the media's sudden curiosity. AIM leaders tried to use Wounded Knee as a stage on which to focus attention on government injustice to Indians. They had only limited success.

Wounded Knee and the events that followed gave birth to several Indian papers, because white-dominated media played the story as they had played the urban unrest in the late 1960s, and Native Americans continued to resent this misinterpretation and other plainly misinformed reporting. One collaborative account about Wounded Knee began:

> The people of the United States, by and large, would rule strongly in favor of native demands at Wounded Knee if they could only find out what happened there. But with the press and television personnel moving along to bigger and better and more violent headlines, with the U.S. Government managing the news emerging from the Pine Ridge Reservation, and with even the reports on the resulting trials of the participants absent from the media, the people of the United States will not have the information on which to base an intelligent judgment. [15]

One difficulty facing the establishment media was that Wounded Knee did not fit prevailing myths held and taught in the United States regarding Indians. Wounded Knee did not coincide with the belief that America was a democratic country where the courts dispensed justice, government agencies dealt benevolently with Indians, and all people had opportunities to match their ambition and willingness to work hard. As the same source said, "Wounded Knee, people say, must be a bad dream—probably done by 'bad Indians,' influenced by 'outside agitators,' and unrepresentative of native people." [16]

Yet, for many Indians, Wounded Knee represented a last-ditch stand, a final plea in the court of public opinion and the arena of equal rights. Witness these comments by Russell Means, AIM leader, regarding media treatment of the life-and-death issues at stake at Wounded Knee:

> Now, this is our last gasp as a sovereign people. And if we don't get these treaty rights recognized, as equal to the Constitution of the United States—as by law they are—then you might as well kill me, because I have no reason for living. And that's why I'm here in Wounded Knee, because nobody is recognizing the Indian people as human beings.
>
> They're laughing it off in *Time* Magazine and *Newsweek*, and the editors in New York and what have you. They're treating this as a silly matter. We're tired of being treated that way. And we're not going to be treated like that any more.[17]

No matter how distorted the reporting, television coverage of Wounded Knee got "the whole world to watch what is happening to the Indian in America," as one Indian on the scene told the *Washington Post*.[18] Thus the takeover helped inform most Americans about things they had not known before: average per capita reservation income—$1,000; average unemployment rate among Indians—40 percent, with a higher percentage at Pine Ridge; a 900 percent greater incidence of tuberculosis on the reservation than in the white population; and a suicide rate twice that of nonreservation persons.[19] Except for a small number of Indian newspapers, the media had neglected to tell those facts to the American public.

They had also neglected, and continue to neglect, to inform the American public about other Indian grievances: that utility companies are being aided by the government in their attempt to take Indian lands that lie over rich mineral deposits;[20] that dams and waterway reroutings are threatening crop and rangelands upon which whole tribal economies depend;[21] that education available to tribal residents is substandard at best and criminal at worst.[22]

Nor surprisingly, Indian journalists have charged the white media with stereotyping. In May, 1973, the *Navajo Times* quoted Franklin Duchineaux, counsel to the United States Subcommittee on Indian Affairs, who said that the Native American often depicted in the press is a sophisticated and intellectual tribal leader. Yet, the counsel suggested, to call on one person and make him stand for or act as spokesman of all Indians is stereotyping at its worst, perhaps because it is at its least conscious level. *Wassaja*, one of two national Indian publications, frequently charges the establishment press with dishonest coverage of Indian affairs. In one article, the editor wrote:

> Information about Indian affairs is meager and largely inaccurate. People need a vast amount of information in order to make intelligent decisions. We need to know what legislation is being readied for action . . . what programs, educational and economic opportunities and experiences of one or another Indian tribe might help the others.[23]

In June, 1975, another incident at Wounded Knee showed that most journalists were unable or unwilling to probe beneath the surface with their questions. Three men, two of them FBI agents, were shot to death on the Oglala Sioux Reservation in South Dakota. Only hours after the shooting the wires were humming with deadline stories reporting that the shooting "stemmed from" the 1973 Wounded Knee disturbances. The shootings were called an "ambush" and the shots were said to have come from "sophisticated bunkers." The misinformation that emerged from these and other reports both developed from and led to more misinformation and stereotyping.

The exact cause of the FBI agents' deaths was never known. No "bunkers" were found. Trials and accusations failed to bring the incident into clear focus. The deaths of the FBI agents brought a massive siege on houses near the death site, and a search-and-destroy paramilitary occupation by hundreds of FBI agents that lasted for months.[24] Press releases by the FBI and other government agencies resulted in the newspaper headline: "FBI Agents Ambushed, Killed by Indians," although no evidence of "ambushing" had been established.

The Native American press has carried frequent accounts of what happened to Indian activists and "sympathizers" involved in the 1973 Wounded Knee occupation and to those suspected or accused of involvement in the 1975 incident. These stories usually were not picked up by the wire services and consequently did not find their way into the white press. Indian activists were beaten, their homes broken into, their families threatened, one of their spiritual leaders harassed and jailed—and the white press remained largely silent.

According to one source, six "Wounded Knee sympathizers" had been killed on the reservation by winter, 1973. In the winter of 1974 people talked of the "murder of the week" on the reservation. At least twenty killings occurred in the first seven months of 1975; it was "a reign of terror—bad before the occupation, but even worse now." [25] The established media gave scant attention to the deaths.

When the Menominee Warriors Society took over an abandoned abbey near Gresham, Wisconsin, in 1975, the media showed up in force and devoted much time and money to covering the incident. There too, however, Indians frequently protested that white journalists were supplying misinformation to their papers. Part of the problem may have come from the journalists' fear of missing good stories or disappointing their audiences. As one Milwaukee television editor put it:

> On several days, very little happened. . . . The question then became whether to report the fact that basically nothing was happening or ignore the story on those days. We decidedly nearly every day that we had to carry some word on the situation, for the sake of those viewers who were interested. [26]

But when all was quiet, reporters stayed around in the event that new developments occurred. Menominee leaders, however, claimed that the reporters could have used their time to obtain adequate background information from individuals whose views should have been heard. [27]

Fast on the heels of the Gresham incident came a series of Indian lawsuits aimed at keeping or regaining lands, mineral rights, and fishing rights promised to Indians in treaties but nullified or at least endangered by subsequent and current developments, legal and illegal. Montanans Opposed to Discrimination and the Interstate Congress for Equal Rights and Responsibilities (ICERR) were just two of the groups mounting massive lobbying efforts against Indian tribal interests. By early 1978, ICERR had chapters in twenty states, mainly in the West and Northeast, areas of the greatest activity in Indian rights. In the spring of 1978, Richard La Course, a prominent American Indian journalist, wrote:

> It's a new political epoch American Indian tribes are entering in the late 1970's. Some call it the "backlash period;" some call it a "state of

siege." Others view it as the forced Era of Treaty Renegotiation. In any case, it's a new ballgame—with consequent new responsibilities for Indian journalists nationwide.[28]

Some of the responsibilities were directed toward Indian audiences and their education for survival. Others were directed toward the non-Indian public, which had to be reached with or without the cooperation of the white-majority media, either by the printed word or by broadcast. Again a good deal of educating had to be done to break through misunderstandings or biases. Said one director of a Native American studies program: "These people [news reporters and editors] really don't give a damn about Indians. We aren't dangerous enough. They think if they just move in on Indians, we'll be forced to give up. Maybe what we need is violence. That's all they seem to understand."[29]

In addition to newspapers, magazines, and the broadcast medium, the book-publishing industry has done its part to cast Indians in a false or negative light. Indian scholars frequently point to the misinformation and prejudice propagated by textbooks dealing with Indians and Indian affairs. *Wassaja* and the quarterly *Indian Historian* regularly publish reviews of current books about Indians. *Wassaja* editor Rupert Costo published *Textbooks and the American Indian*, a carefully annotated study of books frequently used in Indian schools or as authoritative sources of information about Indians. The book, covering historical, sociological, anthropological, and religious studies, as well as basic materials used daily with young people, pointed to some reasons why journalists write about Indians as they do: One learns patterns of perception from teachers, parents, textbooks, and other environmental elements, and these patterns tend to persist beyond one's school days.[30]

As for film, that medium may have more responsibility for creating the current popular image of Indians in this country than all the print media combined. Writers and dramatists, either intentionally or inadvertently, have propagated the stereotypes: the filthy redskin, the noble savage tamed by white refinement and religion, the headdressed warrior who attacks a wagon train, or the swarming redskins attacking the isolated military outpost to the delight of re-run audiences everywhere.

Especially until about mid-century, films reflected largely hostile and negative attitudes in their representation of Indians, who appeared on the screen as bloodthirsty and treacherous. Since 1950 nostalgia or peaceful coexistence has been reflected in the demeanor of Indians in films. Still, today's screen Indian is often a sullen, broken spirit who drinks cheap wine and lives on the handouts of a sometimes benign, sometimes malicious tribal government, or he is the militant Red Power publicity seeker, burning buildings, taking hostages, stealing government documents, or desecrating church buildings.[31]

One writer points out other images, propagated through film reruns, that are still as convincing to a new generation of viewers. The men were lazy, shiftless, unable to conform to white values, not to be trusted. The women were usually quiet, loyal, beautiful.[32]

That the Indians portrayed in most films about Indians have been inauthentic relates directly to the fact that in their creation and production American Indians have been largely excluded. Nor were Indians consulted by the film industry regarding authenticity of plots, settings, and characterizations. Consequently, Keshena writes:

> Movie makers focused on the tribes of the Sioux and the Apache, who thus became the white man's Indian, molded and cast in the white man's mind as he wanted them to be, but projected before the viewer's eye as convincingly authentic. Indians from all tribes were cast in the image of a prearranged reality.[33]

Some few genuine Indian actors surfaced, playing roles that quickly proved the dominance of white heroes: Jay Silverheels, of "Ugh, Kemo Sabe" fame, first appeared as Tonto in the Lone Ranger movies and series. A Mohawk, he also appeared in *Broken Arrow*, *Brave Warrior*, and other films. An earlier Tonto was played by Chief Thunder Cloud, an Ottawa Indian, who appeared in films in the 1920s and 1930s. He was also a radio Tonto.[34]

Only in very recent years, with the emergence of strong Indian actors like Will Sampson and Raymond Tracey, has the image of Indians in film begun to turn away from the degrading stereotypes that formed the material of a half century of filmmaking.

In his own powerfully sardonic way Edward R. Murrow commented in 1958 on the image of Indians in the media. Addressing a national convention of the Radio/Television News Directors Association, Murrow said:

> If Hollywood were to run out of Indians, the program schedules (for television) would be mangled beyond all recognition. Then, some courageous soul with a small budget might be able to do a documentary telling what, in fact, we have done—and still are doing—to the Indians in this country. But that would be unpleasant. And we must at all costs shield the sensitive citizens from anything that is unpleasant.[35]

Ten years later the National Advisory Commission on Civil Disorders, which published the respected Kerner Report, added its own commentary on the plight of America's minorities. It is interesting that the commission failed to mention American Indians explicitly. That failure is itself a comment on the problem. The call for improvement of media coverage of minorities seemed targeted at blacks and Chicanos. But the same criticism could have easily been applied to the media treatment of Indians.

Chapter 15 of the Kerner Report, supposedly well known to journalists and media critics, charged that the coverage of the 1967 civil disturbances contained "mistakes of fact, exaggeration of events, overplaying of particular stories, or prominent displays of speculation about unfounded rumors of potential trouble."[36]

Another criticism by the Kerner Commission was that white-dominated media have not communicated to the majority of their audience—which is white—a sense of the degradation, misery, and hopelessness of ghetto existence: "They have not communicated to whites a feeling for the difficulties of being a Negro in the United States. They have not shown understanding or appreciation of—and thus have not communicated—a sense of Negro culture, thought or history."[37] The Kerner Report also states that "it is the responsibility of the news media to tell the story of race relations in America, and, with notable exceptions, the media have not turned to the task with the wisdom, sensitivity, and expertise it demands."[38]

If this charge is true for black Americans, it is also true for American Indians. How many Americans know of the conditions on reservations or among urbanized Indians? How many are aware of the true story of how Indians came to be dispossessed of their land? How many have any more than a naïve, misleading vision of eighteenth- and nineteenth-century naked savages running through forests whooping and hollering and making off with the innocent children of equally innocent, brave, and honest white settlers? The story of America's birth and its early nationhood is laced with accounts of how white men tamed the wild land, educated the savages, and gradually assumed benign dictatorship over nomadic peoples unable to control their own destiny and unwilling to rear their children as God-fearing, civilized citizens.

Such are the images of Indians throughout nearly two centuries of media "coverage." The neglect and the stereotyping have served the needs of the majority and so perhaps have been inevitable.

It is against this background that we can move to a consideration of the communication efforts of American Indians themselves. Those efforts grew partly in reaction to inaccurate news reports in the establishment media. But in large part the Indian press grew as a natural result of communication problems that only Indians themselves could solve. The story that unfolds in the following chapters concerns Indians' ongoing struggle to communicate—a struggle that has reached life-and-death proportions throughout more than 150 years.

CHAPTER TWO

American Indian Newspapers, 1828 to the Civil War

The survey of American Indian newspapers that starts here opens with an account of early-day press efforts, presenting their development in the context of the social forces that initially prompted the papers and eventually stifled them. Following a general overview, the chapter focuses closely on the first publications, including the *Cherokee Phoenix*, and then looks at several other pre–Civil War publications of the Five Civilized Tribes.

One of the primary tasks of the early papers was clearly educational—to promote among Indians a better chance for successful encounters with a world increasingly populated by whites. Reading those first Native American papers, one senses that their editors were aware of the inevitable: it was only a matter of time before tribal lands were surrounded and stolen. So their people needed to be able to read, write, and converse in the language of the white society in order to stand a chance for survival in the imminent collision of cultures.

Those papers offered their readers in the Indian community news, information, and advertising. They also sounded the alarm when Indians needed to be warned of danger to themselves and their communities. The publications studied here are those owned or managed by, intended for, and speaking for American Indian people. The definition, in theory, excludes publications produced solely by religious or governmental groups, although some of these publications are valuable for the information they offer with regard to the realities of life in Indian country. Indeed, support by religious groups has figured prominently in Indian press efforts through the years.

The early history of white and Indian journalism alike includes some of the same patterns: infrequent publication, primitive format and content, high mortality rates, and minimal staff and resources. What most non-Indian papers in this country did not share was the bilingual and sometimes trilingual nature of several early Indian newspapers, which were printed regularly in Choctaw, Cherokee, or Chickasaw, and eventually Creek, as well as in English. In addition, the existence of Indian papers was imperiled by a whim or policy of government, which might displace or decimate an entire readership before a paper could establish itself.

Another characteristic unique to early Indian publications is that they were usually official organs of Indian tribal governments. Consequently, their editors often shaped editorial policy to promote the interests of the tribes they served. This same editorial shaping operates today in many Indian papers, as we shall see. Then, as now, it created difficulties for editors and tribal leadership. At the same time, precisely because of the tribal subsidy, an Indian paper could generally be free of advertiser pressure and could play a tribal tune, regardless of its unpopularity among non-Indian communities.

Because of the unsettled lives of the tribes, back issues of many of their papers have only rarely been preserved, and it is impossible to state accurately the exact number of pioneer Indian papers that existed at any given period. Carolyn Foreman lists about 250 newspapers established in Indian territory before 1900 and about 320 established in the first decade of the twentieth century. Only a small number of these were Indian papers, however. Some had religious or agency affiliations. Others merely claimed to support Indian interests, many being owned by whites who used Indians as figurehead editors to get around the laws prohibiting non-Indians from owning businesses within Indian nations.[1]

Four of the Five Civilized Tribes—Cherokee, Chickasaw, Choctaw, and Creek—constituted the center of early Indian journalism. Only the Seminoles did not publish newspapers. The Cherokees were the most active. Although many of the early tribal publications were engineered by religious missions scattered throughout Indian country, most were started by tribal leaders. Their educational value was generally recognized by Indian leaders and the white government alike.

The positive role of the newspapers in the life of Indian communities was attested to in 1888 by Robert L. Owens, United States Indian agent at the Union Agency in Oklahoma. He wrote:

I regard one of the chief educational influences operating in this agency as the newspapers of the territory. There are quite a number, and they are beginning to take a lively interest in public affairs and to express their opinions freely, both by correspondence and by editorials. I regard this tendency to public discussion like the sun piercing the clouds. . . . Public discussion will eradicate error and educate the public. It will create intelligent public opinion and moderate. partisanship.[2]

Before its first issue appeared, the paper *Indian Progress* published a description of its aims and policies, in effect summarizing the role that Owens foresaw for the paper. The *Progress* would be a "purely Indian enterprise . . . owned, edited, and printed by Indians," with columns in Cherokee, Choctaw, Chickasaw, Creek, Seminole, and English.

Our columns are open to friend and foe alike for the discussion of the great questions of the day, as we shall claim and exercise the right to entertain and express our views. So we cordially invite those who differ from us to use our columns. . . . The Progress will insist on the faithful observance of every guarantee of the treaties. It will defend the property rights of all the Indians, and aid them in preserving to themselves and posterity the lands they occupy.[3]

The early papers served other functions as well. They advertised schools and hotels, publicized the settling of estates, announced unclaimed letters, ran ads for the return of runaway slaves, printed steamboat schedules and merchants' sales lists, promoted patent-medicine companies, and recorded newly enacted laws. They editorialized for law and order, warned women of dangers to their persons, and encouraged temperance. They also helped build towns by carrying advertisements to attract homesteaders. In general, they informed and supported the Indian nations.

Inspiration such as that behind the *Indian Progress* carried early journalists through the initial hardships of frontier printing. Papers were produced from presses housed in cramped cabins, wagons, tents, vacated schoolhouses, and even open wheat fields.

The papers had an average page size of about fifteen by twenty-four inches and ran between four and sixteen pages. Circulation ranged from a hundred to a thousand, and prices were about one to three dollars a year, often payable in advance. They were of uneven quality and the more established among them sometimes took swipes at the less sophisticated. One critic wrote of a rival paper that it needed "some fixin'" and that the "entire paper has the appearance of having been printed on a hand press and in an awful hurry."[4]

Ads followed frontier style in form and content, and promotions for patent medicine abounded. Two gentlemen named Love and Boyd advertised in one paper that they had "recently purchased and settled upon the improvements, at the well-known Oil Springs, on Hickory Creek." "We wish to inform the afflicted of all Nations," the ad continues, "that we are prepared to take care of man and horse, families, servants, etc."[5]

There were merchandise ads for the general stores. One claimed that a Mr. John James, interpreter at Sutler's Store, was prepared "to wait on his Chocktaw and Chickasaw friends, and sell them goods cheaper than anyone else in the Nation."[6]

The publications generally were financed by tribal governments as well as by outside interests. Papers were often started in boom-towns by real estate companies. Stock companies were also founded to finance newspapers. The Indian International Printing Company, the first Indian stock company, used monies from private investments to support Indian papers. Political parties and church groups also found it useful to initiate or support publishing ventures. Many frontier Indian papers, like their non-Indian counterparts and smaller papers even today, supplemented the work of their small staffs with "ready print," sheets preprinted with news and ads of interest from other regions. They ran these along with their few pages of local copy.

The Oklahoma Press Association was begun in Indian Territory in 1888, when its nine founding editors met in Muskogee. Other press associations that included Indian papers followed throughout the years.[7]

Editorial policies were stated explicitly in most papers. Press directories announced the political affiliations and stances of the papers; but, depending on the directories consulted, a paper could be listed as Democrat, Republican, and Independent simultaneously.

The politically outspoken papers openly invited dispute and bitter controversies. This often led to name-calling, libel suits, and even murder. In defense of the practice, however, one journalist said in an

1871 address: "Take the personalities out of our journalism, and it would go into bankruptcy. Banish the words blackguard, liar, and villain from our newspaper literature, and even the 'good and useful' Greeley would quit the business in disgust."[8]

The papers combined official news, general news, announcements, editorial comments, and serial stories. Comments often accompanied the news, as in this example from a Creek paper: "A short time since, Lem Alexander, who lives near Brooken, was watching for deer when eight wolves came up. He shot into them, killing four and crippling three. Good work."[9]

Special publications were sometimes issued by various printing companies. One of the finest pieces of newspaper work ever put out in Indian Territory was the "End-of-the-Century Edition" of the *Muskogee Phoenix*, published November 2, 1899. The ninety-six-page special included history on the churches, schools, stores, and entertainments, along with vignettes on the leading citizens and major ranches and ranchers.

Indian journalists also produced a number of magazines. About twenty started publication before 1900, initiated or supported mainly by churches or schools. The first magazine, as well as the first periodical issued in Indian territory, was produced by the Cherokees. Called the *Cherokee Messenger*, it was started in 1844 and was printed on the Baptist Mission Press.

Magazines, which ranged in price from one to three dollars a year ("payable in advance"), imitated a New England–style expression with pronounced religious fervor. Their articles focused on temperance meetings, weddings, personalities, sales, and announcements. Some were published by religious groups, others by colleges and seminaries, and others with general audiences in mind.

SEQUOYAH AND THE *Cherokee Phoenix*

In a study of the efforts of the nineteenth-century Indian press, major attention needs to be directed to the pioneering newspapers published by the Five Civilized Tribes between 1828 and 1906.

The Cherokee Nation established the first Indian newspaper,

the *Cherokee Phoenix*, in New Echota, near present-day Calhoun, Georgia. Begun February 21, 1828, the same year Noah Webster's *American Dictionary of the English Language* appeared, it was a bilingual paper, printed partly in English and partly in Cherokee, using the eighty-six character alphabet developed by Sequoyah, a Cherokee silversmith who was also known as George Guess, or Gist.

Commentators give varying accounts of the Sequoyah story.[10] Some contemporary Indian journalists speak of "the Sequoyah legend," but on major points they agree. Sequoyah, a cripple, had served in the United States Army during the War of 1812 against the hostile Creek Indians. He realized that white society possessed in written language a power his people lacked. He was consumed with the desire to bring this power to the Cherokees. Beginning in 1809, he developed symbols for more than 2,000 Cherokee words. He abandoned that approach some time later, developing instead a symbol-for-each-syllable system.[11]

Twelve years after his first efforts he tried to introduce the syllabary to a skeptical village. A Philadelphia merchant, John Alexander, recounted in 1840 what Sequoyah told him had happened. According to Alexander, Sequoyah's fellow Cherokees ridiculed him, or thought he was crazy. Cherokees in Arkansas resisted his efforts to explain the syllabary and to teach its use. But he persisted, promising that some day they would realize he was right.

He wrote letters to his friends, trying to get them at least to come to him, which they did, to find out what the figures meant. Then a breakthrough occurred, unplanned by Sequoyah but convincing to the skeptics. His six-year-old daughter, Ahyoka, had learned to read her father's alphabet. During one "teaching" session with neighbors, he had written out the name of one of them, Turtle Fields. The child, peering out a nearby window, read aloud what he had written. Turtle Fields began to believe.[12]

In another test, this time an official one conducted by five of the Cherokee Nation's "fiercest young men," Sequoyah and one of his older sons were separated, and messages were dictated to Sequoyah and carried to his son for reading.[13] He read them and wrote responses for Sequoyah to interpret. The test went well and doubters began to waiver.

But some final testing was necessary. One scholar explains:

> The leaders of the Cherokees, half persuaded, arranged for a test. They selected a group of young men with sharp minds and sent them to Sequoyah's cabin. At the appointed time, the chiefs assembled and subjected these students to the most rigid tests. When the meeting ended, the scholar was a tribal hero.[14]

At the same time, Cherokees in Arkansas had learned the alphabet and were writing letters to Sequoyah, telling him about the spread of reading and writing. This convinced the Cherokees in Georgia, and suddenly the silversmith was in demand everywhere as a teacher. He wrote out copy after copy of his syllabary, serving as scribe, teacher, and publisher.

As the skepticism gave way, the alphabet was quickly put to wide use, most people learning to read after less than a week of study. A contemporary of Sequoyah wrote in 1828 that throughout the Cherokee Nation young, middle-aged, and old men, as well as women and children, could read. The Sequoyah syllabary had not been taught in the schools. Instead, the people learned from each other, without books, by printing the letters on bark board, fences, and even the walls of houses. He concluded:

> That the mass of people, without schools or books, should by mutual assistance, without extraneous impulse or aid, acquire the art of reading, and that in a character wholly original is, I believe, a phenomenon unexampled in modern times.[15]

Sequoyah's discovery was honored in the autumn of 1823 when the Cherokee Nation voted to present him with a silver medal struck in his honor. Inscribed on one side in Cherokee and on the other side in English, the message read, "Presented to George Gist, by the General Council of the Cherokee Nation, for his ingenuity in the invention of the Cherokee alphabet."[16]

Twenty years later the Cherokee National Council voted to give him, or his widow, in the event of his death, an annual pension of $300, not knowing that Sequoyah had died in Mexico. His widow became the recipient. This literary pension was the first recorded in American history, and the first and only one granted by an Indian tribe.[17]

Seeing the completion of the syllabary and its acceptance by the Cherokees, missionaries were at first opposed to it because of its Indian origins. They finally recognized its value, however, and encouraged the translation of the books of the Bible into the Cherokee syllabary. In 1824 parts of the Gospel of Saint John were translated by a Cherokee named Atsi. By 1825 a Cherokee preacher, David Brown, had completed work on a translation of the entire New Testament.[18]

The progress into literacy was just one indication of Cherokee advancement. A census in 1825, authorized by the Cherokee National Council, showed a population of 13,563 Cherokees, 1,277 slaves, and 147 white men and 73 white women married to Cherokees. It also listed 18 ferry boats, several public roads, 62 blacksmith shops, 8 cotton machines, 31 gristmills, 10 sawmills, 172 wagons, 2,488 spinning wheels, 762 looms, 22,531 cows, 7,683 horses, 46,732 hogs, 2,566 sheep, and 2,943 plows.[19]

The effort to establish a paper grew out of a combination of religious and political needs. On the one hand, the missionaries recognized that the printed word could assist them in "civilizing" and "uplifting" the Cherokees. On the other hand, the Cherokee Nation and its national council knew their people needed an accelerated educational program in order to survive. To fight the white man's encroachment on their homelands, they had to learn to use the white man's weapons. The council hoped to unify opinion in the nation and to gain outside support for the Indians' rights to their homelands. In addition, says one scholar, "the Cherokee nation was a fairly compact unit, which made communication by printed matter comparatively easy. . . . In 1828 the Cherokees may have been more ready to enjoy and benefit from a newspaper than many white communities."[20]

At the same time, Elias Boudinot, a Cherokee schoolteacher, clerk of the Cherokee National Council, and a college-educated missionary, recognized the great contribution Sequoyah's alphabet, or syllabary, had made. Spurred on by support from Samuel Worcester, a non-Indian missionary, he accepted the council's assignment to begin an intensive fund-raising effort to support a newspaper venture. He moved up and down the East Coast of the United States, addressing church and philanthropic groups. On May 26, 1826, he preached at the First Presbyterian Church in Philadelphia. His "Address to the

Whites" was an inspiring sermon, and was perhaps one reason why he succeeded in his fund-raising efforts.

In his remarks, Boudinot described the purposes of the paper as

> comprising a summary of religious and political events, etc., on the one hand; and on the other, exhibiting the feelings, dispositions, improvements, and prospects of the Indians; their traditions, their true character, as it once was, as it now is, and the ways and means most likely to throw the mantle of civilization over all tribes; and such other matters as will tend to diffuse proper and correct impressions in regard to their condition—such a paper could not fail to create much interest in the American Community, favorable to the aborigines, and to have a powerful influence on the advancement of the Indians themselves.[21]

Even before Boudinot's trip, the council had appropriated $1,500 from tribal funds to finance the purchase of a press and types. A decisive move was made in 1827 by the American Board of Commissioners for Foreign Missions in New England. The board announced that it approved a request by Worcester for assistance in the founding of a Cherokee printing press:

> Punches have been cut and types cast after the mold of Guess's alphabet at the foundry of Messrs. Baker and Greene, in Boston. A fount of English types has also been procured, and a press of a very superior kind.[22]

In considering the financing of the press, John Ross, principal chief, had given serious thought to the relationship of the press to its community. In an address to the national council on October 13, 1827, he said:

> The public press deserves the patronage of the people, and should be cherished as an important vehicle in the diffusion of general information and as no less powerful auxiliary in asserting and supporting our political rights . . . the only legislative provision necessary for conducting the press . . . is to guard against the admission of scurrilous productions of a personal nature. . . . The freedom of the press should be as free as the breeze that glides upon the surface.[23]

The new press and type fonts were shipped in a ten-week voyage from Boston to Augusta, Georgia, and then moved by wagon over the final two hundred miles. The press arrived at the Cherokee capital,

New Echota, in January, 1828, and was installed in the new printing plant built there by the Cherokee Nation. The Cherokees later reimbursed the board of missions for its expenses.

At the same time, the general council named Elias Boudinot the Indian editor for the newspaper, textbooks, and other publications, offering him a salary of $300 a year. The council also hired a printer at $400 a year, an eventual source of resentment for Boudinot.

Although Boudinot functioned as editor from the very first issue, he was a close friend of Worcester, who contributed in many ways to the success of the paper. In fact, it was Worcester who drew up and had printed in Tennessee the prospectus for the *Cherokee Phoenix* (the prospectus brought advance subscription payments from as far away as Germany). Reprinted in the first issue, the prospectus stated that the weekly paper would carry laws and documents of the Cherokee Nation; accounts of manners and customs of Cherokees, their progress in education, religion, and culture; news of other Indian tribes "as our limited means of information will allow"; local news; and "interesting articles calculated to promote Literature, Civilization and Religion among the Cherokees." To boost circulation, the editor offered a free subscription to anyone bringing in six or more subscribers "and becoming responsible for the payment."

The four-page *Phoenix* (Cherokee: *Tsa-la-ge-Tsi-hi-sa-ni-hi*) first appeared February 21, 1828. Other issues followed in quick succession, to be read by the eager population. The *Phoenix* was circulated with sometimes only one copy for each village. In the fourth issue, March 13, 1828, Boudinot began publishing the long-standing Cherokee laws. He published regular lessons in spelling, grammar, sentence structure, and conjugation—usually in Cherokee but occasionally in English. The young editor—he was just twenty-seven—acknowledged that the fledgling issues were technically weak. The first issue, he admitted to his readers, was "destitute of intelligence" because of the failure of the mails. It may have lacked news from exchanges around the country (and the world, for that matter), but as Samuel Carter says of the early *Phoenix*:

> Physically the Phoenix stacked up well against the newspapers of New York and Philadelphia, New England and the South. Its four large-

sized pages contained five columns of type in an appropriate ratio of three columns in English to two in Cherokee. Since each of Sequoyah's characters stood for a whole syllable, it required less space to express a thought in Cherokee than in English.[24]

Very little of the content of the paper appeared in parallel Cherokee and English; some was only in Cherokee; some only in English. Samuel Worcester contributed some articles, primarily religious ones, although he needed help in translating them into Cherokee. The missionary's closeness to the paper led to the accusations (refuted in the November 12, 1828, issue) that a white man was the editor and an Indian only the "ostensible" editor. It apparently was hard for some to credit a Cherokee with the journalistic brilliance Boudinot exhibited in the *Phoenix*. In his first editorial, Boudinot announced, "We will not intermeddle with the policies of our neighbors . . . we will not return railing for railing, but consult mildness, for we have been taught that 'a soft answer turneth away wrath, but grievous words stir up anger.'" In closing, he wrote words that are both inspiring and prophetically ironic:

> We now commit our feeble efforts to the good will and indulgence of the public, praying that God will attend them with his blessings, and hoping for that happy period when all the Indian tribes of America shall rise, Phoenix-like, from their ashes, and when terms like "Indian depradations," "war whoops," "scalping knife," and the like shall become obsolete and forever buried "under deep ground."[25]

But Boudinot soon became involved in politics, fighting with print the move of the Georgia government to extend its criminal laws over the move of the Cherokee Nation, and when in the spring of 1828 the U.S. government moved to allocate $50,000 to remove the Cherokees from their mineral-rich lands, Boudinot pointed in print to the reality, based on the actual costs of moving 13,000 Cherokees, their 2,600 homes, stock, and possessions. The expense, he charged, would be $1,783,730. He concluded: "Cannot this sum be put to better use? . . . establish schools in every part of this nation . . . fund a college . . . publish books . . . if it is for the Cherokee betterment. If we fail to improve under such efforts, we will then agree to move."[26]

Meanwhile, Sequoyah himself, who had set the stage for Indian journalism, had moved to Arkansas to spread literacy among the Cherokees there. He maintained his ties with Tahlequah, as one writer tells:

> Every week or two he would saddle his pony and ride up the military road a few miles to Dwight [Mission] to get the latest issue of the Cherokee *Phoenix* that was regularly sent him from Georgia. The miracle of reading in this paper the news of his people in the East, and happenings among the white people, in characters of his own invention, never grew stale. And to see other uneducated Indians enjoying the same privilege as a result of his industry and genius was a source of never-ending gratification to him.[27]

By 1843, the year of Sequoyah's death, more than four million pages of various literature had been printed using his alphabet.[28] This achievement was in addition to the publication of the *Cherokee Phoenix*.

The *Phoenix*, acclaimed throughout the world in its brief lifetime, had subscribers in Germany, Paris, and London. It had sales and advertising agents in Boston, New York, Richmond, and Troy and also in Beaufort, South Carolina, and Statesville, Tennessee, and exchanged issues with such newspapers as the *National Intelligencer*, the *New Hampshire Patent and State Gazette*, *Niles' Weekly Register*, and the *Milledgeville* (Georgia) *Journal*.[29] In the August 12, 1831, issue, the editor noted that non-Indian as well as Indian papers frequently reprinted materials from the *Phoenix*.

Advertising was an important function of the paper, and the *Phoenix* carried ads for "FLOUR for sale low for CASH or HIDES," a boarding school opening, an estate auction, and all the general needs of frontier community readers. Ads were not plentiful though, and money was tight, despite the paper's popularity and fame. Not all subscribers paid on time either, causing the editor to exhort readers: "Thus far, the Phoenix has been a dead expense to the proprietors. It is highly desirable that there should be sufficient patronage to secure it from pecuniary embarrassment in the future.[30]

Throughout its brief history, the *Phoenix* was at the center of Cherokee national life, portraying the standards of its civilization, carrying letters that discussed problems and politics, and reflecting the persistent problem of alcoholism among Cherokees. Many issues featured articles on the evils of intemperance and the joys of sobriety. The *Phoenix* also printed information on the early phases of the controversy over government removal of Indians from their ancestral lands to reservations and Indian territories. This latter controversy, and the political factions within the Cherokee Nation that grew up around it, set the stage for the decline of the paper: it was beginning to be read with increasing wrath by Georgia senators and proremoval lobbies.

A year after its founding, the paper's name was changed, probably to reflect its purpose more accurately. The February 11, 1829, issue bore the new title *Cherokee Phoenix and Indian Advocate*. And advocacy was to be its main role in the troubled months and years ahead.

In 1829, Georgia passed a measure stripping Indians of any right in a court of law. No Indian would be allowed to testify at a trial that involved white men, and no Indian contract or testimony was valid without the corroboration of two white witnesses. A *Phoenix* editorial commented: "Full license to our oppressors, and every avenue of justice closed against us. Yes, this is the bitter cup prepared for us by a republican and religious government—we shall drink it to the very dregs."[31]

A year later Boudinot wrote of the harassment, arrest, and threats of physical harm suffered by members of the *Phoenix* staff at the hands of Georgia authorities. He also protested the postmaster's sale of liquor to Indians. In retaliation the postmaster withheld *Phoenix* mail, including both supplies and exchange papers. Boudinot wrote: "This new era has not only wrested from us our rights and privileges as a people, but it has closed the channel through which we could formerly obtain our news. By this means the resources of the *Phoenix* are cut off. We must now depend, if we continue our labors, upon . . . our patrons at home and abroad."[32]

Earlier that year he had reprinted from the *Portland Christian Mirror* a "Memorial: In Behalf of the Cherokee Indians" that had been signed by more than three hundred persons. He marveled, he told his readers, because

> So universal an expression of sentiment in such a manner is, we believe, of rare occurrence, and is the more to be valued, as it is given by

men of different political parties—the leading friends of the present administration in the town being among the signers. This is magnanimous and patriotic.[33]

Samuel Worcester had been jailed earlier by the Georgia government, which recognized that he was closely involved with the *Cherokee Phoenix* and deeply opposed to Indian removal. He was arrested, along with other missionaries, for refusal to take an oath of allegiance to Georgia, which would have been an avowal of support for the very power that was seeking to disinherit the Cherokees. By an act of the legislature, all white residents were required to take this oath under pain of arrest.

These harassments and legislative acts were, however, only the beginning, and the editor of the *Phoenix* was soon involved in the internal conflict of the Cherokee Nation as it struggled with the problem of settling for removal, along with some monetary compensation, to new and strange lands in the West, thus possibly gaining freedom from white encroachment. On the other hand, there was the strong will of the vast majority of the Cherokees to remain on their homeland, near their hard-earned farms and homes, near the bones of their ancestors, but free from the marauding, land-hungry whites whose depredations the Georgia guard permitted.

The *Cherokee Phoenix* had been established, at least in part, to fight removal. But among the Cherokees were educated and influential people who thought that removal, with all the pain it would entail, was the only route—that it was indeed a foregone conclusion, with only the timing undecided. Gradually, Elias Boudinot came to be convinced that this small majority was right. At the same time, Principal Chief John Ross told Boudinot not to publish in the *Phoenix* any reports of dissension in the meetings of the Cherokee National Council. He believed that such reports would only encourage the enemy by letting him see that he now had a divided people to prey upon. The dilemma the young editor faced was somewhat resolved in a letter of resignation that he printed in the *Phoenix* August 11, 1832:

> I could not consent to be the conductor of this paper without having the privilege and the right of discussing those important matters . . . and from which I have seen and heard, were I to assume that privilege, my usefulness would be paralyzed, by being considered, as

I unfortunately already have been, an enemy in the interest of my beloved country and people.
I should think it my duty to tell them the whole truth. I cannot tell them that we shall be reinstated in our rights when I have no such hope.[34]

In formal acceptance of Boudinot's resignation, printed in that same issue, Ross asked that the new editor of the *Phoenix* reflect the Cherokee people's views, but further urged that controversial views not be presented, in the interest of "unity of sentiment and action." The tension between freedom of the press and the exposure of division in the ranks must have been a difficult one for Ross; it was clearly painful for Boudinot, who remained at the center of the removal dispute. Seven years later Boudinot was to be axed to death by fellow Cherokees for his part in the signing of the 1835 treaty of New Echota that in effect surrendered Cherokee Nation lands to the United States government and set the scene for removal and the Trail of Tears, so named because of the agony and death the removal process caused the Cherokees.[35]

Ross selected his brother-in-law Elijah Hicks as the new editor. He expected Hicks to use the *Phoenix* to fight removal. But Hicks lacked his predecessor's experience and the paper began to falter. Hicks continued to speak out against Georgia's robbery of Cherokee mineral rights, land seizure, harassment of Cherokees, and the impending removal decision. But the power of Boudinot and his literary brilliance were gone from the *Phoenix*. Cherokees, busy and concerned for their survival, found little encouragement and inspiration in the pages of the once-proud *Phoenix*. In addition, the number of articles printed in the Cherokee language declined, and issues appeared with less regularity, their number fluctuating between one and four each month.

The mails again became a problem and, in 1833, Hicks quoted a sign he had seen in a Nashville newspaper office. Dateline "Post Office, New Echota, Ga., June 16, 1833," it directed: "Editors of Newspapers that exchange with the *Cherokee Phoenix*, will please stop sending their papers directed to it in exchange, as it is discontinued."[36] The postmaster gave as a reason for his notice the infrequency of publication. Indeed, following the February 9, 1883, issue, nine weeks went by before another appeared. Two issues were published between April 17 and July 20, and thirty issues came out in the next ten months.

Hicks was a weak writer and editor, and in the last months he was forced to use such almanac copy as "A Father's Advice to His Daughter" and "Cultivation of Peach Trees." Little wonder that interest and readership declined. On May 31, 1834, Hicks announced that he was suspending publication, "say to the last of July, for the purpose of collecting funds." He thanked his readers who had supported the *Phoenix* against the "most wicked policy that the wit of man could conceive to expel the Cherokees from their beloved homes." He concluded: "To our Cherokee readers we would say DON'T GIVE UP THE SHIP. Although our enemies are numerous we are still in the land of the living and the JUDGE of all the earth will impart the means for the salvation of our suffering Nation."[37]

The *Cherokee Phoenix and Indian Advocate* never resumed publication. Born at a time of hope and enlightenment, it ended in a period of tribal uncertainty, dissension, and unrest.

The Cherokee Council in the spring of 1835 resolved to move the press to Tennessee, to establish a new paper. Richard Fields was appointed editor, and Cherokee Principal Chief Ross sent a wagon to New Echota to bring back the press and type. The trip was in vain, however, since the entire operation had been seized by the Georgia guard, led by Elias Boudinot's brother Stand Watie. Subsequent petitions to Washington failed to reclaim the press. According to Ross, from that time not only were the Cherokees denied the use of the press, but they saw it "used by agents of the United States in publication of slanderous communications against the constituted authorities of the Cherokee Nation."[38]

Although the Cherokee Nation was not able to establish another newspaper for nine more years, printing was resumed almost immediately through the work of Samuel Worcester and the American Board of Missions. Worcester moved to the new Indian Territory in the West shortly after his release from prison. He obtained a new press and permission from the leaders of the Western Cherokees to publish at the Park Hill Mission Press (near present-day Tahlequah, Oklahoma), books in Cherokee on literary, religious, and moral instruction.

His first publication and, incidentally, the first publication in Indian Territory, was the *Cherokee Almanac*, which appeared in 1835. While not actually a newspaper, it contained news items, weather predictions, patent-medicine ads, and other items of almanacs. It also carried news of local and Oklahoma territorial events, with the English and Cherokee versions printed side by side on facing pages of the publication. In *Early Oklahoma Newspapers*, Grace Ray says that, although few copies of the *Almanac* have been preserved, it "probably was issued annually, more or less regularly, until the destruction of the printing plant at Park Hill in the time of the Civil War."[39]

At about this time, printing in the Shawnee Sioux language was begun on the Baptist Mission Press by the Reverend Jotham Meeker. In 1834 he printed a hymn in the Shawnee language, using English characters. In March of the following year the *Siwinowe Kesibwi*, or *Shawnee Sun*, was established, edited by Johnston Lykins. This first paper, a monthly or semimonthly printed entirely in an Indian language, was in operation until 1839, then resumed in 1841, and published until 1844.[40]

Ignoring treaties, property deeds, and the sacredness to the Indians of their ancestral homes and burial grounds, the United States government in the late 1830s herded many thousands of Indians westward on forced marches to satisfy the greed of land-hungry whites. These emigrants were not the whooping naked savages of Hollywood. They were civilized and well-established people. Many of their leaders were college-educated; many of them owned large plantations; others were skilled teachers, outstanding craftsmen, successful tradesmen. More than one-fourth of the Cherokees who were removed died on the Trail of Tears, and many of those who survived, died shortly after resettling. Once-wealthy tribes now had nothing. Like others of the Five Civilized Tribes, they arrived at their new "homelands" with only what they could carry.

Late in the same decade the white press, with some exceptions, either supported removal or ignored it altogether. Only a few spoke out, among them the author of the following article printed in the *Montgomery* (Alabama) *Advertiser* and reprinted in the *Southern Advocate*, of Huntsville, Alabama:

The Red Men must soon leave. They have nothing left on which to subsist. Their property has been taken from them—their stock killed, their farms pillaged—by whom? By white men. By individuals who should have scorned to take such mean advantage of these who were unprotected and defenseless. Such villainy may go unpunished in this world, but the day of retribution will most certainly come.[41]

But the surviving emigrants possessed remarkable stamina and courage. By 1839 the Cherokees adopted a new constitution and under John Ross's leadership established a general school system. John Ross also played a leading role in establishing the second and perhaps greatest Cherokee paper. As principal chief (or president of the national council) he issued a message to the Cherokee Nation in October, 1843:

> Deeming it expedient that a printing press should be established . . . to spread abroad a correct knowledge of the state of our affairs. . . . In order that the rumors . . . often circulated through the press in the States by designing demagogues may be corrected, I have in Boston purchased a printing press of superior quality with types, both English and Cherokee. . . . I will resign the whole purchase over to the Nation at the original cost and charges.[42]

The *Cherokee Advocate* and Other Papers

The Cherokee National Council authorized a national press on October 25, 1843. The paper was to be called the *Cherokee Advocate*. William P. Ross, the chief's nephew and a Princeton graduate, was elected editor for a four-year term with a salary of $500 a year. The council also appointed a translator and four printers, each with a salary of $300 a year. A prospectus prepared by the editor said that the *Advocate* would serve to benefit Cherokees and to educate non-Indians. Its objectives were the diffusion of important news among the Cherokee people, advancement of their welfare, and defense of their rights. Ross wrote an editorial in the first issue:

> The object of the Council in providing for the publication of the *Advocate* is the physical, moral, and intellectual improvement of the Cherokee people. It will be devoted to these ends, and to the defense

of those rights recognized as belonging to them in treaties legally made at different times with the United States, and of such measures as seem best calculated to secure their peace and happiness, promote their prosperity, and elevate their character as a distinct community.[43]

Like the *Phoenix*, the *Cherokee Advocate* was to be bilingual and was to use Sequoyah's alphabet. The paper would publish laws and treaties affecting Indians and report on tribal government, education, land claims, crimes and local disturbances, and obituaries of distinguished Indian leaders. It also would carry ads for animal skins, clothing, and fabric.

Ross, who would become the Cherokee Nation's most distinguished statesman as well as journalist, published the first issue of this first newspaper in Oklahoma on September 26, 1844. He gave the paper the slogan "Our Right, Our Country, Our Race" and spread information about the Cherokees to a wide audience, as evidenced by ads that came through such scattered agents as Saxon and Miles, of New York; Tappan and Dennet, of Boston; J. R. Bille, of Philadelphia; and Frank Taylor, of Washington.[44]

In April, 1846, Cherokee agent Pierce Butler, praising the *Advocate* and the work of the Cherokee press, said, "This press has been chiefly instrumental in placing the Cherokees one half century in advance of their late condition; providing an easy and cheap mode of diffusing instruction among the people."[45]

The *Advocate* was a six-column weekly. As the official paper of the Cherokee government, it was financed in part by the government and therefore carried only a small number of ads. It was a general newspaper. The day of the week on which it was published varied in some years, as did its format. War, fire, and lack of money brought the publication to a halt on September 28, 1853. As a precaution against vandalism and other dangers during the Civil War, the press and type were removed to Fort Gibson, where they stayed until 1870.

Another publication had appeared earlier in the Oklahoma Territory. The *Cherokee Messenger* was first produced at the Cherokee Baptist Mission a few miles north of present-day Westville, Oklahoma. Published between August, 1844, and May, 1846, and revived briefly in September, 1858, it was primarily a religious publication edited by a non-Indian; the twelve issues published during its lifetime, all in

Cherokee and English, appeared irregularly. It concentrated on topics having to do with religion and temperance. The first issue described Sequoyah's syllabary and gave instructions for its use. A prospectus printed in the magazine explained its purpose:

> The Cherokee Messenger will be published every alternative month principally in the Cherokee language. To those who read English and thus have access to valuable books and papers, the Cherokee Messenger will, of course, be of little service. Yet for the sake of disseminating useful knowledge among those who are less favored than themselves, and can read Cherokee only, they may wish to patronize our paper.[46]

It would print lessons in geography, translations of both the Old and New Testaments, and such well-known religious works as *Pilgrim's Progress*. "This is the first attempt to give the Cherokees a knowledge of the earth on which they live," the prospectus said, "or any portions of the sacred scriptures."[47]

By mid-century, other Indian journalists had joined the fight, and their ranks swelled. The *Cherokee Phoenix* and the *Cherokee Advocate* had ushered in a fruitful era of Indian journalism. According to one chronicler, within a few years after the tragic removal from Georgia "there were three printing presses in operation in the Cherokee Nation, putting out newspapers, religious tracts, books, and pamphlets by the hundreds."[48]

Soon after the *Advocate* was established, Indian women began making their mark in Tahlequah's journalism world. When it was established in 1848, the magazine of the female seminary was called *Cherokee Rose Bud*. By 1857 the name has been changed to *A Wreath of Cherokee Rose Buds*. The magazine appeared irregularly and carried materials related to the lives and interests of boarding-school pupils, the young womanhood of the Cherokee Nation.

Articles carried such titles as "A Visit to the Fortune-Teller," "The Love of Gain," "Temper," "The Grave on the Hill," "The Dress Is Not the Man," "A Visit to My Old Home," and "The Last Eve of 1856." Most authors signed their Cherokee names or used initials, although in listings of students and hometowns Christian names were used. There was little indication of the turbulence around the country as the young authors wrote of meetings, visits, how Christmas holidays were spent, or which teachers were leaving. Reprints from exchange papers, mostly from other female boarding schools, reflect the same sort of interests.

But in the "Valedictory for the Class of 1857" some hint of their awareness of pending problems for their nation can be found in these words by one of their members: "How close beside each other in this world of ours do joy and sorrow lie; so close, indeed, that often some event bears both upon its wing."[49] Unwitting prophecies like this one were found also in the *Sequoyah Memorial*, established August 2, 1855, at the male seminary at Tahlequah. The *Sequoyah Memorial* had as its motto: "Truth, Justice, Freedom of Speech and Cherokee Improvement." Like the *Rose Bud*, it carried news of the college, a roster of students and faculty and a listing of the courses being offered, in addition to such general news of the day as the scarcity of tobacco, coffee, and sugar "due to the low stage of the Arkansas River." It gained the notice of non-Indian readers, and one particularly poignant passage was found in an article reprinted in Godey's Lady's Book, January, 1857:

> The bow and arrow have been laid aside—the day of bowie knives and pistols is fast passing away. The wilderness is becoming the situation for cultivated farms. This reformation is fast completing; and, should our country remain on the stage of nations until her sons and daughters be competent to manage the future destinies of our nation, we may yet reach the summit of civilization and refinement, when knowledge shall be diffused throughout our country; then and not until then, will our people be a happy and contented people—their motto "progress and freedom"—then will our nation be one of the brightest among the Indians of North America.[50]

Indian journalism was not monopolized by the Cherokees, however. Others among the Five Civilized Tribes were aware of the value of the printed word in the fight for survival in an increasingly white-dominated world. The Choctaws, who had been forced from their homelands in Mississippi in the early 1830s, had their first newspaper in 1848, just twenty years after the first Indian paper appeared.

The short-lived *Choctaw Telegraph* was established by David Folsom for the "advocacy and dissemination of Morality, Education, Agriculture, and general Intelligence." It was a politically neutral "family newspaper" published half in Choctaw and half in English. The Choctaw *Intelligencer* replaced the *Telegraph*, publishing from 1850 to 1852. A bilingual weekly like the *Telegraph*, it was begun in Doaksville (Oklahoma), capital of the Choctaw Nation. It carried weather news, merchandise listings, accounts of court proceedings, obituaries, and general news. Its motto was "Universal Love and Charity Our Shield: Our Only Weapon Truth."

The *Intelligencer's* editors, J. P. Kingsbury and J. E. Dwight, asserted in their prospectus:

> We believe that a newspaper for the Choctaws and Chickasaw people ought to be sustained. . . . We wish to make it a *permanent* paper— useful to the citizens and residents of the Choctaw Nation; and a Channel through which the *people* can communicate with each other on all matters of Public Interest. . . . The paper is designed to be an advocate of *genuine morality*, *sound education*, and *Temperance*, and a source of information in regard to *agriculture*, and the markets, etc., etc., [as well as] history, Indian traditions, manners and customs, and to such other subjects as may be suitably introduced in a Family newspaper. [51]

There followed a request for correspondence from readers for subscriptions, and for other participation in what the editors clearly hoped would be a community venture. The *Intelligencer* carried ads typical of the day: shipments just in from New Orleans and specials on dry goods, saddles, harnesses, groceries, and hardware. Produce was advertised at such prices as: corn, one dollar a bushel; Irish potatoes, seventy-five cents a bushel; sweet potatoes, fifty cents a bushel; eggs, twelve and a half cents a dozen.

Schoolcraft's *Indian Tribes* reported the establishment in 1854 of a weekly newspaper, the *Intelligencer*, at Washita in the Chickasaw Nation. A. J. Hartley of the Chickasaw Nation wrote: "We have a weekly paper of our own, perused by over three hundred subscribers among our own people—a paper brought into existence by Indian enterprise and sustained mainly by Indian liberality." [52] It may not have had a long life or a wide circulation, because the *Chickasaw Choctaw Herald*, which appeared in 1858, announced itself as the first newspaper published in the Chickasaw Nation. The *Herald* was a six-column paper edited by J. T. Davies. Published in English at

Tishomingo City, the capital of the Chickasaw Nation, it carried the slogan "Onward and Upward."

In announcing the paper, Davies and proprietor H. McKinny promised that it would be "what no paper, heretofore established among the Indians, has been . . . a record of the habits, customs, laws and usages amongst the indian [*sic*] tribes" and would be "devoted to Science, Literature, Agriculture, Education, and the advancement of the Arts and Manufacturies among the Chickasaws, and other civilized tribes, . . . as well as news of the day."[53]

The high hopes and noble ideals of the *Herald* were short-lived because Indian journalism was—apparently—halted abruptly in the 1860s. The outbreak of the Civil War forced Indians into another losing situation. Some of the wealthier of them were, or had been, slaveholders. Although their chiefs and leaders had urged a hands-off policy, the common belief fostered in the North was that the Indians were pro-South, pro-Confederacy. It became a handy excuse for those whites who yearned for what little lands and properties treaties had left to the Indians.

During the war years, Indian publications were suspended. After 1865 they would begin again, as the South and the entire nation rebuilt itself. For the time, though, presses were quiet.

CHAPTER THREE

American Indian Newspapers: Post–Civil War to 1960s

Reconstruction in the South was a time for renewed journalistic activity among the tribes there. Printing of the *Cherokee Advocate* was resumed when the presses were returned to Tahlequah. Because the prewar printing offices had burned, the presses were housed in a brick building that was constructed in 1844 to house the Cherokee Supreme Court. The building is still standing. William Penn Boudinot was elected editor of the weekly *Advocate* at a salary of $500 a year. Translators were paid $400 a year. The first issue of the new series appeared April 26, 1870, and Rowell says that circulation in 1871 was 480 for the Saturday publication.[1] The five-column paper continued carrying a substantial amount of material in the Cherokee syllabary.

Advertisements and listings of professional cards were carried in each issue. The June 7, 1873, edition, for example, advertised Joshua Ross, Dealer in General Merchandise; the *New York Tribune*; F. Schurman, watchmaker and jeweler; the advertising agency of George P. Rowell Company; and route schedules for the Illinois Central Railroad. In a self-advertisement in that issue the *Advocate* editor promised:

> the latest information of Indian Matters within the Indian Territory and Elsewhere. The proceedings of Congress in relation to the Tribes will be duly given from Authentic Sources. A Column will be devoted to Agriculture and Stockraising and will be weekly filled with Articles and Items useful to the Farmer and from the Best Authorities and suited to this Climate and Latitude.[2]

A fire leveled the plant and destroyed the presses on December 26, 1874, but in keeping with the symbolism of its predecessor's name, the paper, like the mythical phoenix, rose up virtually from its own ashes. On March 1, 1876, Boudinot reestablished the *Cherokee*

Advocate and reminded his readers of the first Cherokee newspaper. In setting forth his policy, he echoed an earlier Boudinot:

> The *Cherokee Advocate* shall have for its object the diffusion of important news among the Cherokee people, the advancement of their general interests, and the defense of Indian rights; and shall be published weekly, in the English and Cherokee languages; provided nothing of an abusive, personal, or of a partisan character shall be admitted into its columns.[3]

The council also set a one-dollar yearly subscription fee, with the fee to subscribers who read only Cherokee set at fifty cents. Recognizing the need to train typesetters, the council also set aside money to employ young Cherokee males for two-year terms as apprentices.

The *Advocate* adhered to lofty policies, although the behavior of at least one of its editors could be said to have violated them. E. C. Boudinot, Jr., editor in 1887, son of the first editor of the *Cherokee Phoenix*, walked angrily into the offices of the four-month-old *Tahlequah Telephone* to dispute some of the criticisms carried in that paper about him. The resulting dispute left the *Telephone* editor, B. H. Stone, dead of a gunshot wound. Boudinot himself died before he came to trial, but in the interim he continued publishing the *Cherokee Advocate*, issuing in November of that year a series of triweekly "Council Editions." During his editorship Boudinot increased the use of Cherokee to the point that in every issue one full page of the four was printed in Cherokee. The *Advocate* reportage went beyond purely internal matters relative to the government of the Cherokee Nation.

Among the first Indian newspapers to begin publication following the war was one edited by a white man, Thomas O'Bryan, who launched a paper at Fort Gibson (Oklahoma) in 1865. He printed about a quarter of the second page in Cherokee but was "independent of factions or causes, White, Red, North, or South." His four-page *Tomahawk* survived for several years, operating along the following lines:

> The proprietor, like his country being free and independent, and wishing to set an example for his fellow craftsmen, desires it to be distinctly understood that he asks for the support of no man: If you consider the paper worth the money send the cash along and you will

get it—but remember no money, no paper. . . . The Cherokee editions are governed by the same rules.[4]

O'Bryan recognized that Cherokees were interested newspaper readers; like many journalists after him, he took advantage of the market.

In 1872 the Choctaws resumed publishing with the establishment of the *Vindicator*, filling a void in Indian news. While white newspapers carried some columns in Choctaw for the convenience of their readers, their content was alien to the interests of the Indians.

The *Vindicator*, first printed in New Boggy, Indian Territory, moved back and forth between that location and Atoka, interrupted publication for a while, and finally merged with the *Oklahoma Star* in 1877. Its motto was "Devoted to the Interests of the Choctaws and Chickasaws," and it carried the slogan "My people Are Destroyed for Lack of Knowledge."

Late in the first volume it began carrying columns in Choctaw, and its content included advertisements, stories, editorials, anecdotes, advice to the lovelorn, and general local items, as well as news and interpretive articles on major issues confronting the nation. The headlines of one issue are illustrative: A-Tok-A City; Geographical Situation; Prospects for Becoming a Permanent Railroad Depot; Coal Fields and Pine Forests a Source of Wealth.[5] The *Vindicator* favored sectionalism, arguing that the Choctaws would be more prosperous if they owned their properties individually. It also opposed statehood for Oklahoma and the opening of the country to white settlement.

Meanwhile, farther west, the frontier white press was crusading energetically against the Indians, intensifying war fever. In Arizona the press was to help inflame a situation that would end in a massacre of the Apaches at Camp Grant. In Dakota Territory editors would begin demanding vengeance for the Custer debacle. Later on, the Ghost Dance religion, misunderstood and misinterpreted by whites, would lead to the massacre at Wounded Knee. Reports, usually pro-Army, on other Indian engagements further inflamed public opinion and led to anti-Indian decisions in Congress and the territories.[6] In addition to the 1886–87 building of the Atchison, Topeka, and Santa Fe Railroad, the authorized "runs" for territorial settlements and homesteads and the resulting pressures on all sides from and by white intruders forced Indians into militant stances that would be met by further armed violence. But Indian editors kept up the fight. The *Vindicator* took on its adversary, the *Oklahoma Star*. A "Boomer" sheet established by G. McPherson, the *Oklahoma Star* defended the "Oklahoma bills," sensationalized and exaggerated their reports of Choctaw crimes, and pressed with vigor to abolish Choctaw tribal government. Published by W. J. Hemby at Caddo (Oklahoma) in the Choctaw Nation, the *Star* requested that its readers "please keep us posted in regard to thefts, robberies, murders, marriages, deaths, or any other news that may be interesting to the readers of the *Star*."[7]

In 1876 the *Star* was moved to McAlester, and a year later it merged with its opponent the *Vindicator*, which had been having money troubles, to become the *Star-Vindicator*. The new paper's policies toward Indians reflected *Star* policy and often worked in direct opposition to the efforts of Indian leaders. The Reverend J. S. Murrow, editor of the *Star-Vindicator*, gave the paper the motto "Progress Toward Civilization" and listed as distributors the "Missionaries of every denomination in the Indian Territory." Although not pro-Indian, the *Star-Vindicator* carried Chickasaw laws and proclamations. A standing promotional ad promised that the paper would "furnish a medium of information to the five civilized nations of the Indian Territory which they have never before enjoyed."[8] Its profitable advertising section carried ads in the Choctaw language infrequently.

The editor placed paramount importance on Indians making the kind of progress demanded by railroad builders and boomtown developers. In the inaugural issue, January 5, 1876, Murrow wrote:

> To [the *Star-Vindicator*] the Indian people can look as the true exponent of their cause in their upward struggle for progressive civilization. . . . We . . . shall defend them with all the ability of which we may be possessed. We wish, however . . . to be understood as looking forward to an immediate attempt on the part of the Indian people to rid themselves of the reproach of being non-progressive.[9]

Thus he criticized opposition to the opening of the Indian Territory to settlement and of its minerals to development. The next year he offered "Well-Meant Advice" to the members of the Chickasaw legislature with regard to permit taxes levied by the Chickasaws on non-Indians farming in the Chickasaw Nation lands. "You know to whom you are indebted for the fine fields that dot your country from one end to the other," he said. "The white man came in with all the improved implements of agriculture and 'lo, the desert smiled.'"[10] The editor called the tax in question exhorbitant, the result of "an uncalled-for prejudice against a race to whom you are indebted for all you have." He conveniently forgot the forced removal by the federal government forty-four years earlier of Chickasaws from their lands in Mississippi.

In its early months the last page was devoted, sometimes entirely, to what was called the Choctaw Department (Choctaw: *Chahta Anumpa*), edited and translated by Ellis W. Folsom. By 1878 the *Chahta Anumpa* appeared irregularly and with decreasing amounts of space allotted to it. In 1878 the paper advertised itself as "the organ of the Choctaw Nation, and the advocate of progress and a higher civilization. It is published in the center of a rich agricultural region, and is read by Choctaws and white people alike. All its readers are intelligent, industrious, and liberal."[11] The paper continued to publish until 1879.

As if to counter the *Star-Vindicator*, the *Atoka Independent* was started in 1877. A weekly, it was published for the Choctaw Indians by W. J. Hemby; much of the news was in Choctaw and translated into English as well. The *Independent* had substantial advertising revenues, including paid notices for dry goods, wholesale clothing, shoemakers, a steam sawmill, and a new billiard hall. The paper also carried the business cards of physicians, druggists, photographers, and attorneys. Reflecting, as most other frontier Indian papers did, the central role of religion in everyday life, it frequently carried Choctaw translations of hymns. The first months offered little news, but the *Independent* gradually increased its news operation. It was published until 1889, when it merged with another paper.

Meanwhile, it had brief competition from a "Boomer" paper, the *Caddo Free Press*, which was started about March, 1878.[12] Commenting on the *Caddo Free Press*, the *Cherokee Advocate* editor wrote, "The editor of the *Caddo Free Press* is a high-toned gentleman, if he does differ from us a little on the Indian question." The *Free Press* editor answered, "The *Advocate* and the *Free Press* have the same object in view, i.e., the prevention of loss to the Indian people of that which is the dearest of all things, home." [13]

The paper had large advertising sections, well-written editorials, and more local and national news than many earlier newspapers printed for the Choctaw Nation. Although it regularly published the official Choctaw directory and the election returns, Angie Debo writes that the paper was not favored by the Choctaw government, and that its editor "left the Indian country because he incurred the hostility of the Choctaw government by his activities in 1879." [14]

I. W. Stone and Neely Thompson, publisher and editor, respectively, of the *Caddo Free Press*, also issued *Choctaw News* at Chahta-Tamaha, Choctaw Nation. *Choctaw News* was a one-sheet, two-page paper devoted mainly to proceedings of the regular Choctaw Council. Neither Grace Ray nor Carolyn Foreman mentions it in her works, so the *News* may have been in publication only at the time of the council meetings. It carried council minutes as well as such snappy local tidbits as, "Our very efficient Sheriff, J. H. Bryant, is keeping everything quiet and will make it lively for whisky peddlers, if they show their heads." [15]

The October 11 issue reported that the Republicans carried Ohio and the Democrats, Indiana; that the *Caddo Free Press* did "all kinds of Job work on short notice, at the lowest prices"; and that Mrs. B. J. Hampton, who had been "quite sick," was improving.

The next established newspaper in the Choctaw Nation began without a nameplate, because the nameplate was delayed in the mails. *Indian Champion* began in Atoka on February 23, 1884, under the name *Branding Iron*, taken from the many cattle-brand advertisements it carried. The paper was finally named in the fourth month of operation. As the official paper of the Choctaw Nation it had a "Choctaw Department," which was printed in Choctaw in each issue. It ran extracts from letters to the editor, printed church news, local and personal news, school news, and much inspirational material. Advertising at times dominated the front page. Debo says the paper "recorded murders (among the Choctaws) with an unconcern and frequency that is almost incredible." [16] The last issue available in the

Oklahoma Historical Society is dated November 7, 1885, shortly after the Choctaw Nation withdrew its support.[17]

The void created by its demise was filled by perhaps the most important newspaper published in the Choctaw Nation: the *Indian Citizen*. Having purchased several publications, including the *Atoka Independent*, a group of Choctaw citizens began the *Indian Citizen* in 1886 as the only newspaper in the nation. Devoted largely to the interests and concerns of the Choctaw and Chickasaw nations, it was edited by J. S. Standley and Butler S. Smiser. Smiser was a Choctaw citizen by marriage to Standley's daughter. Standley, a Choctaw delegate, was frequently in Washington, D.C., and so could report from the scene. Smiser and his wife acted as editors, and, with the live coverage from Washington, were able to produce a valuable and interesting newspaper. It carried complete summaries of Washington news that affected Choctaws, besides the news of Choctaw government laws, court decisions, and proclamations.[18]

The *Citizen* functioned more as a maker than as a reporter or observer of policy; it also was active in opposing the Indian allotment plan. Debo mentions, however, that, with the increasingly vociferous white population and its support for allotment, the *Indian Citizen* began advocating voluntary division of tribal lands to prevent forced division by the federal government.[19]

The *Indian Citizen* survived well into the twentieth century. It was joined in 1892 by the *Twin City Topics*, which first appeared in McAlester, Choctaw Nation, proclaiming that it was devoted "exclusively to the Choctaw people at large."[20]

The *Cheyenne Transporter*, one of the few newspapers to be published at an Indian agency, was begun in 1878 at the Cheyenne and Arapaho Reservation at Darlington, Indian Territory. A semimonthly publication with, by 1884, a circulation of one thousand, it advertised itself as a journal "overcrowded with home advertisements and will not insert 'patent medicine ads' at any price" and pledged to serve "those who wish to keep posted on Indian and stock news in the Indian Territory."[21]

The *Transporter*, which published until 1886, also gave left-handed compliments to the Indians at the agency in this statement:

"A great change has taken place in the disposition of the Cheyenne and Arapahos to work. It has not been long since it was difficult to get them to work at any price; now they are not only willing but anxious to get employment."[22]

Journalism began later, but with equal fervor, among the Creeks. One influential and controversial newspaper was established by the former editor of the *Cherokee Advocate* in the Creek Nation. *Indian Progress* first appeared October 22, 1975, and in an open letter "To the People" E. C. Boudinot acknowledged the "many questions of vital interest, the character and management of which the masses of the people know absolutely nothing." The *Progress* would try to get out information so that people could make intelligent decisions, it continued, "and not fall an easy prey to scheming demagogues and plausible villains who only live that they may abuse their confidence, plunder their treasuries, and fatten on their substance." It would insist on the rights of every citizen to the rights and privileges accruing to citizenship, would encourage efforts toward a liberal educational system, and would not grind any political ax or allow any favoritism.[23]

In a multicolumn ad that ran the entire length of the third page, the promise was made that "We intend to make the *Progress* the standard of Indian news, so far as it relates to affairs in this Territory."[24] The *Progress* apparently was not welcomed among Indian journalists. A backhanded slap that had appeared in the *Vindicator* was reprinted in the first issue with a response from the *Progress*:

> We look for No. 1 of the *Progress* this week—provided the Creeks don't put a veto on it—*Vindicator*. Never fear, Mr. Vindicator, the *Progress* is not made of the kind of stuff to "veto" worth a cent. If the *Progress* had nothing but the weakkneed support of apparent advocates who are afraid of a shadow or a frown, it might go under.

Again, "Certain parties have been and are yet busy circulating the most mendacious and untrue reports, as to the course that will be pursued, and the objects sought . . . by the publication of this paper." Was it, Boudinot asked, selfish rivalry or fear of exposure that prompted the early criticism? At any rate he concluded, "We are content to await the verdict of the people among whom it is published."[25] The fifteen or sixteen issues published by the *Progress*, before it was suspended by the editors, were full of exciting, somewhat sensationalized news, strong, well-written editorials, and advertising that reflected the flavor of life in Muskogee.

The immediate successor of the *Indian Progress* in Muskogee was the *Indian Journal*, edited by William P. Ross. Its establishment was prepared for when the International Printing Company, made up of Cherokee, Choctaw, Chickasaw, Creek, and Seminole members, was allowed by the Muskogee [Creek] Council to incorporate. This incorporation in 1875 led to the establishment of the *Indian Journal*, one of the most important newspapers in the Creek Nation, and comparable to the *Cherokee Advocate* in significance.[26] Chartered by the Creek Council, the *Indian Journal* was started May 26, 1876, under the editorship of William P. Ross, former *Cherokee Advocate* editor. Its motto was "We Seek to Enlighten," and it carried news in Creek, Choctaw, and English.

The prospectus, published as a full-column ad in several issues, said that the paper would be "devoted to the interests of the Indian race and the Dissemination of Knowledge among them at Home and Respecting Their Conditions Abroad."[27] A major objective was to fight the railroads and their Washington lobbyists, since Muskogee was a strategic point in the first railroad established in Indian Territory. The July 13 issue covered Custer's defeat, using General Alfred Terry's report. The same issue had such departments as "Home and Foreign Gossip," "Fashion Notes," and "News Summary, Personal and Political."

The paper was published daily between October 17 and 20, 1876, for the duration of the Indian International Fair at Muskogee and was thus the first daily newspaper in Indian country. Each issue— printed in English, Creek, and Choctaw and marked "Extra Edition"—was devoted to descriptions of fair activities, ads for local and area hotels and services, announcements of events, and information about exhibits and visitors. The second issue cited the popularity of the daily papers: "The demand for the *Daily Journal* yesterday was unprecedented in the history of journalism." In an 1877 summer issue, the prominent story on page one was "Sequoyah, The Inventor of the Cherokee Alphabet." It was perhaps intended as a reminder of the important fiftieth anniversary soon to occur in Indian country, marking the half-century since the first copy of the *Cherokee Phoenix* appeared.

The *Indian Journal* had moved to Eufaula in 1880, and in 1885 the Creek Council formally resolved to make it the official paper of the Muskogee Nation.[28] It continued to please its readers, maintained a subscription price of $1.50 a year (in advance) and in 1902 reported a readership of five thousand. Advertising abounded, filling most of the front page so that news appeared to be almost a filler around ad copy. There were ads for a bootery, a wagonmaker, a drugstore, a furniture maker, a dry-goods dealer, and others.[29] By 1908 news copy was back on page one, and bold headlines and modern typeface were used with content that included "Notes from Meadow Farms" (timely tips for farmers), "Ventilating the House," "The American Home," and similar items.

The Osage Indians had a newspaper, the *Osage Herald*, which was first issued at the Osage Agency at Pawhuska, Osage County, in 1875. A weekly publication, it came out on Saturdays and carried general local news. One issue contained the 1854 census report, a description of the first female chief of the Osages, an assurance of fat buffalo in the area, and the news that "twenty or more families of Osages are in pursuit of their choicest game."[30]

A Cherokee Nation paper, the *Indian Chieftain*, established at Vinita in 1882, pointed out that it was "devoted to the interests of all Cherokees, Choctaws, Chickasaws, Seminoles, Creeks, and all other Indians of the Indian Territory"[31] and that it was independent and absolutely nonpartisan. Contrary to Cherokee Nation laws that forbade non-Indian ownership of business in the nation, however, it was owned and published by whites, with Indians as nominal editors. Preceded by two unsuccessful newspapers, the *Vidette* and the *Herald*, the *Chieftain* had a wide readership and eventually attracted some illustrious Indian journalists as editors, among them a former *Advocate* editor, William P. Ross, and a descendent of Chief Occonnostolas, Robert L. Owens.[32]

In 1887 an Indian journalist commented on the *Chieftain* in a brief sketch of contemporary Cherokee newspapers:

> At the time the *Journal* became the property of its present owners, the Cherokee nation had two newspapers to which a third has since

been added. Of these, the *Advocate* being a Cherokee national paper was intended to serve only the Cherokee people. The *Telephone* lately established has so far devoted most of its attention to Cherokee politics and other local news. The third paper among the Cherokees, in our opinion the best, is the *Indian Chieftain*, published at Vinita. The *Chieftain* is the only *general* newspaper among those named.[33]

To promote wider readership than was possible with a paper printed in a specific Indian language, the *Chieftain* was printed in English and by 1898 was claiming a readership of more than a thousand. The next year it added a daily edition, with a circulation of four hundred.

The paper dealt with local and national affairs, with business, and with ideas. One issue in March, 1897, contained general news, a major story about an 1893 World's Fair trotting winner becoming available for stud service in the area, and a reprint from the *St. Louis Globe-Democrat* entitled "The Indians Seen in Washington." This latter marveled that the five Choctaws who were entertained in the home of the secretary of the interior were "dignified gentlemen in Prince Alberts" who "not only wore their clothes as if they were used to them, but . . . showed themselves entirely at home in the drawing room."[34] The irony could hardly have been lost upon the readers.

In 1892—a kind of press heyday for the Cherokee Nation—several weekly and daily newspapers were flourishing in Tahlequah. These papers, serving the capital city and circulating throughout the nation and far beyond, included the *Cherokee Advocate* (the official government paper), the *Tahlequah Telephone*, the *Tahlequah Sentinel*, the *Indian Arrow*, and the daily *Capital City News*. Still to come were the *Tahlequah Courier*, the *Daily Capital*. and the *Daily Telephone*, the last printed only during the 1895 session of the Cherokee legislature, in November and December.[35] A brief look at each of these publications will show to some degree the journalistic atmosphere of the Cherokee Nation in the years immediately preceding Oklahoma statehood.

The *Tahlequah Telephone*'s first editor, B. H. Stone, had died following a dispute in his office with E. C. Boudinot, editor of the *Cherokee Advocate*. Established in 1887, the *Telephone* opposed the opening of Indian Territory to settlement and criticized Boudinot and his management of the *Advocate*. Stone claimed to be putting more news and information into his paper at lower cost than Boudinot did. After his death his widow carried on for a time; subsequent *Telephone* editor/publishers maintained the aim of "an Indian Journal; Devoted to the Interests of all Indians."[36]

Little is known about the *Tahlequah Sentinel* except that it was short-lived and was succeeded by the *Tahlequah Courier*.[37] The *Tahlequah Courier*, published by Cherokee Waddie Hudson, was started late in 1892. One issue noted by Foreman reported a robbery of the mail hack from Fort Gibson. The haul was $7.50, taken from registered mail.[38]

The *Indian Arrow*, founded at Fort Gibson by William P. Ross, was owned by a stock company composed of the most prominent leaders of the national political party of the Cherokee Nation. It appeared in 1887 and proclaimed its objectives to be the defense of Indian rights and the diffusion of knowledge, among both Indians and non-Indians, "that the people of the United States might become educated as to the true status of the five civilized tribes."[39] It was moved to Tahlequah in 1890. In 1895 the *Arrow* was leveled in a fire that destroyed much of Tahlequah, but it continued publication until after 1907, when it was renamed the *Tahlequah Arrow*.[40]

The *Capital City News* was established in 1891 as an evening paper to operate during sessions of the Cherokee National Council. A politically independent paper, it was published by the Daily News Company at a yearly subscription price of nine dollars.[41]

The *Cherokee Advocate* maintained its vigilant stance, and on July 25, 1896, Waddie Hudson, editor, commented on the meeting of the International Council of the Five Civilized Tribes set for July 28 for the purpose of forming plans to oppose United States government abrogation of existing treaties. He proposed two courses: "The first and most logical is to fight on lines already explained and advocated and the other course is to make a complete surrender to the boomer and his representative, the Dawes Commission." Taking the first course would require of the leading men, he said, "patriotism, broadmindedness, intelligence and energy, and for this reason, only this class of men should be put forward. If anything is to be done, it must be done on foot quickly and pushed energetically until the fight is won."[42] The same issue contains the full text of an address before the

Indian Territorial Press Association by the acting agent of the Cheyenne and Arapaho Indian Agency. In the address the agent points to the need for outside government of the Cheyenne and Arapaho (and by extension "the Indian") because of the Indian's inability to govern himself.

Just as yellow gold had become a cause of land thievery and dispossession in the 1820s and 1830s, so black gold gave cause for further encroachment by the whites in the 1900s. The *Cherokee Advocate* in 1901 carried formal protests against oil leases. In an open letter from the principal chief that took up most of the front page, the secretary of the Department of the Interior was called upon to refuse the application of the Cherokee Oil and Gas Company for lease renewal, "which in effect would be granting them a new lease and unnecessarily be fortifying their contentions of what they term is a vested right." [43] But the battle lines continued to be drawn, and the Cherokee Nation, like the other Five Civilized Tribes, was divided on how to meet its enemies. Such division affected the *Cherokee Advocate*, in terms of funds, political differences, and the need to meet the interests of a growing non-Indian readership.

The precariousness of the *Advocate* (and other Cherokee newspapers to be discussed later) intensified another concern. Use of the Cherokee language was dependent in great part upon publications using the Sequoyah syllabary. In 1904 only five men could set the type. The fear, generally realized in succeeding decades, was that Cherokee as a printed language would die if the papers were permanently suspended. The Cherokee presses therefore were kept busy. The National Book and Job Printing House at the national capital in Tahlequah printed in English and Cherokee the messages and proclamations of the chiefs, the newsletters from Washington, the minutes of the annual meeting of the Cherokee Baptist Association and of the council meetings, the Cherokee 1880 Census, the tribal political party platforms, and other materials of a national nature. [44]

The *Cherokee Advocate*, the last holdout among the great frontier Indian papers, gradually declined. Its final demise on March 4, 1906, came—as did the loss of lands—by order of the United States government. In December, 1911, J. S. Holden, editor of the *Fort Gibson Era*, purchased the A. B. Taylor Printing Press and the English type formerly used by the *Advocate*. He paid $151. Just a few years earlier the value of the plant had been estimated at $5,000.[45] Two cases of Cherokee type were sent to the Smithsonian Institution. This press, on which from 1876 to 1905 the Cherokee national newspaper and many other publications were printed, was described by the *Daily Oklahoman*:

> Useless, out-of-date, and covered with mould and rust, the plant, type, and fixtures of the old *Cherokee Advocate* . . . was this week sold as junk. With the passing today of all that remains of the old *Advocate*, there passes an institution that perhaps did as much as any single thing toward the uplifting of the Cherokees. It has boasted some of the brightest Indian scholars known to history as its editors. It has preserved peace and it might have declared war. No newspaper ever printed with success, had a policy that was built on as high a plane as was the policy of the *Advocate*.[46]

The press, sold as junk in 1911, is held in esteem today near Tahlequah, at the Thomas Gilcrease Institute of American History and Art, in Tulsa, Oklahoma.

The demise of the *Advocate* was not the end of journalism in Indian country. Many newspapers started before the beginning of the twentieth century continued publishing, and a few new ones appeared. For the most part, however, the first half of the century constituted the "dark ages" of Indian journalism. It was a time of struggling for existence, and its low level of journalistic activity simply reflects that preoccupation.

In the papers that did publish during the period, the great optimism and future orientation that had motivated the earlier papers were gone. Nonetheless, they continued to serve as crusaders and watchdogs. Their names epitomized their roles: *Sentinel, Outlook, Signals*, and others. Some few lasted beyond the decades in which they were born. Most did not, but acted as predecessors for papers published today. All played a role in the emerging consciousness of self and tribe so prevalent among Indian groups today.

The *Cheyenne and Arapaho Carrier Pigeon*, for example, was established on August 15, 1910, at Darlington, Oklahoma, as a hometown newspaper devoted to the "interests and advancement" of the Cheyenne and Arapaho Indians of Oklahoma. A four-page, 8½-

by-11-inch magazine, it carried local news including births, deaths, marriages, visits, reports of farm and garden yields, and so on. It continued publication until April, 1915.

Other and more militant publications came into being around the same time. One, the *Quarterly Journal* of the Society of American Indians (SAI), included works by most of the major Indian writers and scholars. It was published in Washington, D.C., from 1912 to 1916 and was succeeded immediately by another SAI publication, the *American Indian Magazine*, which published as a continuation of the *Journal*, listing the winter, 1917, issue as volume 5, number 4.[47] Both publications aimed at putting into perspective through their thoughtful and at times critical essays the goals and hopes of contemporary Indian America. They were concerned with studying Indian questions and problems in terms of Indians as a race rather than a mere collection of disparate and competing tribes.

At the same time that the *American Indian Magazine* was established, another publication, *Wassaja*, the crusading paper of Carlos Montezuma, was born. In part the result of a split with SAI, and in part the response to the Apache visionary's own concept of journalism, *Wassaja* was started in 1916. Its name meant "signaling" or "the signal," and its slogan was "Let My People Go." Montezuma, a doctor who devoted his life to his people, led the fight for Indian enfranchisement, which came about in 1924. Montezuma used his personal journalistic style to fight for the vote and other Indian civil rights.

Tuskahoman, an "Independent and Indianesque" paper, published "in the interest of the 350,000 Indians in the United States," was started in 1935 in Stroud, Oklahoma. It was an eight-page, eight-column newspaper about Indians and Indian interests, but apparently it was published by non-Indians. It reflected, however, the growing impact that Indian leaders and intellectuals were having upon the consciousness of non-Indian journalists. Translated, its name meant "The Red Warrior," and it maintained a militant, watchful stance.

Other papers begun in 1935 include *Talking Leaf*, still publishing in Los Angeles in the late 1970s and among the oldest existing continuous publications; the *Narragansett Dawn*, established in Rhode Island; and the *Independent American*, published by the Colville tribes in Washington and the predecessor to the current *Tribal Tribune*, which is discussed in a later chapter, as is *Talking Leaf*. The *Narragansett Dawn* was a well-written monthly magazine, published in the interest of the Narragansett tribe. It contained general community news, vignettes on past tribal heroes, announcements of coming events, and such special features as Narragansett words transcribed by a French priest in 1659 and accompanied in the magazine by a pronunciation guide. It also carried poetry and sports reports. In one issue it reported on a track meet and on a silver cup the tribe won for a float entered in the local Chamber of Commerce parade.[48]

The *Indian Speaking Leaf* was started in New Jersey in 1937, followed in 1943 by the *Standing Rock Eyapaha*, established by the Standing Rock Sioux Tribe, Fort Yates, North Dakota.

That same year saw the appearance of *Adhhoniigii: The Navajo Language Monthly*. *Adhhoniigii*, published in Window Rock, Arizona, was printed in Navajo with English summaries. It was suspended in August, 1944, reestablished a short time thereafter, and finally ceased publication in October, 1946, with supplements issued irregularly thereafter. Few publications have published in an Indian language to the extent that this monthly did, and few current periodicals carry any Navajo language at all.

Two different but equally significant Indian publications were established in 1947. One, an individual woman's effort to provide information and encouragement to Indians in California, was *Smoke Signals*, begun in 1947 by Marie Potts, a Maidu Indian whose work will be discussed more fully. The other was the *NCAI Bulletin*, a newsletter of the National Congress of American Indians. As the regular publication of the NCAI, which also issued the magazine *NCAI Sentinel*, it was a crusading paper centered in Washington, D.C., and an important part in the NCAI fight against efforts of the federal government to wipe out Indian reservations under a policy known as termination. The newsletter, an eight-page, two-column publication, reported on work by the NCAI and carried such articles as "Indians of Alaska Betrayed," coverage of the cooperation by the secretary of the interior in Indian timberland seizures, civil-service commission moves to give Indians greater job security, and the problems facing Indian voters.[49]

54

Another *Smoke Signals* was started in Staten Island in 1949, a kind of forerunner of the many current urban newspapers and newsletters serving Indians across the country today.

The next year, 1950, saw the appearance of the *New Cherokee Advocate*. Carried on the nameplate was the message, "Died in 1906—Revived in 1950." The first issue carried the inaugural editorial of the first Cherokee paper and seemed to wrap the mantle of that pioneer about its efforts as it quoted this request:

> Let the public but consider our motives and the design of this paper, which is, the benefit of the Cherokee and we are sure those who wish well to the Indian race, will keep out of view all the failings and deficiencies of the Editor, and give a prompt support to the first paper ever published in an Indian country, and under the direction of some of the remnants of those, who by the most mysterious course of providence have dwindled into oblivion.[50]

Published bimonthly at Tahlequah and Bartlesville, Oklahoma, it lived for four years.

Another newspaper, the *Fort Berthold Agency News Bulletin*, was started at Elbowoods, North Dakota, in 1950. This weekly publication was an 8½-by-11-inch mimeographed paper of sixteen to twenty pages and covered local and area news, art and education, meetings and community comings and goings, stockmen's association elections, and a regular lead article, called "Superintendent's Comments." It was continued until the late 1960s, when the reservation was moved and New Town was established. The paper was succeeded in 1971 by the *Action News*.

Smoke Signals, a bimonthly published by the All American Indian Days Committee in Sheridan, Wyoming, was started in 1954. Other papers established in the 1950s include *Char-Koosta*, established in 1954 in Dixon, Montana; *Ged' Za Dump*, 1955, in Fort Hall, Idaho; *Cherokee Times*, 1954, in Cherokee, South Carolina; *Smoke Signals*, 1956, at Parker, Arizona; *Indian Mailman*, 1957, in Phoenix, Arizona; and *Navajo Times*, 1959, at Window Rock, Arizona.

CHAPTER FOUR

Agency Publications, Then and Now

This chapter focuses on some of the major agency publications from the mid-nineteenth century to the present. Although many of these do not, strictly speaking, qualify as Indian publications as defined in this book, they bear study because they were often, at least in some areas, the only coals keeping alive the spark of tribal and intertribal communication that had been ignited by pioneer Indian journalists. This was particularly true during the first half of the twentieth century—tribal publications were sporadic and often short-lived—when Indians were caught up in an all-consuming fight for survival.

As was the case with early journalism among the Five Civilized Tribes, newspapers and other publications among Indians throughout the country were frequently initiated and encouraged by missionaries and church groups who recognized the power of the printed word and the educational usefulness of the press. Earliest mission efforts focused on publication of biblical and religious works in translation. Their work sometimes preceded publications by Indian tribes themselves and often went far beyond religious topics. According to Debo, such publications were prodigious and resulted, for example, in 30,500 religious tracts published in Choctaw in 1837 alone. Cyrus Byington and Alfred Wright wrote spellers, dictionaries, and grammars, as well as religious books and tracts.[1] In 1845, Samuel Worcester's Park Hill Mission Press published more than 37,000 books and pamphlets—more than a million printed pages. Mostly religious works, they included publications in Cherokee, Choctaw, and Creek.[2]

One of the earliest publications in Indian Territory, and certainly the first all-Indian language publication, was the *Shawnee Sun*, Johnson County, Kansas. In 1841 the Reverend Asher Wright began publishing *The Mental Elevator* (Seneca: *Ne Jaguhnigoageswathah*), a small magazine in the Seneca language. Nineteen issues appeared between 1841 and 1850, printed at the Buffalo Creek and Cattaraugus reservations in New York.[3]

Another publication of the Baptist Mission Press was the *Cherokee Messenger*, printed almost entirely in Cherokee, with a few columns in English. It was started in August, 1844, and continued until May, 1846. An effort to reestablish it in 1858 lasted only a few issues.

The Dakota language soon appeared in print, with the establishment of the *Dakota Friend* (Santee Dakota: *Dakota Tawaxitu Kin*). It was published in Santee Dakota and English and appeared monthly at the Dakota Mission in St. Paul, Minnesota, from November, 1850, to August, 1852.[4] Another Dakota publication, *The Word Carrier* (Dakota: *Iapi Oaye*), appeared in Greenwood, South Dakota, and at the Santee Mission Agency, Nebraska. The founding editor was John P. Williamson, a Dakota missionary, who gave it the magazine format that it retained through most of its existence. The April, 1873, issue, for example, featured a front-page full-color lithograph, two pages in Sioux, and a back page almost entirely in English. It was an instructive magazine as well as a tool for letting benefactors know what was happening at the mission.

The June, 1873, issue, under the headline "Shaking Hands," carried an exchange between the editor of the *Dakota* and the editor of the *Creek Monthly*. The *Creek Monthly* editor congratulated the Dakotas for having "such friends as those who give them this paper." The letter continues:

> We are surprised to see the following in the March number of IAPI OAYE . . . "It is the only other periodical that we know of, any part of which is printed in the native tongue of any American tribe." Has neither the *Cherokee Advocate*, that pioneer of Indian papers, nor its neighbor, the lively *Vindicator*, of the Choctaw, heard of their northern cousin? If they have not, we would be glad to introduce them, but that unfortunately our own reputation with our neighbors is by reputation only.

Iapi Oaye's editor's final comment was, "With a good heart we stand corrected, and stretch out the right hand to our relatives of the sunny south."

The issue carried "Sketches of the Dakota Mission," an ongoing series, as well as Indian agency supply lists in back-to-back Dakota and English, reports on the spring meeting of the Dakota Presbytery, and an informal census report on the Lake Traverse Reservation.

The Niobrara Mission in 1858 issued the first edition of the *Anpao* ("Day Break"), printed mostly in the Yankton Dakota language. It moved to Madison, South Dakota, under the name *Anpao Kin* ("The Daybreak"). Another Dakota publication was begun at the Catholic mission at Fort Totten, North Dakota. *Sina Sapa Wacekiye Taeyanpaha* first appeared in 1892, edited by a Benedictine missionary, the Reverend Jerome Hunt.[5]

While the missionary presses were publishing newspapers ostensibly to serve the Dakota Indians, Dakota Territory non-Indian journalists were publishing a special brand of vitriolic racism. The *Frontier Scout*, for example, established at Fort Rice, Dakota Territory, in early 1865, was edited and published by military officers, and its motto was "Liberty and Union." One typical issue carried a parody of a psalm, in which the Indian was the oppressor and the poor white man the oppressed. Then followed a bitter "story" about the supposed ringleader in "the Minnesota massacre." An editorial, filling all of one page and part of the next, asked "What shall be done with the Indians?" and then proceeded to propose some answers:

> The time to conquer the Indians is to light on their village in winter . . . to catch him at home in the bosom of his family. . . . Men need thinning out sometimes like cornfields. . . . What Indian's life could we offset as of equal value with Lieut. Wilson's? How many Indians could replace the loss of a murdered Jewett, educated in the Athens of America?
> Handle the Indians as you would handle a regiment of undisciplined soldiers. . . . If harsh measures are necessary, and they undoubtedly are, use them unflinchingly; apply the knife in season, and cut out the cancer before it spreads. But whatever the course, let it be steady and uniform; no wavering, no vacillation.[6]

Missionaries tried to counter the spread of such sentiments, both in the United States and Canada. Several publications in Chippewa appeared in Canada beginning in the 1860s. *Petaubun* ("Peep of Day") was started in 1861 at Sarnia, Ontario. An English and Chippewa publication, it was published monthly by the Reverend Thomas Hurlburt. Another, the *Pipe of Peace*, was published from October, 1878, to September, 1879, at the Shingwauke Home in Sault Ste.

Marie, and was an English-Chippewa paper. Kahkewaqonaby, a Chippewa chief whose English name was Dr. Peter E. Jones, edited *The Indian*, at Hagersville, Ontario, from December 30, 1885, to December 29, 1886.

Our Forest Children, a monthly, was started at the Shingwauke Home in February, 1887, and was published at Owen Sound, Ontario, from October, 1890, until the following September. Not until 1896 did Chippewa Indians have a publication in the present United States. In that year *Anishnabe Enamiad* was begun at Harbor Springs, Michigan, by a Franciscan known as Father Zephyrin Englehardt. It was a Chippewa language publication "devoted to the interests of the Franciscan missions among the Ottawa and Chippewa Indians."[7]

The Creek magazine *Our Monthly*, which published between 1870 and 1876, was established at the Tallahassee mission in Wagoner County, Indian Territory, by the Reverend S. W. Robertson. Its purposes were to "give the Creeks parts of the Bible and religious songs in their own language . . . to teach and inform the Creeks."[8] The Creek National Council appropriated funds to finance the publishing of *Our Monthly*, which was printed almost entirely in Creek. The first volume, 1870–72, was handwritten, until the Creek Council donated a handpress for the printing of the publication.

Another influential and widely circulated religious publication of Indian Territory was established in September, 1882. The Reverend Theodore Brewer began *Our Brother in Red* for the Methodist Episcopal Church. In 1883, with a paid circulation of fifteen hundred, it carried news of nearby mission communities, reprints from religious periodicals from across the country, and human-interest articles. Marriages, deaths, church notices, and humor were all treated in regular columns. The publication was changed to a weekly paper in 1887 to meet the increased demands of readers and to accommodate available news and feature material. The paper carried advertisements for schools, railroads, book printers, business firms in the Muskogee area, and regular standing ads for *Our Brother in Red* itself. It was published until about 1900, when it merged with the *Indian Oklahoma Methodist*.[9]

The *Indian Record*, published by the Presbytery of the Indian Territory at Muskogee, Oklahoma, began operation in 1886. It was both a chronicle of mission work among the Indians and an inspirational publication directed toward Indians. It carried translations of hymns and other devotional matter in Cherokee and Creek.[10]

Another Oklahoma publication, the *Indian Advocate*, was started in January, 1889. The Benedictine fathers of the Sacred Heart Mission, Oklahoma, published the paper until the late 1890s. In California the *Mission Indian*, a monthly, was established at the Banning Mission and published between 1885 and 1900.

Between 1894 and 1895 the first newspaper for the Hopis in Arizona was published at the Hopi mission. The *Moqui Mission Messenger* was established by the Reverend C. P. Coe, first in typewritten form and later in printed form.

Other mission publications were established on the west coast of the United States and Canada. The *Youth's Companion*, edited by the Reverend J. B. Boulet, was a monthly magazine for young people, published by the Puget Sound Catholic Missions and written, typed, and printed with the participation of boarding-school pupils on the Tualip Reservation, Snohomish, Washington. The magazine was published between 1881 and 1886.

Kamloops Wawa, a mimeographed Chinook magazine issued irregularly, was published by the Reverend J. M. R. LeJeunne at Kamloops, British Columbia, between 1891 and 1904.[11]

Another British Columbia paper, the *Paper That Narrates*, was printed monthly in the Déné characters designed by the Reverend A. G. Morice and first published in 1891. *Hagaga*, printed in Nass and English at the Aiyansh Mission in British Columbia, was published between 1893 and 1895.

Pro-Indian organizations and Indian rights groups on the East Coast were also getting into the publishing business. The *Indian's Friend*, established in 1888, was published by the New York–based National Indian Association. It was still being published in the 1940s. The *American Indian Magazine*, a publication of the Society of American Indians, was started in 1912 in Washington, D.C. The next year, the *Calumet*, an organ of the Marquette League for Catholic Indian Missions, began publication in New York. It was in print for more than thirty years.[12] *American Indian Life*, published by the

American Indian Defense Association, Inc., was started in June, 1925, in Washington, D.C.

A year earlier the Indian Rights Association, headquartered in Philadelphia, began *Indian Truth*. Initially a monthly, it is today a quarterly publication oriented to non-Indians. Its purpose has consistently been to keep readers informed of current issues in Indian affairs and to acquaint them with the problems of Indians. The current publication regularly includes book reviews, brief news items, original feature material, and resource columns listing individuals and organizations seeking and offering help.[13] Between 1884 and 1935 the Indian Rights Association also issued from Philadelphia the *Annual Report* of the board of directors of the Indian Rights Association.

Bureaucracy a la Mode, an independent newspaper published by Joseph W. Latimer in New York City, took on the bureaucracies encountered by Indians and Indian-oriented groups. His small tabloid was begun in 1924 and published for a few years.[14]

Another publication, the *Little Bronzed Angel*, was started in 1924 at Marty, South Dakota. Produced by the Yankton Sioux Tribe of St. Paul's Indian Mission, it is still in print as a four-page bimonthly paper whose purpose is to keep benefactors informed of mission activities.[15]

In addition to church and Indian interest-group publications written either for or about Indians, journalism among Indian students had a healthy start before the twentieth century. In fact, journalism was stressed in many Indian schools. *Cherokee Rose Bud* and the *Sequoyah Memorial*, described in Chapter 2, were part of the exciting and fertile period of journalism in the Cherokee capital at Tahlequah.

Another early publication, the *Halaquah Times*, was in manuscript rather than printed form, but could be considered a forerunner of newspapers because of its regularity of publication, news content, and circulation of duplicate copies. According to Ray, copies of the paper were handwritten. At deadline time, each student editor made one copy and then had other students at Wyandotte Mission School at Last Creek (Oklahoma) make additional copies. Issues of the *Times* that were published in 1871 carried school, mission, and community news. The paper lasted for at least six years.[16]

Beginning in 1880, the Indian Industrial School at Carlisle, Pennsylvania, published periodicals. *Eadle Keatah Koh*, a monthly, was published from January, 1880, to March, 1882. *School News*, published at the same time, lasted one year longer. It was edited first by a Pawnee student, Samuel Townsend, and then by an Iowa Indian, Charles Kihega. From 1882 to 1887 students at the school published the *Morning Star*; from January, 1888, to June, 1900, the monthly *Red Man*; from August 14, 1885, to July 6, 1900, the weekly *Indian Helper*; and from July 13, 1900 to July 29, 1904, the *Red Man and Helper*, a weekly. Another weekly publication succeeded the *Red Man and Helper* when the *Arrow* was established September 1, 1904.[17]

The *Choctaw School Journal*, which was started in Atoka, Choctaw Nation, in 1891, was a monthly devoted to educational affairs and the Choctaw school system. Most of the teachers in the schools were native Choctaws. All teachers were examined in the Choctaw constitution and in the regular subjects, including United States history and government. Teachers received a salary of two dollars a pupil and were expected to attend frequent teachers' meetings, institutes, and summer sessions. They established the *Journal* as both an extension project and a school public relations venture.[18]

Also established in 1891, the *BIU Instructor* was published for about four years at the Bacone Indian University near Muskogee, Indian Territory. A monthly, it was typeset by one student, Alex Posey, who was apparently its chief contributor. Two years later, also at Muskogee, the *Harrell Monthly* appeared. It was a cooperative publishing venture of faculty and students at Harrell International Institute. A prospectus written ten years earlier had proposed the monthly as one that would be devoted entirely to educational and religious subjects, with no political or sectarian material to be accepted. News from neighboring religious academies would also be included.[19]

The *Indian Guide*, published by Indian pupils of the Wind River Boarding School at the Shoshone Agency, Wyoming, offered its first issue in March, 1896. Another publication, the *Wind River Progress*, appeared at the Wind River Industrial School there in 1908. The *Indian Leader*, the only newspaper for the Haskell Indian Junior College, was started in 1897 at what was then Haskell Institute, in Lawrence, Kansas, as a weekly newspaper.[20] It is still in publication as a bimonthly. Its birth and growth offer an instructive example of Indian school publications.

Haskell's enrollment averages about a thousand but the *Indian Leader* publishes 3,500 copies per issue, with most subscriptions purchased by alumni. As with most Indian publications, copies also go out to the Bureau of Indian Affairs officials, to tribal leaders, and to non-Indians across the country. The *Leader* accepts no advertising, and its entire budget usually comes through BIA funds. It publishes fifteen or sixteen issues during a school year, usually four pages to each issue. The layout, printing, and bindery processing are done by Haskell graphic arts and printing students under the supervision of their instructors.

The *Indian Leader* is more than a collegiate newspaper. It reflects not only the campus life of the current student body but also relevant general information for Native Americans.

Along with the typical college news and reports of campus activities, the *Indian Leader* attempts to showcase Indian history, culture, and opinion. An "Indian History Calendar" is a regular monthly feature that highlights historic events, including such tragedies as Indian massacres by United States Army troops, as well as contemporary themes.

The *Indian Leader* also functions to involve alumni in the life of the college and to provide a forum for Indian students and alumni to present their feelings in the editorials and letters columns.[21]

Beginning in September, 1899, the *Indian Advance* was published at the Carson Indian School in Carson, Nevada. That same year the *Henry Kendall Collegian* was established at Henry Kendall College, later to be named the University of Tulsa. The *Collegian*, edited by Kate White and Anise Sanford, was praised by the *Tahlequah Arrow* as "one of the neatest college papers in the land."[22]

Kendall College News, a monthly, was established in 1904, probably to replace the *Collegian*. It was a news-and-information organ for the college. The *News* also served as an educational tool, with students writing copy, setting type, and working the presses.[23]

Chilocco Farmer and Stock-Grower, "devoted to the interest of Indian education," was a monthly published at the Chilocco Indian

Industrial School, Chilocco, Oklahoma. It was published daily between June and October, 1904, by the Indian Agricultural School at Chilocco, with much coverage of the St. Louis World's Fair. The *Indian School Journal*, printed at Chilocco School, was a monthly edited and printed by students. Like the *Farmer and Stock-Grower*, it was started about 1901. It continued to be published into the 1970s under Bureau of Indian Affairs sponsorship.[24]

The *New Indian*, a monthly, was started in 1903 at the Nevada Training School in Stewart, Nevada. Between June, 1905, and May, 1906, the *Albuquerque Indian* was published by the Albuquerque (New Mexico) Indian School.[25]

Chemewa American, established about 1904 at the Chemewa (Oregon) Indian School, continued into the 1970s, carrying general school news, articles by students, and information of interest to parents and benefactors.[26] *Ganada News Bulletin*, published by the Board of National Missions of the Presbyterian Church, was a glossy eight-page magazine that served the Ganado (Arizona) Mission. Begun in 1935 and discontinued after 1950, it was replaced in 1976 by *Ganado Today*, a quarterly four-page tabloid that included news, art, poetry, and various public relations features. Two other publications, one a college paper, also were originated at the College of Ganado. A yearbook coordinated through the Office of Development and Public Relations, the *Ganado Story*, offered a "record of the academic year for the education institutions located on the Ganado Mission Compound on the Navajo Reservation in Ganado . . . an informational-promotional vehicle designed to tell the story of all the institutions on the historic compound."[27]

Tumbleweed Connection was established at Ganado in 1975 as a four-page monthly. It carried the motto "The Right to Know Is Fundamental" and was the official student voice of the College of Ganado.

At South Side High School in Douglas, Wyoming, students produced the *Indian Paint Brush*, beginning in 1932.

A South Dakota paper, *Woopedah*, was begun in 1934 and continued until 1976. Published bimonthly at Stephan, South Dakota, at Immaculate Conception Mission School, it ceased publication with the transfer of the school's title to the Crow Creek Sioux tribe. A small four-page publication aimed at benefactors and friends of the school, it contained local news, activities of the missionaries, and news items written by students.

Other publications included *Padres' Trail*, a monthly issue at St. Michael's, Arizona, between 1938 and the 1970s; the *Town Crier*, published intermittently, beginning in 1941, at the Zuni Day School in Zuni, New Mexico; and *Wahpetan Highlights*, published at the Wahpetan (North Dakota) Indian school from February 13, 1953, to the 1970s.[28]

Education and agency journalism maintained their importance in the second half of the twentieth century. The publications of Indian groups and agencies tried to meet the needs and challenges of contemporary life, and from the 1950s onward they took a crusading and often increasingly militant stance that reflected both the threats from outside forces and the growing strength and confidence of Indian leadership. Some representative publications are discussed in the following pages.

One of the early Indian-rights publications that would set the pace for crusading and activist journalism in the latter half of the twentieth century was started in 1949. *Indian Affairs*, begun in New York City and later reorganized into a new publication, went to Indians and non-Indians nationwide. It was focused on activities of the Association on American Indian Affairs, on legislation and judicial matter affecting Indians, and on key events and issues related to the survival and well-being of native peoples. Shortly afterward the National Congress of American Indians, formed in 1944 in Denver, Colorado, established *NCAI Sentinel*, a magazine to be discussed in a later chapter, and *NCAI Sentinel Bulletin*, a newsletter that fought the government termination policy beginning in 1953 that aimed at abolishing reservations. Like the first Indian newspaper 125 years earlier, the *Sentinel Bulletin* had an educational and a watchdog role at the time of a life-and-death struggle for tribes.

The climate for crusading Indian journalism was further improved in 1961 with the establishment of the Nation Indian Youth Council (NIYC), an organization dedicated to preserving and enriching traditional tribal communities. NIYC attacks such problems as poverty, employment discrimination, health care, and education. NIYC established *Indian Voices* in 1961 as an activist newspaper that had broad social concerns and carried news of NIYC social-action efforts. It was succeeded in 1968 by *Americans Before Columbus*, which was to report nationally on "what the white media neglect or misinterpret."[29] *Americans Before Columbus* is circulated to every tribal council in the United States and Canada, carrying news of NIYC litigation and doing some investigative journalism often carried in other Indian newspapers. It is published irregularly, more on a "need-to-know" basis than on a systematic time schedule.

One of the goals of the publication in the late 1970s was to help Indian groups deal with the phenomenon of white backlash, a problem that many Indian leaders believed had only begun to be expressed. NIYC attempted to identify the backlash groups and to discover where those groups got their financial backing—and the significance of that backing. Through the pages of *Americans Before Columbus* the editors try to alert readers to the dangers that anti-Indian sentiment holds for tribes and tribal groups.

A similar publication, the *Zuni Legal Aid Newsletter*, was established in 1971 as the official publication of the Zuni Legal Aid and Defender Society at Zuni, New Mexico. This newsletter did on a local level what *Americans Before Columbus* tries to do on a national level. It was an informative, educational, and resources publication that also served as a local legal referral for area Indian residents. Other Indian-issues publications established in the 1970s were *Highlights* (1971), published monthly in Washington, D.C., by the National Tribal Chairman's Association; *Spirit of the People* (1973), a newsletter devoted to Indian child-welfare problems and published by the Association on American Indian Affairs in New York City; the *Northwest Indian Fisheries Commission Newsletter* (1974), from Olympia, Washington; and *Indian Natural Resources* (1977), a New York quarterly of the Association on American Indian Affairs. The last two publications attempt to focus national attention on the facts behind Indian natural resources issues, the actions taken by the courts and government, and the options open to tribes as they formulate strategies and develop conservation programs.

Indian education groups have established several significant publications. Among these are the *Project Media Bulletin*, *Indian Education*, *Indian Education Record*, and *Navajo Area Newsletter*. The *Bul-*

letin was published by the National Indian Education Association in Minneapolis as a continuing study of materials and methods available for use in classrooms. It was the official publication of Project MEDIA (Media Evaluation and Dissemination by Indian Americans), a five-year program funded by the Indian Education Act of 1972 for the purpose of "identifying, acquiring, coordinating, and disseminating evaluations (by Indian people) of Native American media materials." [30] *Indian Education*, also published by NIEA, will be discussed in Chapter 9 on Indian magazine journalism, as will *Indian Education Record*, published in Tulsa, Oklahoma.

The *Navajo Area Newsletter*, originally titled *Navajo Education Newsletter*, retained the strong commitment to education that inspired its establishment in 1971. It was then primarily for Bureau of Indian Affairs employees in the Navajo area, with copies being sent to individuals and institutions interested in Navajo education. It reported special events in the schools, innovations in teaching methods, awards, graduations and other special ceremonies, retirements, enrollment figures, and other news interesting to those involved with some 17,000 students in the Navajo area schools. [31] The change in name occurred with the September, 1977 edition, accompanying a change to a larger size and broader scope that permitted inclusion of news from other BIA branches, representing about 6,000 employees.

Education news also came though the publications issued at high schools and colleges. Sometimes such campus publications are the only Indian papers serving their communities; often they provide Indian students with their first taste of journalism, many of the publications being oriented toward precareer training and recruitment of journalism students. *Rough Rock News*, which began as a mimeographed newsletter in 1966, served the Rough Rock Demonstration School in Arizona, the first Indian school in the United States controlled by the Indian community it served. The newspaper was established to function as both a school and a community newspaper, a characteristic unique to Indian high school journalism. The pattern has no parallel in white journalism. According to the editor, it

> provides a unique view of lifestyle and attitudes of this small desert community that is determined to control its own destiny. Each issue will bring you closer to a people who are committed to keeping their

own language, culture, and identity alive in the face of an increasingly aggressive dominant culture.

The *Rough Rock News* documents the confidence and tenacity of these people whose daily life continues to challenge the values of the dominant society. [32]

The audience of this monthly paper, published during the school year, includes the loyal Navajo community, state and federal politicians, educators, ethnologists, sociologists, American Indian interest groups, "sponsors" of local children, the Bureau of Indian Affairs, and others. It covers school activities, Navajo culture, school-related sports, community news, politics, crime, and "whatever is foremost in the minds of community members." [33] In addition to the work done by the editor and members of the school staff and student body, contributions from community members in either English or Navajo have been encouraged.

Another school-initiated community newspaper is the *Red Times*. It was begun in 1976 as an offshoot of a journalism course taught at Laguna-Acoma (New Mexico) High School under a project called "The Supplementary Course Study," sponsored by the Johnson O'Malley Indian Education Program. The project was initiated because of deficiencies in the education program available to students in the Grants, New Mexico, school system and was aimed at improving offerings relevant to students and their needs vis-à-vis their contemporary challenges. *Red Times*, an eight- to twelve-page tabloid published at New Laguna, New Mexico, has as an audience the inhabitants of the Laguna and Acoma reservations. Its purpose is "to detail the happenings on the reservation, which has heretofore been lacking." Contents include all aspects of education, health, opportunities, job and career preparation, success stories, news of meetings and workshops, sports, editorials, and letters to the editor.

College and university publications have also served a need for their on-campus communities and for alumni and other interested readers. The *Indian Leader*, at Haskell Indian Junior College, Lawrence, Kansas, was discussed in an earlier chapter. Another well-known and widely circulated college paper is *Nishnawbe News*, published by the Organization of North American Indian Students at Northern Michigan University, in Marquette. Established in 1971,

Nishnawbe News is funded by subscription sales, university fees, and contributions of religious organizations. Its prime audience is Native Americans in the United States and Canada, and it aims at increasing awareness of local and national news and events affecting Native Americans, as well as offering a vehicle for Native American expression of opinions, art, poetry, and general-interest articles. It includes Indian-language features, community news, and many photographs.

Other college publications around the country highlighted issues and events that were relevant to their readers but had been overlooked in the pages of the campus press. Some of the papers were more activist than others; some were rather stable financially, and others subsisted on a month-to-month basis with little outside support. In the pages of all these publications, however, and in those of their younger contemporaries at the high school level, was reflected a growing awareness of the editors' Indian identity and a growing dissatisfaction with the status quo as presented (or misrepresented) in the white media. The papers further suggested an increasingly critical media audience among Indians in schools today and a broader base of editorial talent from which Indian community journalism could recruit in the years ahead. It must be acknowledged, however, that only slight credit for successful Indian journalism efforts can be given the schools and departments of journalism on many campuses where the papers publish.

CHAPTER FIVE

The Contemporary Publishing Scene: An Overview

The American Indian press has blossomed into a significant, diversified voice in the past twenty years. Publications in the 1960s and 1970s included newspapers in at least two-thirds of the states, two national papers, scores of Indian high school and college publications, papers by prison culture groups, and several major scholarly and special-interest magazines, as well as print and broadcast news services. The number of newspapers and newsletters changes rapidly, but the list includes a growing number of weeklies, biweeklies, monthlies, and quarterly or irregular publications.

American Indian newspapers and publications, as defined in this book, do not, strictly speaking, include publications produced solely by religious or government groups; however, because papers by these agencies either participated in the pioneer efforts of Indian journalism or filled the void during the early twentieth century, the dark ages of Indian papers, they are touched on here. What they said and where they published are important to the history of the Indian press.

At the same time the list includes some Indian community publications that perhaps should not properly be called newspapers. As we shall see, many newsletters and informal news sheets—the major publishing forms open to groups with small budgets and limited facilities—perform a valuable service in promoting communication among their readers. An impressive number of current newspapers started out as newsletters or mimeographed productions. Some scholars, it should be noted, caution against including new publications on lists of newspapers. Jeannette Henry, of the American Indian Historical Society, for instance, maintains that a paper must have been published regularly for a year before meriting classification as a newspaper.[1]

Among American Indian publications in operation today, some

general patterns are observable, and it is wise to consider these before looking at the individual Indian papers. It is perhaps ironic that the Indian press is almost entirely an English-language press today, although growing numbers of papers are being used to teach tribal languages. Another characteristic shared by most of the papers is that they are anything but profitable business ventures. They usually get their start and often continue to exist through forms of tribal, educational, or governmental subsidy. Some are financially independent, but most are shoestring operations.

Limited funding creates such major problems as erratic publication schedules, erratic formats, and extremely limited staffs. The papers are often crudely (or at least inexpensively) published, some of them mimeographed on legal-sized sheets and stapled together. The most popular pattern for Indian newspapers is the monthly newsprint tabloid of twelve to sixteen pages, closely resembling in format and technical quality many small-town weeklies. Like community and special-interest papers everywhere, many carry small-town gossip and goings-on, recipes, youth activities, weddings, anniversaries and birthdays, graduations, and family visits. In their determination to remain "unbought," many papers carry no advertising. Those with ads frequently limit them to job-related notices or to Indian-owned or -operated businesses. To meet rising costs and make papers less dependent upon tribal subsidies, however, increasing attention is being given to the development of strong advertising programs.

A corollary to funding problems is the isolation of the papers from regional and national news sources, as well as from each other. Efforts to counteract this provincialism have resulted in news services, conferences and training programs, exchanges among newspapers, and experimentation with telex modifications. This sense of isolation and the need for cooperation and support were reflected in a 1974 letter to members of the American Indian Press Association by Harriett Skye, editor of the *United Tribes News* and then president of the association:

> Covering the news in Indian country is a labor of love and wear, reading and running. I know too that those of us in the media are hard pressed financially, often unable to scrape up the necessary funds to

attend meetings, but priority one should be always one of keeping our lines of communication open and sharing with one another as news is happening.[2]

The press association itself grew out of this need to open lines of communication among Indian journalists. Its role in American Indian journalism of the 1970s will be discussed in a later chapter.

Another general characteristic of Indian publications is that the objective reporting purportedly practiced in the established white press is often lacking in Indian newspapers. Stories are written from the Indian point of view, often unabashedly opinionated. Editorials, reader-input columns, and editorial cartoons leave no doubt as to the writer's bias or the paper's stand on issues. But growing numbers of Indian journalists in newspaper seminars and conferences now are calling for more objectivity and professionalism than they find in many publications. Growing numbers of Indian journalists from some of the country's leading Indian newspapers have stressed this need to change. Speaking to their fellow editors at journalism workshops throughout the country, they have been stressing the importance of thorough reporting, intensive research (especially in dealing with complicated issues), and careful analysis in the writing process.

American Indian newspapers still have an acknowledged special mission that they alone can fulfill: correcting or putting into perspective the Indian news that is covered—or ignored—by the majority media. Since much of this altering of perspective directly contradicts the prevailing myths or stereotypes about Indians, the Indian perspective itself is often read as biased or unobjective.[3] During an Indian journalism conference, for example, Richard La Course, regarded by many of his peers as a major leader in Indian journalism, called the newspaper "a vehicle of Indian intelligence," born out of need and needed more than ever today.[4] La Course, a Yakima-Umatilla and former editor of the *Yakima Nation Review*, acknowledged the danger that journalism, especially in tribal publications, might degenerate into a training ground for political life. This danger is a real one, because so many of the editors become involved in the political issues and, like their non-Indian counterparts, can be lured into higher-paid, more secure positions. Too many instances of this could lessen the credibility of the papers among the readers they serve. La Course called for *objectivity*, not *advocacy*, in Indian journalism, echoing growing numbers of his colleagues.

According to La Course, areas of interest need to be built into the Indian newspaper's organization for regular treatment. These include legal affairs, education, health, politics, entertainment, local personalities, politics, tribal society and culture, intertribal cultural news, the interracial environment (reservation borders are peripheral zones of violence), and government.

Government news coverage is divided into the areas of tribal government, county government, state government, and national government—beyond the coverage of the Department of the Interior.

Interest in heritage is another characteristic of the newspapers. More and more they feature photographs and stories dealing with tribal traditions and legends; they also emphasize coverage of council meetings and efforts to reestablish pride in the Indian heritage. Growing numbers of papers act as preservers and teachers of tribal languages. In some cases these languages have only recently been developed into written form. The papers, dedicated to survival of tribal identity and pride, are catalysts for more than physical or political well-being, important as these are. Indeed, D'Arcy McNickle sees the newspapers as the decisive force in bringing into being an enduring policy of self-determined cultural pluralism.[5]

Another general characteristic of the papers is their promotion of the welfare of Native Americans. Sometimes they function as alternatives to the white-oriented press, but often they are the only papers read by their communities. Consequently they tend to be cause-oriented, frequently conducting gutsy, irreverent investigations into situations that affect Indians adversely in their relationships with the white-establishment society and its power structures.

One editor described the role of communication and the communications media in Native American communities. Calling communication "the most powerful and essential tool with which to protect all which can so easily be buried by the plow of progress," she pointed out neglect of Indian concerns by the mass media.[6] Investigative reporting of these concerns requires money and journalistic skills, unavailable to many small Indian communities, she said, and "well-heeled" media corporations have provided, at most, superficial coverage of Indian problems:

> Because it is primarily a business—and secondarily a means of communications—American journalism has developed most fully in areas which affect, or are of interest, to most people. However lamentable to isolated minorities, this is basically a healthy fact of journalism, enabling it to remain free of outside influences. . . . Indian population is scattered mostly in sparsely populated areas. Indians are not, therefore, a significant market for newspaper sales or for advertisers in the more powerful and competent media of this country. . . . Coverage of news affecting and about Indians has been sporadic, overall incompetent, and does not hold promise for much future improvement by the general media. Many areas of government . . . have had a fairly free rein in actions relating to Indian tribes, without most of the checks and balances normally provided by a vigilant press.[7]

La Course underscored the fact of non-Indian media misrepresentation:

> I think the central problem, as defined both by Canadian and American Indian people, is that nobody really understands what the special citizenship status is of Indians. Hence we have ignorance . . . stereotypes . . . racism. These problems cause the loss of Indian land and create deep human havoc in Indian families, resulting in all the psychological and social woes which we know that Indian people suffer.[8]

He said that journalism needed to "direct a flow of information to Indian people," empowering them to make wise decisions affecting their future. And a broadcast journalist added, "I think that communication is probably one of the most important occupations for Indian people in the future."[9]

The conviction, as La Course noted, is shared by Indians in Canada as well. The editor of *Indian News* wrote, in 1977: "The emergence of Indian journalism has been developing slowly but surely. Entering like a lamb—meek, shy, often 'squeaking along'—it is evolving into a real voice of the people. It is, admittedly, however, having a very difficult birth."[10]

Partly because of its developmental problems, and partly because of its wish not to ape the failings of the white media, much Indian journalism ignores longstanding white journalistic traditions.

Style, format, and approaches to reporting reflect both the lack of training of staffs and the need to look Indian. Many editors, Indian or non-Indian, are untrained or inexperienced in journalism, although some have worked for other newspapers or held various other media-related jobs. Extensive research across the country showed that in the mid-1970s a major proportion of editors of Indian newspapers were non-Indians.

The need to hire non-Indians as editors and staff people is directly related to the lack of visible incentives for young Indians to pursue journalism as a career. The pay is abysmally low. Tribes, in most cases, do not or cannot allocate competitive salaries that would attract top editorial talent. So the incentives to long hours of thankless work must be related to something other than money. Most editors interviewed in the mid-1970s said that they had few successful role models to hold up to young Indians making career choices. The powerful papers these young people might read carried no Indian bylines and had no Indian editors. The broadcast outlets they watched featured few if any Indians. Editors accused the white-dominated media and educational institutions of the same lack of interest in prospective Indian journalists as they demonstrated in regard to the needs and problems of Native Americans generally.

A forceful editorial in the *United Tribes News* once argued that the press was a "wellspring of power" and that good Indian journalists were needed to direct this power. It read in part:

> We need diligent, trained Indian journalists on reservations and in urban Indian centers to report in depth the problems stifling Indians and Indian tribes, problems which the established press skates over or smilingly ignores. We need the pressures and strength [that] objective, cogent Indian journalism can bear on those officials in positions of authority.[11]

At least one journalist has traced part of the responsibility for recruitment of Indian journalists directly to tribal leaders. Tanna Beebee, a product of the minority broadcasting internship program of the Columbia Journalism School, frequently urged tribal leaders to encourage young Indians to get into journalism and to get some training themselves in the basics of the media, so that they could cope in a more adequate way with representatives of the white media.

Discouraging as the current picture may seem to some persons, other Indian journalists are optimistic. Frank Ray Harjo, addressing the American Indian Press Association annual meeting in 1974, said, "I think that . . . there's a new confidence and a new desire to speak the truth in a very comprehensive fashion with the confidence that today it will actually be heard." [12]

In keeping with the special mission of the newspaper in Indian country, editors often are actively in the news they report. This involvement can be demonstrated by watching the career of one newspaper, established in 1974 and replaced by another in 1976. *A'tome*, published by the Northern Cheyennes out of Lame Deer, Montana, was a crusading biweekly paper that took on religion, traditional education, and government land deals. It was begun as a free-distribution publication with a Teacher Corps grant. Later it was tribally funded, with press-run costs covered by revenues from ads. In a rationale drafted to support fund-raising requests, the editor spelled out the paper's objectives:

> 1. To meet the threat of strip-mining with communications.
> 2. To encourage in all ways the retaining of tribal cultural values. To strengthen the human individualism inherent in such traditionally stable social systems.
> Auxiliary objectives include the following:
> 1. Establishing a viable business for the economic benefit of twelve reservations—both in profits of the business and jobs it will provide.
> 2. Training of Indian people for jobs in specialized communication fields.
> 3. Improving personal communication ability for people being trained professionally, as well as among the general Indian leadership.
> 4. Information is a powerful weapon . . . to provide as much of this as possible in any field affecting the well-being of people.
> 5. Improving the future lot of Indian people by interceding and promoting greater understanding and sympathy among the general public. [13]

With some modifications to meet the particular problems and needs of particular Indian tribes and communities, these objectives still ring true for most Indian publications.

A'tome also did investigative reporting in such areas as alcoholism, stock-grazing rights, the inadequacies of penal and rehabilitative systems, violations of Indian civil rights, and ecological damage threatened by pending coal and water rights decisions. In 1975 the editor wrote:

> Some estimates project an influx of 400,000 people on and around the now-isolated Northern Cheyenne reservation. Cheyenne population is now under 3,000. What will happen . . . to the chokecherries women still pick to make pudding . . . Where will a man go to pray at sunrise? . . . Applying standarized yardsticks to such areas as sanitation, for example, will mean the end of dried meat as Indians know it. And yet, for hundreds of years, the Cheyennes have been curing meat in this way (thinly sliced, air dried) using it as a dietary staple, while enjoying physical well-being.[14]

A'tome focused heavily on the welfare and activities of young Indians and on the quality of education. Profiles of teachers and accounts of school athletic events were carried in each issue. Readers were also informed of curriculum and program developments at the schools, of who was attending what college, and of the achievements of individual students. The paper was actively involved in discussions about the propriety of the begging letters sent by a religious order running a reservation Indian school and about who should control the school.

Financial problems in 1976 closed the paper; it was replaced shortly afterward by a new publication, *Tsistsistas Press*, about the same size and with many of the same investigative, participatory, and activist qualities of its predecessor.

One major issue, and one that still confronts Indian newspaper editors today, was addressed in the 1968 Indian Civil Rights Act. This document contains a fundamental guarantee of freedom of the press for Indian tribes, as carried in the United States Code. It states that individual tribes are not allowed to make or enforce laws prohibiting freedom of religion, speech, press, and so on. It emphasized that freedom of expression within reasonable limits excising obscenity, libel, and slander applies to all people, whether or not they happen to live on or off reservations. Countering some arguments, the document stated:

> The inclusion of free speech, press, and assembly in the Indian Bill of Rights has caused many tribal spokesmen to complain that these

principles are not part of traditional culture and should not be applied to Indian society. They have argued that tribes are not ordinary governments, but are close-knit, familylike groups, and that the exercise of free speech in this atmosphere would lead to the disruption of discipline and the breakdown of tribal life.[15]

Congress, however, decided that Indians should be entitled to the same freedoms as other Americans and banned tribal governments from wholesale infringements on freedom of expression. According to the document, a tribal government could not prohibit the distribution of a newspaper it disapproved of or prevent assemblies for the purpose of expressing opinion.

As noted earlier, however, many tribal governments subsidize newspapers. Tribal councils or governments hire (and fire) editors. In addition Indian journalists are aware that the tribes they serve are under siege from many groups outside the tribe: landowners fearing Indian sovereignty and land-title claims, white Americans mistrustful of people they neither know nor understand, United States government moods and whims that could affect tribal lands and futures. Journalists also recognize that persons in any kind of authority are sensitive to the images of themselves that appear in the media. There is a tendency among Indian leaders to consider the Indian newspaper more as a house organ for the tribes than as a medium for exchange and analysis. For this reason, among others, there have been incidents of tribal governments firing editors for critical reporting or seizing whole press runs because of controversial contents.

Editors around the country have acknowledged the tension they experience between free expression of ideas and loyalty to the good name and best interests of the tribe. When tribal leadership (or segments within a group) need to be criticized, many editors admit to being torn between self-censorship and the concept of a free marketplace of ideas. As one editor said: "Yes, this is a mouthpiece for the tribe. Maybe I'm knuckling under sometimes, but when you think of the greater good, you do it."

Another editor, whose paper was controlled by the board of directors of an intertribal corporation, said in an interview, "When it comes to leading strong campaigns, we must tread very carefully." The paper was discontinued not long after the comment was made.

On the basis of this brief overview we can turn to a consideration of some of the specific publications that make up the contemporary American Indian publishing scene. For purposes of organization only, in the following chapters they are divided into four categories: (1) national publications, (2) tribal and intertribal publications, (3) regional publications, and (4) magazine, special-interest, and agency publications. The picture is current only through 1978; the needs of each community continue to change quickly. What follows is simply a cross-sectional look at Indian journalism at one point in its varied history.

CHAPTER SIX

National Publications

Indian journalism in the late 1970s was epitomized in two national publications, *Wassaja* and *Akwesasne Notes*. Because the papers and their editors have often differed in approach to news and current issues, they offer a view of varying philosophies among Indian peoples. They also represent both ends of the financing spectrum of Indian publications.

Wassaja, an urban-based paper edited and written by experienced journalists and researchers, was associated with the Indian Historian Press, publishers of the *Indian Historian*, a respected quarterly journal. *Wassaja* was not initiated by or associated closely with any individual tribe or group of tribes. Developed from its first issue as a professional national newspaper, it always had a healthy financial base.

Akwesasne Notes, on the other hand, was established as the official publication of the Mohawk Nation largely because of the need among Mohawks in New York and Ontario to be apprised of specific governmental policies that could have adverse effects on them. The paper grew almost by accident into a national militant and activist publication. Reservation-based, it has concentrated heavily on reservation-related problems. It has been accused at times of being an arm of the American Indian Movement, of publishing slanted and sensational articles, and of being nonprofessional. The paper's staff viewed itself as being motivated by causes rather than profit, and the financial base of the *Akwesasne Notes* has been (by most publishing standards) shaky.

Wassaja

Wassaja, published in San Francisco, has been a monthly publication with a circulation of more than eighty thousand. It has promoted self-determination, education, and Indian rights. It has dealt with such major national news affecting Native Americans as water and land rights, treaty violations and other Indian legal matters, education of youth and adults, and activities of the Bureau of Indian Affairs. It also has covered native history and culture, the works of significant Indian scholars and artists, and Indians in the news because of specific controversies.

Wassaja's first issue, in January, 1973, urged Indians to "inform yourselves about your water rights." It called on urban Indians to "mount a campaign of information to the public, to the press, radio, television." As an object lesson in why such a campaign was needed, it explained one currently threatening problem:

> Loss of water will destroy Indian land, culture, and economy. The San Juan–Chama Project diverts water from the Navajo river, dumping it into the Rio Grande for the use of non-Indians, to the detriment and utter destruction of the Indian tribes. . . . all these have been perpetrated by local and federal governments, by big ranching interests and sub-division speculators. This has been done with governmental connivance and governmental refusal to act as responsible agents for the Indian tribe.[1]

The next issue provided the reader with a map of the areas concerned.

Wassaja editor Rupert Costo started his journalistic career as a youth apprenticed to a small community newspaper. His wife, Jeannette Henry, editor of the *Indian Historian Press*, was a veteran of newspaper and public relations work. They frequently urged cooperation among Indian newspapers and journalists, pointing out problems facing the Indian media. Good newspapers were needed across the country, but few professional Indian papers existed.

In an advertisement in a 1975 issue the editors wrote that the paper covered current news with an understanding of historic and cultural background. They went on: "Know about education, economy, legislation, the arts, health, the beauty and literature of the Indian world. The Indian learns about Indian life through *Wassaja*. He learns how to cope with modern life by reading how other tribes manage . . . through *Wassaja*."[2]

From the start *Wassaja* worked to live up to its name, which means "the Signal," and was dedicated to Dr. Carlos Montezuma, who early in this century fought for Indian rights and was credited with eventually winning Indian suffrage in 1924. Montezuma, an activist publisher, had started a short-lived paper, also called *Wassaja*, that called for Indian unity in the suffrage cause. The original paper carried the slogan "Let My People Go." Today's *Wassaja* altered that slogan to read: "Let My People Know." On one extremely crowded letter page, the editor suggested that perhaps the paper's slogan should be changed to "Let My People Speak."[3]

Costo pictured Montezuma as an activist publisher who "showed the world that Indians can become doctors, engineers, scholars, and who demanded self-determination for the Native Americans." Costo continued:

> It was Carlos Montezuma who started a broad water struggle on behalf of his tribe, the Mohave-Apache, as well as the Pima and Papago people. He was able to stop the selling of the Indian land and water for more than 15 years . . . Wassaja, the Chicago doctor who visited his people frequently, who fought for them, who set an example for them in their struggle for the right to live. . . . Around this man, in his day, there were developed many groups of fighting Indian people, from southern California to Arizona. They called themselves "the Montezumas."[4]

And of Montezuma's followers he said, "These Wassaja people believe that holding on to the reservation is as sound an idea as it was when Wassaja fought for it." Carlos Montezuma's Indian name was Wassaja, and the current newspaper had, in its content and orientation, modeled itself after his activism. Costo may have been thinking of Montezuma as well as the Indian people whom he as a journalist wants to inform and motivate, when he wrote: "Today, perhaps, groups of Wassaja Indian fighters should take up the fight for the right to self-determination, not only for a better life for our people, but also for the continued existence of Natives as a race, as a culture, and as a people."[5]

The first issue of the paper set a tone of aggressive reporting with its major story, an article about water rights headlined "Indians Face Genocide." An editorial in that inaugural issue underlined the *Wassaja* philosophy: "We want, we need, and we must have decision-

making power on all levels: planning, training, organization, direction, and evaluation of our government, our programs, our funds,
and our lives . . . today, and in the future. *Wassaja* is dedicated to this
goal."[6] It went further in 1976, commenting on the performance of
the mass media in their approach to Indian problems and the role that
Indians must play in correcting such stereotypical concepts:

> Mass media have the ear of the general public, and even most of the
> Indian people. They are propagandizing their own brand of policy and
> approach to Indian issues. Should the Indians ignore them? If we do,
> we risk everything. Because the moulding of public opinion depends
> upon accuracy and factual information. Editorials represent the posi-
> tion of newspaper owners, the radio and television owners, and gener-
> ally the upper echelon of dominant society.

Wassaja invited the readers to respond to these editorials.[7] A fighting,
investigative newspaper, *Wassaja* has carried information on wrong-
doing, named names, and faced issues.

In 1974 the American Indian Press Association (AIPA) gave
Wassaja the Marie Potts Journalism Achievement Award, the highest
honor in Indian journalism, for its investigative reporting of a California organization gathering money in the name of Indian newspapers without any apparent benefit accruing to those papers. The
AIPA said of *Wassaja* that its investigative reporting "laid bare an area
of exploitation little known and never before examined by an Indian
newspaper, and received wide reprinting by other Indian editors,
thereby widening the impact and influence of the investigation."[8]

An activist newspaper, *Wassaja* had activist editors. Not content to report on the news, the editors were sometimes involved in
making the news. Such was the case when they published a landmark
study of books on American Indians, a study of Indian history, social
studies, literature, and related textbooks used in Indian schools and
elsewhere.[9] The study took on some established favorites as well as
new works that claimed to make use of new findings and research.
They found error, distortion, and misinformation similar to those
criticized in earlier parts of this book. *Wassaja*, in a regular feature,
kept a running report on new titles, publishing criticism and some
praise.

In another example Costo, as president of the American Indian

Historical Society, called for a full-scale investigation of violations of Indian treaties. His demands were covered as a news story in the April–May, 1973, issue. This was followed by a special eight-page supplement titled "Indian Treaties: The Basis for Solution of Current Issues." The supplement was so thorough as to include the names of all those who signed an 1869 treaty. In January, 1976, the paper's lead story reported a fire that claimed two lives in the San Francisco Indian ghetto. An investigative, interpretative piece, it described the building as it existed before the fire and continued: "Hugging forlornly close by are stores, light industry, garages, and the ever-present bars. The building contained the lives of people who somehow managed to survive, making the best of a rotten deal." [10] Also featured in the same issue was an angry, critical story about the excavation of Indian grave-sites by anthropologists and relic hunters. Another issue that same year reported on continuing investigation into a fake Indian publication and a supposed media employment agency charging exorbitant fees and producing no results for the job-seeking Indians it purported to serve.

Besides reporting on issues and problems rarely and poorly treated in the white press, *Wassaja*'s editors are trying to improve the journalism profession. Costo and Henry see a dearth of trained Indian journalists and an implied refusal by media and schools to do anything about this situation. A goal of *Wassaja*, therefore, has been to serve as a training ground and a kind of apprenticeship program. Another aim has been to "set an example of what could be done" if tribes or groups committed themselves to the development and support of good newspapers. In addition *Wassaja*'s editors acknowledge the need for a national news service and a good national daily newspaper for Indian Americans. [11]

The intent to share information with other papers and to promote communications among Indians across the country was demonstrated in a policy spelled out in one issue of the paper: "Indian newspapers and periodicals are welcome to reprint materials and information from *Wassaja*. We ask only that you credit this paper." [12] Indeed, this sharing and use of information has been crucial to several smaller publications. Papers without the staff and contacts built up by such experienced newspapers as *Wassaja* need the help—and frequently reprint articles in their entirety.

Wassaja, as a part of the American Indian Historical Society, has also participated in the International Work Group of Indigenous Affairs, which provided news of Indian people in South America and other countries with significant Indian populations. This small news service was centered in Copenhagen, Denmark.

Low staff salaries have helped the paper, an attractive tabloid, to be self-supporting. No public advertising and no public funds have been solicited or accepted by *Wassaja*, although the latter were available to it. According to Costo, such a policy was pursued to ensure the absolute independence of the paper.[13] Advertisements in the early issues were mainly for publications put out by the Indian Historian Press. Since June, 1974, ads have been expanded to include employment opportunities, educational grants, fellowships, Indian-related services and products, and so on.

Circulation started in the first issue with fifty thousand, but the second issue claimed eighty thousand, and that figure held constant for several years, although some subscription data have cited a figure of sixty thousand. Initial circulation efforts relied on reader contact: "If you will send us the names of friends or those who you think should receive *Wassaja*, we will be glad to send them a complimentary copy of this newspaper. Indian tribes and organizations receive *Wassaja* free."[14] Subscription rates were set at ten dollars a year, with a special fee of five dollars for Indians who could not afford to pay more. The paper was the hub of the Indian Historian Press, which has published twenty-five books to date. But it had frequent difficulties reaching its readers or potential readers. According to the editor: "*Wassaja* has been unable to get on the news stands. Nor will stores, airports or other mass circulation areas accept an invitation to carry the paper at *any* price."[15] The editor also cited difficulties with the Internal Revenue Service and with various postal agencies that "held up delivery for more than a month, and regularly 'lost' bundles."[16] Their complaints mirrored those of other editors in several parts of the country.

Akwesasne Notes

"We never intended to start a newspaper," wrote the editor of *Akwesasne Notes* in the paper's fiftieth issue.[17] The national publication began as an 8½-by-14 inch offset reproduction of clippings reporting on the December, 1968, blockade of the international bridge between Ontario and Cornwall Island, New York, the major site of the Mohawk Reservation. Editors were protesting Canadian restrictions against free border crossing for native peoples, guaranteed by the Jay Treaty. The bridge divided the reservation, and so in effect native peoples were being penalized for moving about on their own property.

The first few issues—circulation was nine hundred—were put together at the Antioch-Putney Graduate School, in Putney, Vermont. The next base of operation was an old mobile home that doubled as a traveling van, allowing staff members to visit subscribers and get firsthand information for articles.[18] Then *Akwesasne Notes* moved to a combination home and barbershop, and finally into its first permanent quarters, an old house in Hogansburg, New York.

According to the founding editor, Jerry Gambill, its early days were disrupted by various harassment techniques. One such, a night raid in which bricks and bottles were thrown, was apparently motivated by anonymous accusations that the paper was recruiting Puerto Ricans and blacks for a massive takeover of the reservation. The IRS and FBI put the area under surveillance, and Gambill (renamed Rarihokwats when he was adopted as a citizen of the Mohawk Nation) was arrested in 1969 by a task force composed of the United States Border Patrol, state troopers, and Indian police. He was jailed, refused bail, charged with illegal entry into the United States, and threatened with deportation.[19]

Rarihokwats, whose Mohawk name means "He uncovers buried facts," was a citizen of Canada who came into this country to work with the Mohawks on Cornwall Island. Court decisions eventually allowed him to remain in the United States working with *Notes*. He left the paper in 1977.

The same postal problems that had afflicted *Wassaja* also beset *Notes*. Of a series of mailing conflicts in 1973 the editor wrote:

> All of this occurred at a critical point in native history—the story

of what really was going on at Wounded Knee, 1973, did not get into the mails until early April when postal officials confided that the application (for mailing privileges through the two new sponsors) was in the Postmaster General's office, and pressure by several senators shook it loose.[20]

The mailing problems in 1973 did not end the paper's experiences with disruptive efforts. In 1976 several instances suggested that the activist newspaper was still recognized as a fighter for unpopular causes and peoples and a target for harassment. In one instance an anonymous letter was published in *Nishnawbe News* of Northern Michigan University, the largest Indian-student newspaper in the country. This letter, apparently planted, bore what *Notes* editors saw as the earmarks of the FBI's COINTEL program or the CIA's Operation Chaos, designed to cause disruption, destruction, and possible violence in groups considered by the agencies to be subversive or dangerous.[21]

According to the letter, *Akwesasne Notes* was a communist organization, peopled with drug pushers who were living off welfare and, through the paper, making money that they were saving up so that they could leave for Russia. In another instance a free-lance investigative reporter for a *Notes* article was the object of an unsigned letter accusing her of treachery against the American Indian Movement and urging that she be assassinated to prevent further damage—and to punish her. Similar letters were sent to the *Notes* staff, who in turn sent them on to United States senators for action.[22]

The paper's growing circulation brought an increase in the number of pages in each issue and reflected its sophistication and nationwide prominence as a fighting, alternative paper. From the original 900 in 1968, circulation jumped to 7,000 in 1969, 18,000 in 1971, 56,000 in early autumn, 1973, and 81,000 in early summer, 1976.[23]

Readers were asked to send in stories with photographs on events across the country, which would help cut production costs, and to sell the paper at powwows and other Indian events. These hawkers could sell the paper for fifty cents and then return thirty-five cents to *Notes*, paying only for those papers actually sold.

Akwesasne Notes has been the center of a growing publishing operation that has included native calendars, books, posters, and pamphlets. These publications helped support the newspaper, which has been circulated free of charge.

Besides the publishing work, paper and staff were supported through sales of herbal smoking mixtures, stamps and buttons, and records and tapes of Indian music. *Notes* also acted as distributor for basketry and artworks executed by artists in Akwesasne, New York, and in other areas. Contributions from readers constituted the mainstay of the paper, however. Some were small, some large, like that a Connecticut woman who donated land and a house in the Adirondacks. Some readers gave time, equipment, or small items. Except for university mailing sponsorship, staff insurance coverage, and subsistence costs for one staff volunteer paid by the United Methodist Voluntary Service, the paper was independent of outside grants. In 1978, however, it told its readers that the Youth Project of Washington, D.C., a public foundation under the Internal Revenue Code, had "agreed to take *Notes* under its wing as a research and educational project," thereby giving tax-exempt status to monetary contributions.[24]

Part-time helpers, Indians and non-Indians, have come to Akwesasne from around the United States and from other countries to supplement the efforts of the paper's volunteers. They help with correspondence, filing, mailing, and other small but time-consuming tasks. Others help with planting, harvesting, woodcutting, spring cleaning, construction, painting, and similar odd jobs necessary to support the *Notes* community.

The staff gardens provide food for the commune at Akwesasne, and its column "How It Is with Us" notes its progress, prospects, and problems. Under this column the staff includes lists of things it needs and hopes that readers can donate: tools, lamps, snowshoes, a 35mm camera, the services of an attorney. The motive was to set up a way of living and sharing that was rooted in traditional Indian ways of life. The sharing has gone both ways. In the summer of 1976 the *Notes* staff gathered volunteer farmers, carpenters, technicians, and other helpers, along with supplies and money, for a June caravan to Guatemala. Their mission was to assist in planting and general recovery work in

San José Poaquil, a Cakchikel pueblo of Guatemala, following the devastating earthquake in that country. *Akwesasne Notes* suspended operations for the summer, and most of the staff traveled to Poaquil in an effort initiated and funded by *Notes* and its traveling communications group, then called White Roots of Peace. Renamed Voices from the Earth in 1977, the group, numbering between six and sixteen persons, traveled cross-country twice each year, conducting seminars and workshops, craft shows, film screenings, and cultural presentations and logging more than 400,000 miles as of autumn, 1978.[25] The group's activities mirror the crusading, activist nature of the paper, openly biased in favor of the rights of Indians.

Notes reports on the efforts of the American Indian Movement and other causes and on the violation of treaty rights and other injustices suffered by Indians today. Stories rarely found in the white press informed readers about harassment and atrocities visited upon Indians in South Dakota, efforts by militant or activist white groups in Montana to quash Indian land claims, and international disregard of large-scale mercury poisoning on reservations in Ontario.

Akwesasne Notes has been accused of being an arm of the American Indian Movement, partly because of its heavy coverage of AIM activities in the mid-1970s. The editor commented in response:

> Some readers assume that *Notes* is an American Indian Movement newspaper. True, we have printed lots of news about AIM, but unless the movement of native peoples has an independent critic, it cannot grow. Furthermore, if communications for an entire movement get centered in one organization, if that organization runs into trouble, the whole communications effort suffers.[26]

As even a quick review of Indian papers shows, the contents of *Akwesasne Notes* have often found their way into smaller papers across the country. *Notes* has encouraged the reprinting of its material, requesting only acknowledgement of sources. It also has encouraged action on issues and problems reported and discussed in the paper. Sometimes it has suggested specific actions: writing letters to particular legislators, voting in upcoming elections, boycotting products or areas, and reading specific publications.

The tabloid, which averages forty-eight pages, has been published five times annually, calling itself "A Journal for Native and Natural Peoples." Its editions have been designated "Early Spring" and "Early Autumn," for example, relating to the calendar in terms of seasons rather than months. Regular features in *Notes* include center-fold posters of famous Indians or Indian scenes, poetry, original art, calendars of historic events, announcements of Indian meetings and conferences, letters from readers across the country and around the world, and guides to resource material. Many of its articles are written to condense, clarify, or refute information found in established papers. Many of these articles and other features, including essays, editorials, and book reviews, come in from volunteer correspondents across the country.

High journalistic quality earned *Notes* the Robert F. Kennedy Memorial Foundation Journalism Award Citation in 1972, as well as the 1972 Marie Potts Journalism Achievement Award. Again in 1974 it was nominated for the Marie Potts award on the basis of its work in covering the 1973 occupation of Wounded Knee, South Dakota, and the social, political and economic conditions that led up to it. *Notes* initiated, supported, and published a book-length account, *Voices from Wounded Knee, 1973: In the Words of the Participants*, which was published in 1974 and revised in 1975 and 1976. In 1976 the World Council of Churches Special Fund to Combat Racism also acknowledged the excellence of the publication, giving it a cash award.

Although *Akwesasne Notes* and *Wassaja* have been in some obvious ways quite different publications, their similarities have been more important in American Indian journalism of the 1970s. Both have been speaking to a nationwide audience, native and nonnative alike. Both have dedicated themselves to addressing issues of vital— some say ever-growing—importance to Indian peoples. Both have cut across tribal, ethnic, and geographic boundaries to fill an information void.

Succeeding chapters will look at the other levels of coverage of Indian affairs by the Indian press. We turn first to tribal and inter-tribal publications, which have formed the bulk of Indian publishing activity in recent years.

CHAPTER SEVEN

Tribal and Intertribal Publications

The focus of this chapter is on newspapers and newsletters published either by individual tribes or as the cooperative projects of groups of tribes. Most Indian journalism falls into these two categories. Most currently publishing papers began in the late 1960s or early 1970s. Some have taken hold, establishing themselves as credible, influential publications. Others have died. The papers discussed here as current publications existed as of 1978, the 150th anniversary year. Given the volatile nature of Indian publishing, some have doubtless perished since then. The papers under consideration in this chapter provide a good view of what was happening in Indian-country publishing through the 1970s.

TRIBAL PAPERS

The tribal newspaper acts as a community newspaper, promoting understanding of the workings of tribal councils; concerning itself with local education, health and welfare; and functioning as a "letter from home" for tribal members living elsewhere. The tribal newspaper, usually a monthly tabloid, takes a more intimate approach to its readers than does a national publication, carrying accounts of everyday life and the doings of its community. What follows is a sampling of such tribal papers.

Arizona has had two strong weekly newspapers, the *Navajo Times*, serving the Navajo Nation from Window Rock; and *Qua Toqtii*, at Oraibi, an independent paper serving the Hopi people.

The *Navajo Times*, the older of the two, was started in 1959, funded by the Navajo Tribal Council. Although the paper officially became independent in 1972, it has retained its relationship with the council, thus experiencing many of the problems associated with its role as an official publication. For example, the *Times* has been accused by tribal members and by editors of other newspapers of being a "mouthpiece," an uncritical conduit of the party line rather than a free journalistic agent at the service of all factions within the Navajo Nation. One of these critics, the independent protest paper *Dine' Baa Hane*, wrote:

> A journalist's responsibility is to keep a check on the equal balance of power by governmental agencies on behalf of the public. Apathy breeds corruption such as censorship and nepotism, as you will see.
>
> The *Navajo Times*, the largest of the "Indian" newspapers, is governed by policies and resolutions passed by the council and heartily endorsed by the Administration. It more or less acts as a dispersing agent for the power-structure, whereas *Dine' Baa Hane* tells it the way it is, short of sensationalism.[1]

Such accusation notwithstanding, the *Times* has maintained a healthy balance of hard, in-depth news and interesting local copy. According to its business manager, the paper has been self-sufficient, which has given it a good deal of independence and security.

Published in two sections, it has operated as the only paper in Window Rock, functioning as a source of information, entertainment, and advertising. A frequent insert into the *Times*, the *DNA Newsletter* (a publication of the Navajo Legal Services staff), has been a referral-information publication. Regular features of the *Times* deal with politics (tribal and national, as they affect Navajos), education, and health issues. The paper also carries editorials, cartoons, letters to the editor, sports, comics, and poetry, often militant in tone and directed at tribal consciousness and pride. Nonlocal news sources include correspondents at the center of activities involving Indian issues, the Associated Press, United Press International, and exchange papers. The circulation of the *Times* has reached fourteen thousand.

Qua Toqtii, on the other hand, is an independent, privately owned operation with no ties to the Hopi tribal government. It was started in 1973. The paper's aim has been to help Hopi people become more aware of the issues facing them vis-à-vis white society. Local and national events and issues are covered, from the quality and accomplishments of Indian boarding schools to heritage, land-ownership issues, and problems encountered daily by Hopi people. The goal is to "educate our young and old, as well as anyone interested in Indian-related news."[2]

Other Arizona papers include the monthly *Fort Apache Scout*, published in Whiteriver, Arizona, since 1961. The official paper of the White Mountain Apache Tribe, it is funded by subscriptions, advertisements, and tribal funds, and it carries local news, nutrition, education, sports, history, letters to the editor, schedules of meetings, notices of workshops, powwows, church schedules, and general community features.

Newsletters, many of them funded through Community Action Programs, serve tribes throughout the United States. In Arizona the *Fort Yuma Newsletter*, a monthly established in 1965, serves as a general community news vehicle. Mimeographed, it carries information on tribal business, education, nutrition, money management, and local events.

The *Mountain Ute Echo* in Cortez, Colorado, was begun in 1976. *Smoke Signals*, a monthly published in Parker, Arizona, for the Colorado River Indian Tribe, celebrated its nineteenth anniversary on July 4, 1974. The *Pima-Maricopa Record*, Sacaton, Arizona, is the successor to the *Gila River News*, established in 1962.[3]

The *Southern Ute Drum*, official publication of the Southern Ute Tribe centered in Ignacio, Colorado, is a biweekly tabloid publication. Started as a newsletter in the early 1960s under the Community Action Program, the *Drum* features community news, bilingual bicultural education, local news, council news, a column by the council chairman, and general area Indian news.

Like many other Indian papers, the *Drum* has an readership made up largely of area residents but including also such out-of-state subscribers as libraries, officers in the Bureau of Indian Affairs, state government officials, and interested non-Indians. Also like other papers, the *Drum* has published, amid some differences of opinion on whether the paper should be merely a house organ, the official voice of the tribe, or a community newspaper. If the latter, it would carry balanced commentary on tribal government and engage in discussion of all issues vital to the members of the tribe without sidestepping sensitive or controversial issues.

Mittark, the Wampanog tribal newsletter, is published at

Mashpee, Massachusetts. It carries the Indian name of the great supreme sachem of the tribe, Lorenzo Jeffers, who devoted his life to the needs and the rights of the Wampanog tribe. *Mittark* was started in 1977 as a monthly.

Several newspapers were started in Minnesota in the 1970s. One, which has been influential and helpful in the establishment of others, is *Ni-Mah-Mi-Kwa-Zoo-Min*, (formerly *Ni-Mi-Kwa-Zoo-Min*) the newspaper of the Cass Lake Chippewa tribe. The paper was formed in 1973, with sporadic publication its first year. In 1974 it began appearing as a regular monthly tabloid, tribally funded, and by 1977 it had a circulation of twelve hundred.[4] It is a general community newspaper that served the six Chippewa reservations at Red Lake, Fond du Lac, Grand Portage, White Earth, Nett Lake, and Cass Lake.

Ni-Mah-Mi-Kwa-Zoo-Min ("Speaking of Ourselves") was launched, said the editor, as an "experiment in communication—to let Minnesota Chippewa tribal people know what programs, opportunities, and plans are available through their tribal organization."[5] It was conceived "in response to requests from Tribal people, from organizations and agencies with which the Tribe is in contact, and from departments within the Tribe itself."[6]

The paper is tightly written in traditional journalistic style. Its stated editorial policy reads in part: "We are seeking contributions from individuals of the six member reservations of the Minnesota Chippewa tribe. . . . Letters for publication should deal with issues and conditions, not personalities. We will grind no axes."[7] It carries local commercial advertising, including such regular features as news items, household hints ("At Home—At the Range"), items of organizational interest, legal briefs ("Legislation to Watch For"), tax information, job openings, a powwow calendar, and an elementary course in the Chippewa language ("Here's How to Say It"). "Other Voices" is a periodic column made up of items summarized from other papers. "Silver Notes" carries accounts of accomplishments and anniversaries of older tribal members.

Like most Native American newspapers, *Ni-Mah-Mi-Kwa-Zoo-Min* concentrates on education and and the welfare of young people. Articles on schools and school athletics programs appear regularly, with attention focused on alternative education and self-determination for Indians.

The paper, although it is the official organ of the Minnesota Chippewa Tribe, is frequently pinched financially. Free distribution is the rule, but, like other Native American publications, the paper often publishes appeals for financial contributions.

An editorial column entitled "Win Some . . . Lose a Few" discussed the generally precarious financial status of Native American newspapers. Listing papers that recently had folded and some that were "having problems," the editor, Betty Blue, stressed the role of the press in the Indian community. She quoted *Wassaja*:

> An effective system of communication is the most serious need of the Indian people. Most of us believe we had better communications before the Europeans came than we have now with all the sophisticated and technological developments of newspapers, radio, and television. Misinformation is regularly disseminated. Misinformation and misrepresentation can regularly be found in the mass media. We still don't know the truth of current events, their underlying causes, their effects on people and the true situation of the Indian people themselves.[8]

Blue also wrote:

> In order to take advantage of the opportunities available—college, adult vocational training, economic development, local business development—Indians have to *know* what is going on. But most Indians cannot yet afford to subscribe to a paper of their own. So provisions have to be made to keep the news-oriented, Indian-edited papers going to the Indian community.[9]

Another newsletter initiated through the Community Action Program is *White Earth Reservation Newsletter*, which serves the White Earth Chippewa residents. Established in 1975, the newsletter is aimed at a general circulation. Its goal is to keep people informed about the activities on the reservation, with coverage of such topics as history, general news, upcoming events, and children's news.

De-Bah-Ji-Mon ("Telling News"), was started in June, 1977, for the Leech Lake Reservation of the Minnesota Chippewa tribe. Its first issues were four-page tabloid inserts in *Ni-Mah-Mi-Kwa-Zoo-Min*.

The purpose was to keep readers up to date on reservation programs, projects, employment needs and opportunities, and social activities. Articles featuring poetry, hobbies, recipes, child care, the history of the area, and the activities of local people were included in the publication. It was financed by the Leech Lake Reservation Business Committee.

In Mississippi, the Choctaw Indians established *Choctaw Community News* in 1971. A twelve-page, five-column tabloid, the paper is published in Philadelphia, Mississippi, and appears twice a month. Its circulation in 1977 was close to four thousand. It succeeded the earlier *Chahta Anumpa*. With the motto "Progress Through Self-Determination," it carries articles on health and nutrition, covers such injustices as the conditions of the jail (used mostly for Indian and black prisoners), and reports on the accomplishments of students and teachers in local schools and on the action of the tribal council.

Tsistsistas Press was started in March, 1976, for the Northern Cheyenne Tribal Council in Lame Deer, Montana. A biweekly tabloid, it carries on its masthead the slogan "We Are Here to Serve the Northern Cheyenne Reservation." Contents include tribal council news, community news, a "History and Culture" section, editorials, articles on education and the environment, and interpretive and investigative reports.

The paper and its staff are activist in style. At one point in disputes over tribal council decisions to lease Northern Cheyenne lands for strip mining, the paper sponsored a bus trip to strip-mining sites in Navajo country so that members could see the impact of such mining on the land. At another time the staff sponsored workshops in photography and film processing. The classes were open to all interested tribal members, both as a skill-training opportunity and as a way of interesting people in participating in work on *Tsistsistas Press*.

In early August, 1978, the paper gave lengthy interpretive coverage to the tribe's confrontation with the Bureau of Indian Affairs over coal leasing, air quality, water rights, oil and gas potential, and the legal aspects of these and other Northern Cheyenne concerns. The same issue gave photo coverage of a July powwow on the reservation and of the "Longest Walk," in which more than 120 tribes walked between California and Washington, D.C., to protest anti-Indian activity throughout the country. It also carried an editorial calling for support and prayer for an upcoming Sun Dance ceremony.

The pattern for the paper had been set by its predecessors: *Morning Star News*, a Community Action Program newspaper started in 1967, and *A'tome*, a crusading biweekly paper that took on religion, traditional education, and government land deals.

Established on February 14, 1974, *A'tome* was begun as a free-circulation publication with a grant from the Teacher Corps. The paper was later funded by the tribe, with press-run costs covered by revenues from a well-rounded assortment of advertising that included classified ads, job announcements, full-page grocery displays, and other paid inserts. It has been sold in stores in towns on and around the Northern Cheyenne Reservation.

Among the paper's major investigative concerns are alcoholism, the penal and rehabilitative systems, stock-grazing rights, violations of Indian civil rights, and ecological damage threatened by pending decisions on coal and water rights. The paper has been actively involved in discussions about the propriety of fund-raising letters sent by a religious order that ran a reservation Indian school and about who should have control of the school.

The first tribal newspaper in New Mexico, the *Jicarilla Chieftain*, appeared on January 8, 1962, at Dulce, New Mexico. It carried the motto "Dedicated to the Future and Progress of the Jicarilla Apache Tribe." The masthead also told readers that the paper was intended to be "Independent in Politics, Optimistic in Disposition, Impartial in Religion, Published so that the Jicarilla Apache Tribe May Have a Spokesman and a Champion."[10]

Appearing every other Monday, the *Chieftain* worked gradually toward weekly publication. As a self-supporting enterprise, the *Chieftain* has given heavy coverage to local news and also has covered national news related to the needs and interests of the Jicarilla Apache tribe, or to other tribes with some proximity to Dulce. It reprints from exchange papers, and some of its articles have appeared in other Indian papers. In 1977 the editor, Mary F. Bacca Polanco, who had established the paper and worked with it until 1970, returned to edit it once again. Her hope, she told interviewers, was to get more Apaches into journalism and ultimately to get Indian journalists to work together nationally. Active in the American Indian Press Association, she wanted to see more national investigative journalism by Indians for Indians.[11]

Other, younger publications in New Mexico include *Cochiti Lake Sun*, Cochiti, New Mexico, and the infrequently published *Zuni Tribal Newsletter*, established in 1960 and reestablished in 1970. The latter is a mimeographed publication for which various departments at the Zuni Tribal Office have taken turns gathering news and information each month. The *Newsletter* also carries local and general news and information.

In New York the Seneca Indian Nation has been served by *Si Wong Geh*, a weekly publication established at Irving in the 1960s to inform residents of the Cattaraugus Indian Reservation of current events and activities, to provide current announcements of tribal statements, and to serve as a means of arousing public opinion. A successor to the earlier *Cattaraugus Indian Reservation Newspaper*, it is funded through subscriptions and through the social services agency at the reservation. Another New York paper, *O He Yoh Noh*, ("People of the Allegany"), was started in 1969 at Salamanca to meet the information needs of members of the Allegany tribe separated by the relocation necessitated by the building of the Kinzua Dam. Contents of *O He Yoh Noh* include general local news, senior-citizens news, sports and recreation, and weekly devotional material. Information comes in through letters and from other Indian papers, local newspapers, and telephone calls.

Two weekly newspapers are published in North Carolina. The *Carolina Indian Voice* is published every Thursday in Pembroke by the Lumbee Tribal Publishing Company. Dedicated to "The Best in All of Us," it began publishing January 18, 1973. A nine-column, large-size paper, it emphasizes general local news and events from the Lumbee perspective. It carries politics, wedding news, school news, church and religious messages, editorials, and letters to the editor, and is financed through subscriptions and advertising. In 1976 the editor called its purpose "To build a common bridge between the Lumbee Indians and the rest of the world."

Another weekly, the *Cherokee One Feather*, is published by the Tribal Council of the Eastern Band of Cherokee Indians in Cherokee,

North Carolina. Begun in 1969, it is primarily local in coverage, with such regular features as education, sports, social and cultural events, Cherokee language, community welfare, and tribal council action. The motto of the paper, reminiscent of that of the first Cherokee newspaper, is "To Strive, to Seek, to Find, and not to Yield." *Cherokee One Feather* is a five-column, twelve-page tabloid supported by subscriptions, display and classified advertising, and tribal funds.

The *Turtle Mountain Echo*, the newspaper of the Turtle Mountain Band of Chippewa Indians, was started in 1973 at Belcourt, North Dakota. It first appeared in magazine format but by 1974 had become a full-sized biweekly tabloid. It is financed by subscriptions, advertising, and funding through the tribe's adult-education program. Like many of its Indian counterparts, *Echo* (the only newspaper in town) emphasizes getting local news to the people, covering the schools to promote community involvement in education, and supporting Indian-owned stores and businesses. By 1975 its circulation was six hundred. Its letters-to-the-editor column draws lively participation, and much Indian artwork is used on the covers and inside pages. *Echo* performs the function of a local bulletin board, reprinting tribal council notes and giving news of weddings, school accomplishments, and job notices.

Elsewhere in North Dakota, the Devil's Lake Sioux Tribe established *E'Yanpaha* ("Reservation"), at Fort Totten in early 1976. A duplicated newsletter, it carries the minutes of tribal council meetings, items of national and local interest, tribal business notes and information, and such topical items as "Estimating Your Retirement Check." Another newsletter, the *Action News*, was started in 1971 to serve the members of the Fort Berthold Reservation. A project of the Community Action Program, it succeeded the *Fort Berthold Bulletin* and features community news, job announcements, church news, and information on services offered by reservation and extension programs.

The *Cherokee Advocate*, direct descendant of the nineteenth-century Cherokee newspaper, was started in February, 1977, in Tahlequah, Oklahoma. The monthly tabloid is aimed at all registered Cherokees and oriented to issues and policies affecting Cherokees. Regular contents include local news, letters, editorials, features,

"Cherokees in the News," sports, a monthly calendar, job announcements, and coverage of national news, housing, education and Indian rights. *A-Ne-Geh-Ya* ("Women's Pages") feature articles on nutrition, recipes, fashions, and general homemaking. The *Advocate* was preceded by the *New Cherokee Advocate*, *Cherokee Newsletter*, and *Cherokee National News*.

Another Oklahoma newspaper, *Hello Choctaw*, was established in 1969 by the Oklahoma City Council of Choctaws, Inc. It was discontinued a few years later, but was reestablished in 1975 by the Choctaw Nation. It is published in Durant, Oklahoma, with funding through tribal subsidies. An eight-page two-column tabloid, it is both tribal and national in scope because tribal members (estimated at one hundred thousand descendants of the twenty thousand Choctaws enrolled in 1906) are scattered across the United States. For this reason very little nontribal news is included in *Hello Choctaw*.[12]

Muskogee Nation News, a bimonthly established in 1975 in Muskogee, Oklahoma, ceased publication in early 1977 because of financial and organizational problems. The *Osage Nation News* began publishing in Pawhuska, Oklahoma, in February, 1977. Published through the Osage Media Center and the Osage Office of Native American Programs, it is a five-column, twelve-page tabloid containing general information and items of interest to Indians. Although financed through advertising, subscription, and tribal funds, it is free to tribal members and Indians living in the Osage Nation.

Various South Dakota publications serve the tribes there. One, *Sota Eya Ye Yapi*, established in 1976 by the Sisseton-Wahpetan Sioux Tribes of the Lake Traverse Reservation, is published as a supplement to the local *Sisseton Courier*. Subscriptions are available for non-*Courier* subscribers. As a four-page, five-column tabloid, it reaches many non-Indian readers with local and national Indian news, general human-interest features, and the "Chairman's Corner" by the tribal chairman.

Other forms newspapers have taken are exemplified in the *Sioux Messenger*, a small tabloid monthly published by the Yankton Sioux tribe in Wagner, and by the *United Tribes Newsletter*, published monthly in Pierre. The latter covers local, state, and national news having to do with people and programs that affect the Indian community and Indian traditions.

At Fort Duchesne, Utah, the *Ute Bulletin*, started in 1960, is published by the Uintah and Ouray tribes. An eight-page, four-column tabloid in 1977, it features education, health, housing, employment, and promotion items, and many letters to the editor that reflect reader interest in both the paper and the issues it covers. The paper has no editorials.

The state of Washington has had several strong newspapers that were and are published by tribal and intertribal groups. *Makah Viewers*, established in February, 1977, succeeded an earlier paper, the *Makah Newsletter*, started in 1955. *Viewers*, a bimonthly publication, is an eight-page, four-column tabloid. Its readership is the Makah tribal members near Neah Bay, and its purpose is to "better inform our community of local happenings, Makah Council actions, fishing, education, and law and order and legislative decisions affecting Indian people."[13]

Regular features include council activities, legislation, culture, history, and such small community events as weddings, visits, birthdays, and other social activities. *Viewers* is the only paper in the Neah Bay area.

Nugguam, established in 1965 by the Quinault Indian Nation, is published twice monthly at Tahola. It functions as a "letter from home" and is directed at getting tribal news to nonreservation Indian people. It carries political, local, general, and sports news.

Another small Washington newspaper, the *Klallam Monthly*, was started in 1973 at Little Boston as a mimeographed four-page newsletter. It carries local information. Most of its early coverage was devoted to working out a law-and-order code in anticipation of the "Trident Impact"—possible white encroachment in connection with the building of the Trident missile base on nearby Hood Canal.

Another Washington paper, *Rawhide Press*, published by the Spokane tribe in Wellpinit, is a monthly tabloid that has won several awards for news reporting and writing. It is the successor to the *Smoke Signal* and *Northwest Indian Times*.

Rawhide features include news and "Tribal Council Briefs," a column on schools called "From the Superintendent's Desk," a community calendar, a column on state politics called "Capital Scout," and a collection of information and news from and about Indians of many regions called "Bits and Pieces." Selected Spokane legends, entitled "From the Past" and reprints of treasured photos, usually under the headline "Do You Remember?" serve to preserve and reconstruct history and heritage, as do "Through the Years" and "Speelya [Coyote] Stories."

Rawhide Press carries brief lessons in the Spokane language, only recently developed in written form by scholars of the University of British Columbia. Other regular features include question-and-answer columns on social security, court records and probation hearings, obituaries (under a standing head), and news on extension and school programs.

Because most readers of the paper are tribal members, emphasis is on local and tribal news, informative features, and articles of interest to tribal members living on and away from the reservation. Circulation figures have reached fourteen hundred, with copies mailed to thirty-two states and Canada. Readership, however, was set at more than seven thousand, based on surveys conducted by the editor.[14]

One of the largest and most impressive tribal newspapers in the country is the *Yakima Nation Review*, established in May, 1970, to serve the members of the Yakima Nation. The biweekly, twenty-four page tabloid, published in Toppenish, carries national Indian news, local and tribal news, a ceremonial calendar, interpretive and investigative reports on issues vital to the welfare of Yakima and Northwest Indians, and a legislative digest of Indian legislation before the Senate and the House. In addition, the paper, which serves as the sole community newspaper, carries a police log, a safety corner, obituaries ("Walking On"), a "Student World" page, news of education and educational achievements by Yakima youth, many letters, and reprints of work by tribal artists. Financed through subscriptions, display and classified advertising, and subsidies from the Yakima Nation, the paper is printed on tribal printing presses.

In Wisconsin, tribal publications include a monthly newspaper and several newsletters. The *Menominee Tribal News*, established in

1976, is published from Keshena as a monthly tabloid. The paper aims at giving tribal members "access to all viewpoints and information on tribal affairs that affect our lives." It tries to be a "progressive and objective instrument," to "unify" the tribe, "preserve our culture and traditions, exercise our freedoms, cultivate peace at home, and give us an insight to help control our own jealousies, prejudices and mistrust."[15]

The *News* covers local news, tribal news, housing, education, health, personal items, sports, and general small-community news. It includes claims and legislation affecting Menominees and carries obituaries, job notices, recipes, some advertising, and photographs.

Other Wisconsin tribal publications are *Kali Wisaks*, a mimeographed newspaper published twice a month by the Oneida Tribe of Indians; *Quin A' Month A?* ("Are You Well?"), published monthly at Bowler by the Stockbridge Indians; and *Red Cliff Tribal News*, published every two weeks at Bayfield and used mainly to let tribal members know of job openings.

INTERTRIBAL NEWSPAPERS

Intertribal newspapers are those that include news and information about several tribes and are directed by representatives of various tribal councils. Although one person functions as editor of the publications, he or she is in effect employed jointly by the tribes, usually through intertribal cooperative governing procedures. Some intertribal papers serve reservation Indians. Others serve urban populations and are independent of tribal councils.

Smoke Signal, a bimonthly published from Sacramento, California, for the Federated Indians of California, is one of the early modern publications, beginning in 1947. It is aimed at informing California Indians of issues and events affecting them and at promoting cooperation. Its motto is "In Unity There Is Strength."

Smoke Signal's first editor, Marie Potts, a Maidu Indian revered across the country for her pioneering journalistic efforts, was honored by the American Indian Press Association when it named for her its most prestigious award for journalistic excellence. She was also honored by the state of California when the entire second floor of State Office Building Number One was dedicated in her honor.

Although it is a simple, legal-sized, mimeographed publication, *Smoke Signal* exemplifies the best ideals of Indian journalism, ideals that Indian journalists today try to emulate. Mrs. Potts died in 1978, but the paper has continued, carrying announcements and commentary on the government's Indian programs and news of general interest to the Indian population of California.

A relative newcomer to the Indian journalism scene, the Idaho publication *Sho-ban News* was started in 1970 and reestablished in 1976. A tabloid, it is published twice a month by the Shoshone and Bannock tribes through the Fort Hall (Idaho) Business Council. It carries general local news, information on national and governmental events and decisions affecting Indians, editorials, letters, sports, announcements of meetings, and general community features.

The *Camp Crier* is a weekly published at the Fort Belknap agency in Harlem, Montana, by the Tribal Council of Assiniboine and Gros Ventre in cooperation with the Extension Service of Montana State College. Founded in 1969, it had a circulation in 1977 of about 750 (with 350 paid subscriptions), but surveys showed a weekly readership of between 8,000 and 10,000.[16]

The *Camp Crier* is governed by directors who are closely involved with the policy and business of the paper. Office management is under the supervision of an extension agent for the Fort Belknap Reservation.

For the most part the paper's content is a series of notices and unconnected little stories of events in various areas on the reservation. There is an informal, chatty tone to the paper, as evidenced by the tribal news accounts of who visited whom, who was "seen dancing in the Frontier Club," where the potluck dinner would be held, and who was ill or in the hospital. Practical suggestions on how to keep carpets clean, how to repair furniture, or how to start garden plants indoors are also run regularly, as are local ads, extensive listings of job openings, educational opportunities, and achievements of reservation members. Sports reports and the prominently displayed "Cook's Corner" appear in each issue.

The paper also keeps tribal members informed about legislative issues, running the full texts of pertinent documents having to do with tribal housing, education as it affects Native Americans, the reclassification of state highways, and the civil rights of former drug abusers.

Char-Koosta is the biweekly paper of the Salish, Pend d'Oreilles, and Kootenai tribes of the Flathead Reservation. An earlier short-lived version having the same name was founded in 1954 and revived briefly in 1962. Headquartered in Dixon, Montana, the paper was organized to carry tribal news, including the full minutes of all council meetings, and to report the viewpoints of council leaders on current issues.

In addition to reporting on tribal government, *Char-Koosta* has been an alternative to the white press, which often ignores or is neutral to Indian problems. In one issue, for example, it explained the potential effects of various pending forestry and land-management proposals. In others, it carried a series by the tribal economic development planner on buying a home or property, reported on issues and candidates before the voters in reservation school-board elections, and discussed eligibility and voting procedures.

A health-and-hygiene column, "Good Medicine," has carried the home telephone numbers of community health representatives and articles on such wide-ranging topics as alcoholism, accidental poisonings, safety belts, vaccinations, and skin tests for tuberculosis. A series by a botanist teaching on the reservation was focused on the uses and medicinal values of native plants. Similar articles told how to tan hides and smoke salmon. Regular features include reminders of the dates of various game seasons, listings of new tribal members, tales from Kootenai tradition, and brief lessons in the Salish language.

Investigative pieces in *Char-Koosta* have been concerned with land and mineral rights and the dangers to those resources both from outside encroachments and from tribal mismanagement. One issue was headlined "Can Tribe Play Market With Saw Timber?" and looked at alternatives for preserving and yet profiting from tribal forest lands. Another issue reviewed a 119-year-old government treaty that in effect signed away vast acres of tribal rangeland.

Subscriptions are paid by the tribes, and yearly subscriptions for nonmembers were $3.60. The 8½-by-11-inch paper, printed on tribal offset presses, usually runs sixteen pages.[17] Photographs and line drawings are used extensively throughout, and the magazine format is kept informal through the use of ragged-right margins. Ads are for Indian businesses only.

Another Montana newspaper, *Wotanin Wowapi*, was started in 1969 by a Vista worker and was reestablished by the tribal council in 1971 as a mimeographed, stapled publication. By 1977 it had grown to a twice-monthly, sixteen-page tabloid printed on the tribal press. A successor to the earlier *Eyapi Oaye*, it is intended for Sioux and Assiniboine tribal members on the Fort Peck Reservation and is funded by subscriptions, advertising, and tribal-council subsidies. Much space is devoted to news from the tribal executive board. Other regular features include "Looking Back," a collection of old-time pictures of the reservation and its people; "Killing Time," a puzzle of some variety in each issue; and profiles of interesting reservation residents. The paper also has reported on the impact of energy problems in the Fort Peck area, tribal industry, Head Start and other federal education programs, and job opportunities. Like many other Indian papers, *Wotanin* also carries a full page of "Indian News Notes" from across the country, usually focused on Indian-rights litigations, activities of national Indian organizations, and Washington decisions vis-à-vis Indians. News came through releases from colleges, other newspapers, the Department of the Interior, and local organizations.

The *19-Pueblos News*, established in 1973 at Albuquerque by the All-Indian Pueblo Council, serves small tribes in the area. It is a monthly eight-page tabloid. The *News* is directed at Pueblos, at government, and at congressional people. It covers education, bilingual and bicultural efforts, news of the All-Indian Pueblo Council, fiestas and other social events, voter information, servicemen's appointments, and general current events. Reader response has been minimal, partly because of the wide geographical area the *News* tries to cover and partly by the feeling, expressed by some readers, that the paper is a council mouthpiece and hence not an effective news and communication vehicle.[18]

Another paper that attempts to walk the delicate line between mouthpiece and public information vehicle is the North Dakota paper *United Tribes News*, a monthly tabloid begun on October 8, 1974, by the United Tribes Educational Technical Center. It serves the five tribal groups belonging to the United Tribes of North Dakota Development Corporation: the Standing Rock Sioux, the Lake Traverse Sisseton-Wahpeton Sioux, the Turtle Mountain Chippewa Cree, the Fort Totten Devil's Lake Sioux, and the Fort Berthold Three Affiliated Tribes.

The *News*, published at Bismarck, North Dakota, carries news from all the tribes and tribal sessions, focusing on education, curriculum, and control of the schools. Environmental concerns also have been central, with in-depth and interpretive reporting on hunting and fishing rights and legislation affecting those rights. The editor, Harriett Skye Meeches, also took to the airwaves with Indian issues for several years on a talk show called "Indian Country," discussed in Chapter 10.

Like many other Indian papers, the *News* concentrates on such health issues as alcoholism and drug addiction, the practices aimed at their prevention, and documentation of their dangers and effects. Indian business successes are chronicled, as are athletic achievements.

The *News* follows the pattern of other community papers in running such regular features as the "Student of the Month" column, accounts of graduation honors and speakers, Indian poetry and art, vignettes on local artists and businessmen, "News Briefs," and items of interest from various tribal groups, including weddings, anniversaries, and other celebrations.

The sixteen-page tabloid has made good use of photographs, skillful cartooning, and reprints from other Indian papers. It follows an earlier paper, the *Standing Rock Star*, published at Fort Yates.

The Cheyenne-Arapaho tribe in 1967 established the *Cheyenne-Arapaho Bulletin*, a successor to the *Carrier Pigeon*, which was started in 1910. The *Bulletin*, a monthly five-column tabloid mandated by the tribal constitution, is published at Concho, Oklahoma. It carries information on local and national events, job opportunities, training programs, educational opportunities, and health and social services.

The only paper in Concho, the center of the Cheyenne-Arapaho Reservation, the *Bulletin* serves all the functions of a community paper, running information on weddings, anniversaries, high school graduations, youth activities, ground breakings, and so on. It uses pictures of tribal officers, old people, young athletes, powwow princesses, and other persons of note.

The *Confederated Umatilla Journal*, serving the Cayuse, Walla Walla, and Umatilla tribes, is a tabloid published since 1975 in Pendleton, Oregon. Its circulation in 1977 was two thousand in forty-two states. The stated purpose of the paper is to reach concerned people, both Indian and non-Indian, to inform them and share the issues and interests of Indian people, and to provide the Umatilla Indian Reservation with local and national news. The slogan under the masthead emphasizes this goal: "Only an informed people has its future in its own hands."

Regular features in the paper include columns from the tribal attorney and various tribal chairmen, a health page, news of the Bureau of Indian Affairs, sports, news from across the Northwest, and items of interest to reservation people. "Beautiful People," focusing on photographs from the past, and "Umatilla Vocabulary" are efforts to bring the history and language to life.

The paper also performs a public service through its profitable classified-ads section. Other sources of funds are from display advertising, subscriptions, and Title 638 (the Self-Determination Act) moneys.

Another Oregon paper, *Spilyay Tymoo*, was started in March, 1976, and published as a biweekly tabloid by the Confederated Tribes of Warm Springs. Its purpose is to present to the people an objective and informative view of reservation activities as well as national and state news pertinent to the tribe. Land and water resources, youth and education concerns, local events, religion, and sports are all covered. The editorial page has had an open forum in which members of the public could express their views on any subject relating to reservation activities. "We print the truth with accuracy and impartiality and try not to mislead the readers," the editor wrote.[19]

The *Indian Voice*, a monthly tabloid published at Sumner by the Small Tribes of Western Washington, serves sixteen tribes and is sent to twenty-two tribes throughout Washington and to twenty-seven tribes in Oregon. Established in 1969, within seven years it was reaching a readership of more than 12,500.

Like many tribal newspapers in the Northwest, the *Indian Voice* covers natural resources and financial news, such as news of Indian-treaty fishing rights and violations, land-grab attempts affecting Indian country, the work of the Northwest Indian Fisheries Commissions, and grants to Alaskan natives.

Unlike many other Indian papers, the *Voice* has established a consistent advertising program, including an Indian consumer-habits survey. In one issue the editor reported, "Indian consumers are in the mainstream of American buying habits for the middle-class and industrial payroll segments of the general population."[20] Because of this pattern, he pushed for regional and national advertising efforts by Indian newspapers. The *Voice* has had healthy advertising revenues, one indication that market surveys could be profitable for more Indian papers.

The *Tribal Tribune*, a sixteen-page monthly tabloid, is published at Nespelem by the Colville Confederated Tribes. Printed at the tribal printing plant, it is the tribal council's voice, aimed at keeping non-reservation members informed about Indian-related issues that major media do not cover, as well as information on activities at the reservation. Regular features of the *Tribune* include fishing and mineral rights reports, tribal finances, education, Indian poetry, profiles on Indian artists, a Community Action Program column, "Council Briefs," "Enrollment Office Reports," and "History in Pictures." The last feature covers tribal and area legends and history. Like many other tribal papers, the *Tribune* also carries local weddings, accomplishments, obituaries, and announcements concerning health and social services.

Another intertribal publication, the weekly *American Indian News*, is published as a newsletter at Fort Washakie, Wyoming, through the Office of Native American Programs. It serves the Shoshone and Arapaho tribes with information and news relevant to their interests.

CHAPTER EIGHT

Regional Papers

In a kind of middle ground between tribal or intertribal papers and Indian national papers lie the several regional Indian publications that are directed to state, regional, or urban audiences. These papers extend the idea of community beyond tribal bounds, invariably striving to respond to the needs and interests of a larger Indian community.

The more noteworthy regional papers are discussed here. The list is not necessarily complete; Indian journalism is too fluid an enterprise to permit of precise cataloging.

Because of its geography and the nature of its native Indian population, Alaska has perhaps the largest number of Indian papers that are circulated statewide. The state's most widely circulated and most influential Native American paper, the *Tundra Times*, was established October 1, 1962. The American Indian Press Association named this excellent weekly the most outstanding Indian newspaper for 1973.

The twelve-to-sixteen-page tabloid has had a rather erratic and sometimes precarious existence because of financial problems it shares with other Indian newspapers. It was initially underwritten by a donation from a retired Massachusetts physician, who pledged $35,000 to the newspaper in 1962. The need was for an information medium that would bring before the public the potential dangers to environment and heritage from Atomic Energy Commission (AEC) developments in the northwest Arctic. The founding editor, Howard Rock, an Eskimo and a graduate of the University of Washington, had a frustrating experience with the *Fairbanks News-Miner*. When he had tried to do an investigative piece on the consequences of an atomic blasting project in Alaska, he found that the AEC had reported, through the Associated Press, that there was no radiation danger involved in the blasting. But, in fact, radiation contamination directly linked to the blasting had already been discovered in the food chain. The AEC tried to stop his investigations, and the paper failed to support him.[1]

Approached by Native Alaskans to begin a paper, he did so, working in primitive offices, threatened and harassed with unusually high utility bills and telephone service cutoffs. But the AEC eventually bowed to the pressure of exposure created by his vigilant newspaper.[2]

Other accomplishments can be attributed to the *Tundra Times*, such as bringing about a moratorium on filing land-claim settlements when white firms were claiming the settlements on Alaskan lands already claimed by natives. Following an issue that reported on the plight of the inhabitants of Pribilof Island, the Bureau of Commercial Fisheries labeled *Tundra Times* editors communists. These native hunters had to exchange their sealskins for goods at the government store at government rates, and as a result were reduced to a semiservitude existence. Eventually, the *Times*—by exploring the plight of the Native Americans—induced some white newspapers to do the same, and also to carry positive news about these peoples.[3]

The motto of the *Tundra Times* is Voltaire's famous response to Madame du Deffand: "I disapprove of what you say, but I will defend to the death your right to say it." The paper, financed by subscription and advertising, carries ads from local companies, airline firms, and out-of-state organizations. The paper moved from Fairbanks to Anchorage in 1978. It has continued under various editors since Rock died in 1976.

Most of the paper's subscribers are native leaders, government agencies, and other newspaper editors, as well as a few interested whites. Instead of carrying social and local news, the paper concentrates on government agency activities and meetings, business transactions affecting the environment and the native people of Alaska, and reports on discriminatory practices against Native Americans of Alaska. Investigative and interpretive reporting focuses on significant legal developments and environmental problems. Proceedings are fully reported as the *Tundra Times* maintains a strong role as an environmental and governmental watchdog.

The Voice of Brotherhood, a statewide paper, was started in 1954.

A monthly, it was published at Juneau, with funding from subscriptions, from advertising, and from a group called the Alaska Native Brotherhood and Sisterhood. The organization was founded in the early 1900s as a religious and philanthropic enterprise whose stated purpose was to

> assist and encourage the Native in his advancement from his Native state to his place among the cultivated races of the world, to oppose, discourage, and to overcome the narrow injustice of race prejudice, to commemorate the fine qualities of the Native races of North America, to preserve their history, lore, art, and virtues, to cultivate the morality, education, commerce, and civil government of Alaska, to improve individual and municipal health and laboring conditions, and to create a true respect in Native and in other persons with whom they deal for the letter and spirit of the Declaration of Independence and the Constitution of the United States.[4]

A message on the *Voice* nameplace read: "A Monthly Publication Intended to Be a VOICE Concerning the Native Population of Alaska. We Hope to Create Interest, Concern, and Action Within the Native Culture." The *Voice* dealt with the problems and accomplishments of Alaska's native people in schools, in the art world, in cultural achievement, and in business. It discussed medical and health problems, as well as religious and political issues.

Another Alaskan publication, established in 1974, is the *Bering Straits Aglutuk*, a joint monthly enterprise of the Bering Straits Native Corporation (BSNC) and the Norton Sound Health Corporation in Nome, Alaska. The paper was directed at stockholders of the BSNC, as well as at persons in government and in the private sector. It carried information on stock ventures, environmental issues, and regional traditional culture, in addition to instructions to stockholders and tips on health and safety. The *Aglutuk* was not localized, since most of the thirteen corporations (of which BSNC is one), founded under the Alaska Native Claims Settlement Act, have their own quarterly publications.

A smaller, more regional publication, the *Caribou News*, a biweekly tabloid, was started in 1977. Its primary audience was the native population of northwest Alaska, and it aimed at informing the communities of local and national events of local impact. Published at

Kotzebue, Alaska, it was a successor to the earlier *Kotzebue News*. The *Caribou News* covered subsistence hunting and fishing, local and community events, and issues pertaining to education and transportation. That the paper was a community venture is clear from an early comment by the editor acknowledging the assistance of twenty-two individuals, some of whom contributed to the paper by donating furniture, supplies, and the use of a darkroom.[5] The paper devoted more than a third of its space to advertising.[6] These Alaska papers have been replaced by several others, most associated with native regional corporations (see Appendix C).

Papers of statewide circulation were published also in California, Michigan, Utah, and Washington. The *Tribal Spokesman*, established in Sacramento, the California state capital, began in 1968, to provide information to California Indians on state and federal services available to them: housing, education, health, and emergency assistance. In general the paper tries to inform Indians of relevant state and federal legislation. Funding comes from subscriptions, foundations, and other private sources.

The *Michigan Indian*, a bimonthly, 8½-by-11-inch stapled newsletter, is published by the Michigan Commission on Indian Affairs in Lansing. Although it is a government publication, the newsletter lives up to its name, providing considerable information about activities of Indians around the state and nation, announcing events and job openings, and offering a number of instructional articles, such as one listing a person's legal rights in the event of an arrest. Also included is information on official actions and regulations from the commission as well as from health, education, and employment sectors of government. The paper has a circulation of about twelve hundred and no subscription price, because funding comes from the state. Most issues run about fourteen pages.

The *Native Nevadan*, published by the Inter-Tribal Council of Nevada, is a monthly tabloid of eight to twenty pages. The paper, published at Reno, gets its funds partly from subscriptions ($2.50 a year for non-Indians), advertising, and the United States Office of Native American Programs. It was started in 1964, carrying news of three Nevada tribes on twenty-four reservations and in small communities. Interestingly, about half of the subscribers live out of state, with some copies going to foreign countries. The *Native Nevadan* offers a substantial number of columns of local, state, and national news; features on Indian achievements, personality pieces, and motivation in education and business; and a large sports section. Pictures, used throughout, enliven the paper.

The *Utah Indian Journal*, a monthly started at Salt Lake City in 1977, was established for the stated purpose of providing communication among the Indian tribes of that state. A cooperative venture, it involves the University of Utah, the Utah Native American Consortium, the Utah Division of Indian Affairs, and the Utah Board of Education. It serves as both a point of identity for urban Indians and a unifying and supporting vehicle for Indians statewide.

The *Northwest Indian News* at Seattle serves the Indian and non-Indian communities of the state of Washington as well as subscribers in nearly thirty-five states and several foreign countries. Billed as "the Largest Urban Indian Newspaper in the Northwest," the monthly tabloid, begun in 1960, has for years been considered one of the strong Indian voices in the United States. It is published by a group called Indians into Communications, a nonprofit group dedicated to recruitment, training, and placement of Indian journalists. The paper has been a training ground for Indian journalism students at area colleges and universities. *Northwest Indian News* may well be the only Indian regional publication with this specific recruitment and training system, partly because neither governmental nor private groups have shown much interest in funding such programs.

The paper focuses on local news and issues and aims at top-quality, professional coverage of Indian points of view. But it goes beyond local boundaries to cover issues pertinent to all Indians. For example, one issue carried comprehensive listings of Native American artists and crafts persons who have worked or lived in the Pacific Northwest. The *News* also features arts, poetry, health and relevant government news, and some local investigative efforts. The paper carries some advertising and has an annual subscription rate of five dollars. Like most Native American papers, it has faced a constant struggle to stay alive. In 1975 the *News* publications director, a non-Indian who had worked first as a Vista volunteer and later as a paid staff member, pointed to the dearth of interest and support for programs to recruit and train Indian journalists. He wrote: "To date I have found little realization on the part of those who profess to be concerned with social movements that a minority press can truly be a force for social change. I am hopeful that these views can be changed, however, and it is one of my primary concerns."[7]

On the East Coast, a statewide newspaper, the *Wabanaki Alliance*, was started in Maine in 1977. The paper is a tabloid with offices in Orono. Its purpose, according to the editor, is to inform members of the Indian communities of the state on matters affecting their lives, as well as to serve as a forum for Indian opinion. The paper also attempts to provide coverage on topics of interest to Indian and non-Indian readers. It had an especially timely and urgent purpose when it was founded, in view of the Maine Indian land claims then in the courts.

Urban papers, newspapers designed to serve urban Indian communities, are or have been published in about twenty United States cities, most of them with comparatively large Indian populations. Here is a look at many of them, listed by state, containing information that had been gathered either firsthand or by letter through 1978.

Talking Leaf, which bills itself as the only Indian newspaper in Los Angeles, is a successful, graphically bright monthly tabloid that was started in 1935. It carries news of the Los Angeles Indian Center, as well as local, state, and national news and announcements for the Indian community. Its purpose, according to its editor, is to promote a positive image of the Indian community.[8] As for financing, it is a "non-profit operation produced solely by revenue generated from subscriptions, advertising, and contributions." It varies from eight to twelve pages with a yearly subscription price of seven dollars. In recent years the paper has adopted a magazine format, its first page devoted to a photograph and a bottom-of-the-page index called "Inside Talking Leaf." In 1978 the paper claimed a paid subscription list of seven thousand. Features have included sketches on outstanding American Indians, a calendar of events, poetry, comics, and an occasional clever spoof, such as a full page in one issue devoted to "The

National Indian Inquirer," announcing "$500,000 to every Indian," "John Wayne named to head BIA," and in the "Psychic Predicts," a comment that "All Indian land will be returned in November, 1985, but the world will end January 19, 1986, at 7:30 P.M. (about 8:45 for Indians)."[9]

In San Diego, *Take Ten*, a tabloid, was started in 1972. It carries local and national news, poetry, and a variety of features of interest to San Diego Indians. The paper is distributed free, with funding coming from the Federal Office of Native American Programs.

Redletter is a monthly publication put out by the Native American Committee, Inc., a Chicago-based nonprofit group. Originally an 8½-by-11-inch stapled sheet, the *Redletter* later took shape as a four-page typed tabloid. Although some national items are listed, the paper has focused on activities of the Native American Committee. Its stated purpose is to promote a positive image of Indians.

The *Iowa Indian* began serving the Indian population of Sioux City, Iowa, in 1973. Like the *Redletter* and many other urban publications, the *Indian* has a scope that was intentionally limited. This newsletter, an 8½-by-11-inch stapled sheet, publishes information about the city's library system and its Indian projects, with funding by the State Library Commission of Iowa. In addition some local and national news concerning Indians is carried, "since they probably wouldn't receive it through any other local source," according to the editor.[10]

Nish Nau Bah, a monthly four-page tabloid, is published by the Indian Center of Topeka (Kansas). Another newsletter put out by an agency, this publication carries word of the activities of the center, as well as general news of interest to the city's Indian community. It also includes features on the Potawatomi history and language.

The *Circle*, a publication of the Boston Indian Council, is a lively twelve-page monthly tabloid that covers local, state, and national news of interest to the Boston Indian Community. Started in 1976, it is funded by subscriptions, advertising, and the office of Native American Programs. The intent of the paper, as stated by its editors, is to inform the Indian community in Boston of the services provided by the Indian Council and to increase the awareness of Indian and non-Indian people of Indian affairs in New England and the nation.[11] One regular feature of the paper is a continuing account of the status of various Indian land-claim cases on the East Coast, especially the Passamaquaddy-Penobscot claims in Maine.

Indian Viewpoint, a monthly tabloid supported by a Duluth Indian Action Council grant, was published at Duluth, Minnesota, for two years, between 1973 and 1975. Editor Ray Murdock, who also produced a television program of the same name as the tabloid's, viewed the paper as a training ground for young Indian journalists as well as a communications vehicle for reaching the Indian community of Duluth and beyond.[12] Although the paper folded, Murdock predicted that Indian papers generally would continue to be published, serving as an alternative press "until large circulation papers accept the fact that all papers cannot remain lily white" and commented that there existed "conscious and unconscious resistance to including Indians in media, with no attempt either to train or to cover Indians."[13] Another urban paper in Minnesota is *Wig-I-Wam*, a Minneapolis newsletter sponsored by the Division of Indian Work of the Greater Minneapolis Council of Churches. Financing is from the churches and from individual contributions. The publication, a monthly 8½-by-11-inch stapled sheet with a predominantly local readership, was started in 1969. In purpose (as stated on the cover) the paper is dedicated to the welfare and advancement of Indian youth, and hopes "to create leadership in our fight for self-determination."

In Kansas City, Missouri, the *Heart of America Indian Center Newsletter* was established in 1972. Although designated a newsletter with local, state, and national news of interest to Kansas City Indians along with announcements of programs and special events, the monthly publication has many newspaper features. A monthly, its funding is from the Office of Native American Programs.

The *Hi-Line Indian Alliance Newsletter* serves the Indian community of north-central Montana and surrounding areas that are involved in the Montana United Indian Association. It started in 1975 at Havre as a monthly. The newsletter informs its readers of news of the Indian Center along with job openings and health referrals. Funding is through the Montana Indian Association.

The *Helena Indian Alliance*, published monthly in legal-sized sheets by the Helena Intertribal Alliance, was started in 1969. The newsletter confines itself to local events and programs.

Buffalo Grass is the publication of the Missoula Indian Center. The monthly 8½-by-11-inch sheet covers national and state issues affecting Indians, together with such community news as employment opportunities and legal information.

The *Winnebago Indian News*, Winnebago, Nebraska, is a weekly paper serving the area's Indian community. It is published by the Nebraska Indian Press, with subscriptions at three dollars annually. It was started in January, 1972.

In New York City, the American Indian Community House publishes a monthly newsletter for the New York Indian community. Funding for the newsletter, which was started in 1975, is through the Office of Native American Programs. Although its emphasis is on community affairs, the publication—which has no formal name— also carries local and national news briefs as well as government information.

The Oklahoma City *Camp Crier*, an eight-page monthly tabloid, is the joint project of the Native American Center, the American Indian Training and Employment Program, and the Indian Health Project of Oklahoma City. Established in 1975, it was offered free for three years and then at a subscription rate of five dollars a year. Government information is featured along with local, state, and national news; sports; arts; and calendars of coming events.

Another urban Oklahoma paper is the *Tulsa Indian News*, a monthly tabloid with a focus on information about Indian activities and programs as well as guidance and referral services. The paper was started in 1973 as an arm of the Tulsa Human Services Agency and was funded by the U.S. Office of Economic Opportunity.

The *Tacoma Indian News* is another community newsletter that has expanded into a full-fledged paper. Established in September, 1976, it became a professional tabloid using pictures and copious art. Subscription rates were set at one dollar a year. In addition the paper has carried advertising and has received some funding from the Office of Native American Programs. It includes local, state, and national news of interest to Indians, along with governmental information, job and school notices, and sports.

In Wisconsin, the Milwaukee Indian News established a four-page monthly tabloid in 1976. Funds for the publication, which is distributed free, have been provided by the Indian Urban Affairs Council. The paper covers news of the council as well as some national and local issues of interest to the Milwaukee Indian community. Also included are poetry and a calendar of events.

Another recent Wisconsin effort is the *Wisconsin Inter-Tribal News*, which calls itself a "Monthly Newspaper of Indian Country Issues." It was started at Ashland in 1978 by the ten member tribes of the Great Lakes Intertribal Council: six bands of Chippewas, Potawatomis, Oneidas, Winnebagos and Stockbridge Muncees (Mohican). The paper is edited by Walt Bresette, a Chippewa who worked for the public information office of the Intertribal Council. It is distributed statewide, its news directed both at members of the affiliated tribes and at non-Indians throughout the state and the upper Midwest.

In Washington, D.C., the American Indian Society (AIS) of Washington began publishing a monthly newsletter in 1966. The simple four-page newsletter has been limited almost exclusively to describing the activities of the organization. Many of the four hundred subscribers are members of AIS, living either in Washington or scattered throughout the country. The publication is supported by an annual subscription of two dollars and various fund-raising efforts.

A final group of publications to be discussed is Indian magazines and publications for professional groups. We turn now to these.

CHAPTER NINE
Magazines and Specialized Publications

In addition to newspapers, print journalism in Indian country
also includes magazines, specialized publications, and newsletters. This chapter discusses some thirty such publications covering a
wide range of interests, causes, and communication needs. Those
included here were selected because they represent a broad spectrum
of Indian magazine journalism. As with newspapers, the list of magazines discussed as currently publishing is valid through 1978.

The publications are grouped here according to five areas of
interest: historical-cultural, advocacy, professional, educational, and
prison culture-group publications.

A major historical-cultural publication, *Indian Historian*, is a
quarterly produced by the American Indian Historical Society, based
in San Francisco. *Indian Historian* has graphically illustrated the goals
of the society, which are "to promote and develop the culture, education and general welfare of the American Indians; to inform and educate the general public concerning the history, languages and general
status of the Natives as original owners of this land."[1]

Besides establishing the magazine in 1964, the society has also
held workshops for classroom teachers, evaluated textbooks, and
placed the issue of textbook correction on a national plane. It prepared pioneering curricula for educators in the areas of Indian studies;
founded and organized a regular convocation of American Indian
scholars, held every four years; and established and maintained the
Indian Library and Archives, where noted scholars have worked.
Other publications established through the Indian Historian Press
include *Wassaja*, the national newspaper described earlier, and the
Weewish Tree, a magazine of Indian America for young people. The
latter magazine, begun in 1971, is published six times a year and is
written by Indians, Eskimos, and Aleuts, both adults and children. It
has carried fiction, poetry, history, puzzles, pictures, and humorous

120

articles. Its circulation has climbed steadily past ten thousand. Contents of *Indian Historian* have included historical, anthropological, and sociological studies by leading Indian and non-Indian scholars; reviews of films and books about Indians or with Indian-related themes, and literature and art by American Indians.

Indian America was started in 1967 as a mimeographed newsletter called *American Indian Crafts and Culture* and was 'directed at a predominantly non-Indian readership of "Indian" hobbyists. In 1974, however, the scope and purpose of the quarterly began reflecting the growing politicization of Indian readers. Later issues have contained articles on the use and abuse of Indians in the United States by the stamp and currency establishment, current views on archaeology and the invasion of Indian mounds and burial places, news from across Indian America ("The Indian Way"), critical reviews of books on Indian topics, Indian recipes, and calendars of events throughout Indian America. One reader's response to the newer format was as follows:

> As a hobbiest and student of material culture, I'm still impressed with the craft articles. I find the increased scope not only refreshing, but necessary to keep in perspective the hobbiest's role. These are political times, and this forum is vital to the complete understanding that must come in order for everyone to communicate, to live, and to create together in peace.[2]

Another Indian crafts-oriented publication, the monthly *Whispering Wind Magazine*, also begun in 1967, is published in New Orleans, Louisiana. The readers are "primarily those interested in National American crafts, powwows, dancing," and it aims to present Indian arts, crafts, and traditions both past and present. The twenty-four-page offset publication contains such regular features as *Sa Kan* (contemporary Native American news highlights), book reviews, record reviews, and calendars of coming events. It is funded by subscriptions and advertising.

Other publications combine the historical-cultural approach with a concern for environmental awareness. *Many Smokes*, published in Klamath Falls, Oregon, is the unifying link among small groups across the country, groups visited by its editorial board members in frequent trips and brought together often in seminars and workshops. Regular features have included interviews with medicine people, editorials, book reviews, news from across "Indian Country," hints on survival in harmony with nature, poetry, a powwow calendar, and classified advertising. One issue also carried the following message:

> We all share our Earth Mother with many other spirits—those of four-leggeds, wingeds, and other two-leggeds. . . . Some people now seek to move away from an attitude of possession. The bounty of Mother Earth was meant for all. In this time of drought, it is good to put water out for the wild creatures. To contribute toward their well-being is part of living in a balanced and sacred manner.[3]

A fourth publication, *Tsa'Aszi*, the quarterly magazine of traditional and contemporary Navajo culture, is produced by Navajos at Ramah, New Mexico. Widely circulated and extensively used as a primary resource, it includes interviews and information on weaving, foods, ceremonies, art, hunting, and other topics.[4] A similar publication, *Clan Destiny*, the bimonthly publication of the Seneca Indian Historical Society, is centered at Irving, New York. It contains news, legends, poetry, and spiritual teachings. Although not crafts-oriented, it focuses on the original life and customs of Indians as the natural peoples of the United States and its organizes its materials around the first-people theme.[5]

Predominantly literary magazines also place increasing emphasis on Indian rights and growing self-awareness. *Sun Tracks*, published at the University of Arizona by the Amerind Club, has been issued annually since 1971. Its purpose is to promote literary expression among Indian people, offering an outlet and an inspiration. It has invited readers to "share your concern about contemporary Indian existence in the form of artwork, poems, stories, essays, or any other creative work you would like to have published."[6]

Woloch Pi, published through the Sioux City (Iowa) Public Library, is a small literary magazine. It grew out of the Indian Library Project of the Sioux City Public Library, which sponsored an Indian Writing Contest for Native American residents of the city in 1976. Monetary prizes, contributed by a local television station, have been awarded in age categories of youth, adolescent, adult, and elders, with all entrants required to offer proof of at least one-quarter Indian blood. *Woloch Pi* contains the first- and second-place winners in each category and provides a forum for the thoughts and talents of otherwise unknown writers. It also demonstrates the efforts being made among urban Indians to retain their native culture in the collision with modern society. Such publications also help set the stage for increasing political and legal activity by tribes and national Indian groups.

At the heart of Indian advocacy efforts is *Indian Law Reporter*, a scholarly monthly established in January, 1974. Published in Washington, D.C., it has been financed through subscriptions and the contributions of private foundations. It is published by the American Indian Lawyer Training Program, a private, nonprofit organization. The *Reporter*'s main purpose is to transmit and discuss current developments in the field of Indian law. For example, a typical issue carried recent court decisions, a survey and analysis of Indian legal developments, proceedings in the United States Supreme Court, legal opinions, litigation and status reports, and a cumulative topical index.[7] In this format the *Reporter* has been useful as a resource document and a continuing history of the development of Indian law in the United States. The magazine has developed a working relationship with the National Indian Law Library (NILL) in Boulder, Colorado. Each month all items in the *Reporter* are categorized according to a comprehensive index of Indian law developed by NILL and are assigned acquisition numbers where appropriate. Complete copies of court decisions, pleadings, and briefs, compiled and edited each month, are forwarded to NILL, and from there they are available free of charge to Indians or at a nominal cost to non-Indians.

Another law publication, *American Indian Journal*, was established in Washington, D.C., in 1975 by the Institute for the Development of Indian law.[8] A thirty-two-page monthly magazine, it has been funded by subscriptions and through memberships in the institute. It focuses on Indian history, Indian law, and current legislation and federal administrative actions affecting Indian people. The *Journal* functions as a means of providing information on new developments and ideas relevant to Indians in their efforts toward self-determination. It is easily read and well-documented.

The readership for the *Journal* includes Indian governments, individuals, and organizations across the country, as well as colleges and universities, law schools, federal and state agencies, members of

Congress, religious organizations, and other Indian publications. Some regular features of the magazine include a Washington report, results of current legislation and related Capitol Hill action, federal agency plans, and Supreme Court cases relating to Indians. It also includes periodic book reviews. Most authors are attorneys, professors, researchers, or students, and most articles are solicited from persons known to be doing research in relevant fields.[9] The *American Indian Law Review*, published by the College of Law in the University of Oklahoma, Norman, Oklahoma, is another legal periodical. It covers topics in Indian law, such as hunting and fishing rights, mineral rights, taxation, education, and BIA matters—anything that touches the lives of Indians in legal matters.

On a more local level, the *Zuni* (New Mexico) *Legal Aid News* interprets legal developments affecting New Mexico Indians, suggests resources helpful to Indians, and announces programs and services available through the Zuni Legal Aid and Defender Society. Other specialized publications related to law and Indian rights took such material as that included in the *Indian Law Reporter* and gave it local application. For example, the *Northwest Indian Fisheries Commission Newsletter*, established in Olympia, Washington, in 1974, is a multilithed 8½-by-11-inch publication that interprets legal decisions as they affect Indian fishing rights in the Pacific Northwest. Information comes from Indians themselves, from the consulting biologists and specialists on fishing and natural resources, and from federal agency representatives. A major use to which the newsletter has been put is as background for Indian newspaper editors in the affected regions.

A related publication, *Indian Natural Resources*, is a bulletin of the Association on American Indian Affairs. It was started May 1, 1977, with a circulation of five thousand. A quarterly with free circulation, *Indian Natural Resources* emphasizes important federal, state, tribal, and corporate actions; significant research contributions relating to water and fishing rights; federal management of tribal resources; and tribal efforts to protect mineral and water rights. It serves as a reference collection of sources for further information and provides a forum for discussing policy issues of both immediate and long-range concern to Indian tribes and to the general public. The editor, quoted in another publication, pointed to what he called an urgent nationwide need for a comprehensive and accurate source of information concerning Indian natural resources issues, the actions of state and federal governments and of the courts, and the options available to Indian tribes as they formulate their own programs and strategies for resource protection, conservation, and development.[10]

Indian Family Defense, also published by American Indian Affairs, was started in 1974. A quarterly, it is an eight-page newsletter devoted to Indian child-welfare problems, with a nationwide circulation of three thousand Indian and non-Indian readers. One issue carried such stories as that of a Chippewa woman who had fought for three years to regain parental rights terminated by a Montana court; of Apache families deceived into placing their children through a "Christian" foster agency; and proselytizing efforts of one church that centered upon removing Indian children from their homes and placing them in "Christian" homes in order to work for the children's "redemption."[11]

Americans for Indian Opportunity, established in 1969, publishes the *AIO Report* from Washington, D.C. The *Report* has been published irregularly as an annual report and as a publication geared to special conferences and workshops on Indian development. Issued as supplements to the *Report* are fliers titled *Red Alert*, with news of job opportunities, federal deadlines for funding proposals, newly published resource materials, legal developments relating to Indian rights claims, educational opportunities, and related announcements.

Oklahomans for Indian Opportunity (OIO) was established in Norman "to tell the story of how Oklahoma Indians are learning by doing, . . . helping themselves, . . . helping others." Its newsletter carried news of small business successes, jobs, educational achievements and opportunities, Indian-owned enterprises, health and preventative medicine, and generally upbeat messages. The OIO has discontinued the newsletter because of a duplication of its information and the information received from other Indian newsletters and is now embarking on the publication of a journal (projecting three issues a year). Iola Hayden, who has been the director of OIO since it began in 1965, describes the new journal as an effort in resource development, "to provide models for the effective use of social services, grants, and educational opportunities available to Indians."

A final advocacy-style publication, the National Tribal Chairman's Association *Highlights*, began with NTCA's establishment in 1971. The association developed, as a *Highlights* article recounts it, "partly, as a result of growing tribal frustration with then-leadership in the Bureau of Indian Affairs, and partly because of other major events which had occurred over the past several years."[12]

Intentionally or not, those major events had been successful in convincing Indians across the country that the BIA was unresponsive to the needs and problems of reservation-based Indians. An organizational meeting in Billings, Montana, in February, 1971, resulted in the formulation of fifteen basic concepts for a new government policy. These fifteen concepts included the necessity that Indian leaders redefine their goals, objectives, and relationships vis-à-vis federal agencies; that Indian leaders provide impact for federal program planning regarding Indian needs; that there be a greater coordination among agencies serving Indian populations; and that program priorities be realigned with priorities set on the reservations instead of in Washington. *Highlights'* purpose is to report on the success of tribal leaders in putting these concepts to work. As a twelve-page, three-column monthly magazine, it accomplishes its tasks through the use of background material, interpretive reporting, on-the-spot coverage of events, and news items from across the country.

Professional publications, another category among the specialized magazines and periodicals of Indian country, serve the particular communication needs of Indian professional groups.

A single issue of a magazine for Indian media people appeared in 1978. Called *Red Current*, the publication was the work of Richard La Course, then editor of the *Yakima Nation Review*. The magazine was billed as a quarterly, but publication proved infeasible after the first issue. That issue, a tabloid, was twenty pages long. It contained news and analysis of developments among Indian media people. Advertisements were almost exclusively for Indian-oriented media products.

Also appearing in 1978 was the *White Cloud Journal*, which carries results of research on American Indian and Alaskan Native mental health. The journal is published by the White Cloud Center at the University of Oregon Health Science Center. White Cloud Center was sponsored by the National Tribal Chairman's Fund. Managing editor of the quarterly is Ann Goddard, a Cherokee-Shawnee. The publication was to be directed to Indian and non-Indian mental health researchers.[13] Subscriptions were set at twelve dollars annually.

Another professional publication is the four-page *Newsletter of the Association of American Indian Physicians*, published in Oklahoma City. Established in 1973, it is aimed at persons interested in upgrading Indian health. It is a quarterly sponsored by the AAIP general fund. One issue included such features as "Washington News," "Update on Public Law 94-437" (Indian health-care delivery), and assorted news items related to health care and American Indians. The *Newsletter* functions both as an information service and as a unifying force among Indian physicians.

With similar goals, *Indian Courts Newsletter* is published in Washington, D.C., by the American Indian Court Judges Association. Begun in 1971, it functions as a journal reflecting the affairs and personalities of American Indian justices. The *Newsletter* helps identify and define issues facing Indian people in terms of the individuals who sit on the bench.

Indian Travel Newsletter is a businessmen's publication, designed to acquaint travel-industry executives with American Indian and Alaskan Native tourism facilities and activities. Established in 1972 in Lakewood, Colorado, it is an attractive, four-page quarterly publication of the American Indian Travel Commission. The *Newsletter* has focused on Indian tribes, tourism facilities, economic predictions and recommendations, tips for camping, achievements of the AITC, tips on effective publicity for tourism and recreation facilities, and a regular column, "Marketing Tips." One issue of "Marketing Tips" discussed news-media relations. Another discussed cooperation with such related industries as airlines, travel agencies, car-rental companies, bus companies, and local business organizations.

The aim of the *Newsletter*, like that of the two previously mentioned professional publications, is public relations. Each group uses its publication to unify Indians of its particular profession and to present a professional picture to non-Indian colleagues. Although they are small and few in number, these newsletters are important, because they promote economic independence for Indian America.

Working toward the same end through education, several specialized publications have made an impact through their consistent coverage of the problems and accomplishments of Indian schools and educators. *Indian Education*, established in 1970 in Minneapolis, is a twenty-four-page magazine. Published by the National Indian Education Association, it is designed to further the NIEA goal of better educational opportunities for Indian people everywhere. As the executive director wrote in the March 1977, issue, "Education is the key to our heritage and to the preservation of our culture." [14]

With this concern in mind, the editors focus the magazine on such issues and problems as educational testing policies and their impact on students of varying cultural backgrounds, the difficulties of measuring educational effectiveness, Bureau of Indian Affairs budgeting and its impact on Indian education, and materials and resource assistance available through NIEA and related groups. The three-column magazine uses many photographs and Indian designs. It also reprints many articles from Indian newspapers, chiefly from the *Yakima Nation Review*.

A satellite publication, *Project Media Bulletin*, is devoted to specialized areas within the NIEA, and, like *Indian Education*, it is illustrated with photos and artwork throughout. Also like *Indian Education*, it is dedicated to developing educational environments that promote among Indian students a healthy self-concept and a pride in their own history.

Another education magazine, *Indian Education Record of Oklahoma*, was begun in Tulsa in September, 1975, by the Tulsa Indian Youth Council. A monthly, it has focused on educational issues and Indian educators in Oklahoma. It includes articles on statehood and Indian sovereignty, the Indian Education Act of 1972, activities of the Tulsa Indian Youth Council, a series on contemporary Indian educators, and achievements of Indian students. The *Record* voices the continuing strong concern for improving the educational opportunities of Indians as demanded by tribal and urban Indian groups across the country. The magazine's motto, printed in each issue on the title page, reflects that concern; it reads, "First Americans Should Be First in Education."

Publications are also produced by the more than twenty Indian culture groups in prisons in nine states, with wide-ranging coverage that varies in style, content, and approach. These newspapers and newsletters have been outlets for expression and vehicles for unity. *Lakota Oyate-Ki*, published by the Lakota Club of the Oregon State Penitentiary, was established in September, 1969. It is published twice a year, with an international readership estimated at half a million readers, in an effort to interest readers in the cultural, religious, social, and ceremonial rights of Indian prisoners. An editorial described the magazine's function:

> to promote the culture, heritage, and traditions of our people, and to instill within the Indian prisoner positive goals and ideals that will give him the knowledge to confront the many problems that he will be faced with after he is released. Also, we hope to make our people aware that the problem of one Indian is the problem of all Indians, and it is only through a united concern that our people will be able to walk in balance once more.[16]

Material comes from Lakota Club members, from members of the Ms. Lakota Club at the Oregon Women's Correctional Center, from outside correspondence and letters to the editor, and from exchange papers. Regular features have included poetry, legends and prophecies, editorials and questionnaires, news and events among inmates, sports, and photographs of club activities. The fifty-two-page, two-column mimeographed magazine is generally well written and interesting.

A smaller prison publication, *Indian American Folklore Group Newsletter*, is a relative newcomer. A six-page dittoed monthly, it is published by the Indian American Folklore Group at the Minnesota State Prison at Stillwater. Poetry, fiction, sports, and records of releases, paroles, and new incarcerations are carried. One issue also carried a lengthy report on a prisoner grievance involving apparently unfair searches of visitors and disciplinary action against prisoners who protested such searches.[17]

Four Winds, established in 1970, is the monthly magazine of the

Confederated Indian Tribes Council at the Washington State Penitentiary at Walla Walla. A thirty-page dittoed production with a circulation of three hundred, it promotes unity among the Indian inmates at the pentitentiary. Its readers include Indian and non-Indian inmates and persons outside the prison, in addition to agency, state, and national officials. It covers Indian cultural activities inside the penitentiary, letters from readers, sports, stories concerning Indian culture and history, humor, poetry, artwork, and news of released Indian prisoners and their successes. Like other prison culture-group publications, as well as the other magazines and periodicals discussed in this chapter, *Four Winds* represents an effort to use print communication to further unity and self-determination.

These publications, some of them admittedly very unsophisticated, have met many of their aims, as attested to by their continued existence and the increasing numbers of groups using them.

Another avenue of communication, broadcast journalism, likewise is being recognized as a community builder and a powerful ally. This new communications wave will be discussed in the next chapter.

CHAPTER TEN

Broadcasting in Indian Country

Broadcasting is in many respects ideally suited to the communication needs of American Indian peoples. If skillfully used, the electronics media can be important ingredients in bringing together a group of people who share common problems and common concerns. Communication can help form community, and in some parts of Indian country broadcast communication probably can serve that role better than any other medium.

Radio—the spoken word carried afar—blends well with the tradition of oral communication in Indian culture. Much closer than whites to a strictly oral civilization, many Indians have a greater affinity for the spoken word than for the written word. And among some of the poorer, less educated Indians in the United States, for whom becoming literate is an uphill fight at best, the spoken word often provides the only link to the outside world.

Television may be an even better medium than radio in this regard. Nothing short of actual physical presence can rival television in its sense of involvement, of immediacy, of bringing near that which is spatially dispersed. For people of an oral background television adds the opportunity to take into account the gesturing and body language that accompany speech. Through television the visual cues that are an integral part of speech can be transmitted. Tim Giago, an Oglala Sioux who heads that tribe's broadcasting company, believes that television is the most natural of all the media for Indian use. As a visual medium, it is tied closely to Indian tradition, says Giago.[1] In his television programming Giago has found that older, more tradition-oriented Indians seem to take naturally to television.

Despite their inherent advantages, however, radio and television have several major disadvantages that have interfered with their widespread development by Indians. Radio stations—not to mention television stations—are often prohibitively expensive to set up and to operate. They require highly trained and usually well-paid technicians to get them going and keep them going. The investment in time, manpower, equipment, and technical ability is large, especially when contrasted with the resources needed to start and operate a tribal newspaper.

A financial disadvantage of a different sort is that owners of existing media outlets often have a vested interest in keeping competing stations off the air in a given market. In terms of establishment versus Indian stations, the fight for the Indian advertising dollar has allegedly been the motive behind such opposition in more than one case in recent years. Given complex FCC regulations that affect broadcast-license proposals, such opposition can be effective in slowing the license-granting process, if not blocking it entirely.

Some people, notably scholars of sociology and anthropology, speak also of a cultural problem in the imposition of the electronic media on a traditional culture. The argument has long been advanced that such exposure could only work against the preservation of that culture.[2]

At least one recent study has applied this thesis to the effects of radio on the Navajos living on the Ramah Indian Reservation in northwestern New Mexico.[3] The reservation has operated its own radio station since the early 1970s. The author of the study suggests that the exposure to the "new" medium has, instead of preserving an oral heritage, "militated against strengthening the Navajo's cultural awareness and appreciation."[4] He concludes that radio has simply hastened the acculturation of the Navajos into the larger society.

That argument, a familiar one to Indian scholars and media professionals, draws fairly strong reaction. Richard La Course, a Yakima whose studies span close to two centuries of Indian communication efforts, acknowledges that acculturation is and has been going on for many years. But La Course distinguishes between acculturation and assimilation: Indians have had to modify their culture by contact with the white culture, but they have not become absorbed. The adaptation of the "white man's media" to the Indians' needs is, La Course argues, yet another instance of such acculturation.[5] And Jerry Elliott, an Osage who works as a *NASA* engineer and is promoting satellite-communications projects for Indians, cites Darwinian theory in his refutation of the argument:

> Unless you adapt to your environment, you die. I am not less an Indian because you teach me how to use a computer. Using a computer does not mean that I have to change who I am. Survival is the name of the game. And survival means to adapt. . . . Maybe you have to give up some of your old ways, but you can still be an Indian person.[6]

Despite the financial, political, and philosophical difficulties inherent in their moving into the electronic media, by the mid-1970s American Indians were recognizing the power of the airwaves and the need to adapt them to their own purposes. The recognition was coming from many quarters within Indian culture—not only from media professionals but also from tribal officers and national spokesmen. Even members of the law profession saw the need, as witnessed by an article in the *American Indian Law Review*. As the writer of that article stated:

> The needs of Indian communities resulting primarily from a language barrier, partially from a barrier of isolation of Indian groups on reservation areas, and from the highly specialized nature of Indian information and culture, are best satisfied by the broadcast media. . . . Assertive movements by Native American groups to seek broadcasting licenses in order to, in good faith, fulfill needs and interests of the Indian communities must be made in order to encourage Indian broadcasting to the extent required to satisfy the necessities of Indian communities across the United States.[7]

Indeed, by the late 1970s that recognition of a need had turned into widespread and growing interest in the media, with strong activity on several fronts. Several Indian-owned radio stations were on the air, film and videotape were in use in Indian Centers throughout the country, and proposals for TV stations were in the works in at least three places. Indians were moving into satellite communications and had begun to organize into larger media blocks by way of a broadcasting consortium and even a media watchdog enterprise.[8]

The first involvement of Native Americans in broadcasting came not with station ownership but with programming offered over established stations. The earliest radio efforts go back to the 1930s in

Alaska. Some programming for Indians of the Southwest was started during the 1950s. But most Indian-oriented radio broadcasting started in earnest only during the 1970s—most of it within the past few years. Nor has the development been in a straight-line fashion: some programming goes for several months or years, then dies out, sometimes to be replaced by other efforts, sometimes not.

A profile of Indian broadcasting shows that it has made its greatest inroads, as might be expected, in geographic regions of (1) fairly high concentrations of Indian people or (2) Indian-native peoples spread over a large area. In the United States that translates into Alaska, major parts of the Southwest, the Far Northwest, and parts of the Great Plains, especially the Dakotas. The profile also shows that much (though not all) of the programming has been produced by Indians. Many broadcast-media efforts throughout the country have been along the lines of one-hour (usually Sunday morning) public affairs programming geared to helping stations meet their FCC-mandated public-interest program requirements. Much of this programming is of a religious nature, some of it with a strong dose of proselytizing. Some establishment stations have gone considerably further, however, offering Indian-oriented programming of significant quantity and high quality.

An extensive survey conducted in 1977–78 identified about a hundred such broadcasting outlets in the United States (the vast majority of them white-owned) that were then offering regularly scheduled Indian-oriented programs. About fifteen percent of the stations were television, the rest AM or FM radio, either commercial or public. Their offerings ranged from a five-minute weekly newscast to a total schedule of Indian-oriented programming.

Programming varies from news and information to culture and entertainment, from public affairs to contemporary or traditional music—paralleling the range of content found in any cross section of the establishment media. A notable difference, particularly apparent in stations devoting longer blocks of time to Indian-oriented programming, is that those stations allot significant periods of time to announcements of all sorts, both public and private. That points up a special function of broadcasting in Indian country—a bulletin-board function.

Indian broadcasting has reflected the bilingual knowledge of many Indians in the country. Much programming alternates between English and the local native language. Some stations broadcast the same information, first in one language and then in the other; others supply different programming in each of the two (or more) languages.

The survey and subsequent interviews revealed a high degree of expressed concern from both white and native broadcasters for more Indian involvement in radio. Quite a few stations listed as carrying regularly scheduled programming said that they were hoping to increase the amount of such coverage. Speaking from the perspective of white broadcasters, several said they had found a lack of Indian interest in broadcasting, both as program listeners and as program producers-announcers. A fairly typical comment in this regard was that offered by one white station manager: "Despite our usual and frequent requests to Indian leaders, we get only promises but no programs on a regular basis."[9]

A more balanced assessment of the problem of increasing Indian involvement in radio came from another manager. He wrote, "Radio may be invaluable, but so far it's absolutely alien to them."[10] He reported that, before a recent tribal election, he had offered ten minutes of free air time to each of sixteen candidates. Not one had taken him up on the offer. Whether it was the medium or its controllers that was alien to the Indians is a question that was not explored.

Even on stations owned by non-Indians which devote large quantities of time to Indian broadcasting, the question of access to the airwaves has continued to raise problems. The owners, being responsible for programming, almost universally keep a strong hand on programming policies, as well as on employment practices that determine which Indians will be hired. These owners stressed that they had to contend also with the reactions of non-Indians to Indian programs. Quite a few white broadcasters reported negative or hostile audience reactions from their non-Indian listeners.

Most of the white-owned stations that go beyond the one-hour weekly public-service broadcasting employ Indian announcers, newscasters, disc jockeys, or show hosts or a combination of all of these for the programs. Several station managers mentioned that their Indian announcers, nearly all of whom receive their training on the air, had gained considerable popularity among their people as a result of the media exposure. Some announcers had parlayed their popularity into elected positions as tribal councilors or even as tribal chiefs.[11]

The difficulty in holding on to good Indian broadcasters was also prevalent. As one Alaska broadcaster stated her case:

> We have difficulty employing and keeping Native persons in broadcasting. The corporations created by the Land Claims Act, the Alaska Pipeline Project, and other expanding opportunities provide an effective brain drain away from broadcasting. Also, the profession does not pay as well as others.[12]

The problem of access to establishment-licensed airwaves and the fact that non-Indians determine Indian programming have been factors behind the move toward native-owned media outlets. Also impelling such a move was the growing need in the late 1970s for Indians to make their voices heard in an increasingly hostile era. The reaction to so-called Indian privileges was growing, and Indians saw the need to offer a rebuttal that would be heard.

But the move toward involvement in their own media outlets was not simply one of reaction. It was a natural progression, an organic development into new media needs and forms. In large part the development was an outgrowth of expanding communication and community needs of Indian peoples. Indians simply need their own media voices, not someone else's.

Against that history, December 10, 1977, became something of a landmark in the history of Indian media development. It was on that day that radio station KMDX-FM began broadcasting at Parker, Arizona. It was the first commercial radio station in the country owned and operated by an Indian. Owner Gilbert Leivas, one of the members of the Colorado River tribes who live in the area, fought several legal battles to get the station on the air. Within a year Leivas was "nearly" back off the air, driven out of business by the station's inability to generate or collect advertising revenue.[13] No loans were forthcoming either. Despite these problems, however, the station had made broadcasting history.

Several other Indian-owned and operated stations had been on the air before, but KMDX-FM was the first commercial operation.

One of the more noteworthy noncommercial radio operations is KTDB-FM, Ramah, New Mexico, mentioned earlier. As the first Indian-owned and operated noncommercial station in the nation, it has become a sort of model for noncommercial Indian radio. Its primary audience consists of the Ramah Navajos and about two thousand other Navajos. Since the main Navajo reservation sprawls north and west of Ramah, the station reaches only a small corner of that area. So the Ramah Navajos have a distinct location that is served by their own station. They also form their own distinct community—although, in the tradition of Navajos generally, they too are spread out over many miles.

It is partly because the community is so scattered that radio has had a natural role to play at Ramah. The station fast became the de facto newspaper, telephone, and bulletin board of the community, filled with announcements and messages of every conceivable kind.[14] Public health immunization schedules are listed, and tribal business affairs are publicized. Individuals send messages to their families, a man complains about cattle grazing on his land, and someone else asks his friend to be home at a certain time for a visit. The school district, the Bureau of Indian Affairs, and the tribal police are all regular users of the airwaves. Announcements are made in Navajo and English or both, as required. Announcers are all bilingual and overall the station carries about 60 percent Navajo and 40 percent English broadcasting. In addition to the bulletin-board function, KTDB carries local, state, national, and world news in both languages. KTDB took its call letters from Te'ochini Dinee Bi-Radio ("Radio Voice of the People"). It went on the air in 1972.[15]

The All-Indian Pueblo Council ran station KIPC-FM for about a year in the mid-1970s. The station, broadcasting from Albuquerque, New Mexico, was set up to serve a confederation of Pueblos throughout the area.

The Rosebud Sioux tribe brought station KINI-FM onto the air at St. Francis, South Dakota, in 1977, and by mid-1978 the Zuni Tribe in Zuni, New Mexico, had station KSHI-FM on the air.

KSUT-FM is the radio voice of the Southern Ute tribe of southwest Colorado. Tribally owned and operated, it went on the air in mid-1976. The noncommercial station broadcasts in stereo during daylight hours. Broadcasting is in English and Ute. The programming is largely local, with some National Public Radio and other tapes to supplement local efforts. It includes news, public affairs, homemaker programs, Indian and non-Indian music, announcements, interviews, and discussion programs designed for the informational needs of the people of the Southern Ute Reservation.

KEYA-FM, another public station, was licensed to the Couture School Board, Belcourt, North Dakota. The school board is part of the Turtle Mountain Band of Chippewas. About three hours of Indian news and public affairs progamming is offered each week. The station went on the air in 1975.

KRNB-FM, another noncommercial station, went on the air to serve the Makah Reservation Indians in northwest Washington in 1975. It features local, state, national, and international news and information, along with educational and entertainment programming.

Several other small stations have made an occasional appearance, such as KNCC, a station run by the Navajo Community College in Tsaile, Arizona. KNCC, a ten-watt station, is student-run and operated during the school year. Other stations were in the planning stages. For instance, the Yakima Nation was making ambitious plans for putting an FM operation on the air, as were the Oglala Sioux at Pine Ridge, South Dakota. The Menominees in Keshena, Wisconsin, were likewise preparing the groundwork for an FM station there.

Among non–Indian-owned radio stations that run Indian-oriented programming, several have distinguished themselves in playing important roles in Indian communications.

KNOM, Nome, Alaska, represents a unique broadcasting effort that has to be considered on any list of minority programming. The station, on the air since 1971, has been a nonprofit enterprise owned by the Roman Catholic Diocese of Northern Alaska, but has offered negligible religious programming. Rather, its eighteen-hour daily schedule has offered a full complement of news and information, instruction, music and other entertainment, public affairs, and Eskimo or Indian features. With a hefty ten thousand watts of power, the station covers an area of 200,000 square miles, reaching an estimated thirty thousand Eskimos and Athabascan Indians living in about ninety villages scattered throughout western Alaska.

Like other Indian or Indian-oriented stations, KNOM has filled a vital bulletin-board role as well. According to KNOM surveys, more than half of the people in its vast broadcast area listen to the radio more than eight hours a day, and 80 percent list radio as their prime or only source of news.

News is a big part of the broadcast day. The general manager wrote, "Emphasis is on local, regional, and state news, with as many Native-related subjects and interviews as possible, to encourage Native listeners to take an active interest in events which affect their lives."[16]

The station was started and run by a volunteer staff, with 60 percent of its operating funds coming from individual contributions. It covered an area in which nearly half the listeners (48 percent) were below federal poverty levels, 37 percent have completed fewer than six years of school, 64 percent of the families have at least one alcoholic member, and the suicide rate is twenty times the national average.[17] The manager offered this rationale for the station's existence:

> The reason for KNOM . . . is to bring Western culture closer to the Native in a non-threatening manner, to stimulate an interest in education, to teach specific means of improving health, sanitation, and general lifestyle, to encourage the retention of cultural tradition and to wrap the entire package in a bright, entertaining manner that will maintain the listener's attention, promote his receptivity to the material, and make him feel better about being alive.[18]

Far south of Alaska, stations in Arizona and New Mexico serve similarly impoverished peoples, bringing them what for many is their sole contact with an outside world. The vital role that radio can play among the Navajo people led one non-Indian broadcaster at Farmington, New Mexico, to make it a commercial success as well. Farmington lies at the eastern edge of the main Navajo reservation, which covers vast stretches of Arizona and New Mexico. For about twenty years Jim Gober, partner and general manager of station KWYK, carried considerable Navajo-language programming. By the mid-

1970s more than half the day's programming was in Navajo. Gober claimed an audience of eighty thousand Navajos and was able to persuade large numbers of merchants to advertise in the Navajo language. He found that car dealerships and related industries were most responsive and pointed out studies showing that Navajos spent 25 percent of their incomes on private transportation.[19]

In selling advertising directed at Indian audiences, Gober had to take a unique approach. Radio ad rates are conventionally determined by standard rating services that attempt to define and determine the size of a station's audience. But most such services are set up to measure metropolitan areas. That and other problems prevent any accurate tabulation of Indian audiences scattered over a wide geographic area. So Gober at one point conducted his own audience survey by having car-repair servicemen note the dial settings on the radios of Navajo autos and pickups coming into their shops. He was able to use the highly favorable results as selling points with potential advertisers.

KGAK, Gallup, New Mexico, is another non-Indian station that has had commercial success with Indian programming. From its beginning in 1953, the station has carried about thirty hours of Indian programming weekly—most of it in Navajo, but some in Zuni to serve the Zuni Pueblo Indians south of Gallup. The station, the first to broadcast in Navajo, has won the Peabody and DuPont awards for its Navajo program concept. The "Original Navajo Program" features news, public affairs, announcements, a thrice-weekly "Navajo Homemaker" program (focusing on nutrition, prenatal care, and hygiene), and Indian as well as country and western music. The Zuni format is similar, except for more soft rock than country and western music.

Gallup's KYVA also broadcasts about fifteen hours weekly in Navajo. Indian news, music, public affairs, music requests, and dedications have been a part of the station's bill of fare since it went on the air in 1959. Here, too, the information-entertainment function has been successful financially for its white owners. In Taos, New Mexico, station KKIT carries one hour of news every evening, music, and announcements in the Tewa language of the Taos Pueblo. The local

Indian announcer supplements news with occasional wire-service stories of interest to Indians.

Throughout Arizona, with its vast reservation lands—primarily Navajo, Hopi, Hualapai, Fort Apache, and Papago—are several other white-owned radio stations that feature significant amounts of Indian programming. The most notable of these have been KCLS, Flagstaff; KDLJ, Holbrook; and KINO, Winslow.

The remainder of Indian-oriented programming on non-Indian radio stations in the United States is scattered through other states, especially Alaska, Oklahoma, Montana, North and South Dakota, Washington, and, to some extent, Utah, Colorado, and Minnesota. The pattern reflects in fairly direct ratio the sizes of Indian populations in the various states; however, none of the white-owned stations in any of these states except Alaska regularly offers more than one or two hours of Indian-oriented programming.

As for television, Indian-owned outlets were still in the planning stages in the late 1970s. But Indian-owned and operated television is thought to be fairly imminent in Alaska, where native groups are negotiating for satellite-transmission facilities; in Arizona, where the Navajos are fast developing their film and videotaping capabilities and planning a television station; and in Allen, South Dakota, where the Pine Ridge Oglala Sioux Broadcasting Company is planning to start programming before the end of the decade. Several longer-range projects likewise are under consideration, as Indian tribes and urban groups look toward their media needs of the 1980s.

Some of the more prominent people and television shows during the middle and late 1970s are discussed below. Ron Holt, a Nez Perce, produced a monthly half-hour show called "Indians in Progress" for the Montana Television Network, an affiliation of stations in Billings, Great Falls, and Missoula. Holt lived on the Montana Crow Reservation. The program, whose primary audience consisted of Crows and Northern Cheyennes, included news, interviews with Indian leaders on current issues, and cultural programs.

Francis Montoya, a young San Filipe–Isleta Pueblo Indian, was public affairs director for Albuquerque's KOAT-TV, for which he produced a variety of programs. He was serving as host on "The First

Americans," a biweekly Sunday morning talk show that had been started earlier by Oglala Sioux Tim Giago. Montoya also was coordinating "Pueblo Voices," another open-format show that he said he wanted to build into the Southwest's strongest Indian voice.

Most of any significant Indian-oriented programming produced in Oklahoma during the decade was the work of Sammy White, a Kiowa in Oklahoma City who goes by the media name of Tonekei ("Rushing Water"). He writes a weekly column for the *Oklahoma Journal*, which serves the Oklahoma City area, and among the programs he has produced was the weekly "Tribal Voices from the Land," which ran on the Oklahoma City educational-television station on Sundays.

Other Indians have also been at work in television. Among them were Ray Murdock, who broadcast a weekly program called "Indian Viewpoint" on WDIO in Duluth, Minnesota, and Harriet Skye, editor of the *United Tribes News* of North Dakota, who produced "Indian Country" for KFRY-TV in Bismarck, North Dakota, biweekly on Saturday afternoons. Giago had a version of "First Americans" on KOTA-TV, Rapid City, South Dakota, for several years.

Gerald One Feather, then treasurer of the Oglala Sioux, and a non-Indian named Tom Katus teamed up to produce a series on KOTA-TV called a "Red-White TV Dialog." The two traveled around the state interviewing Indians and non-Indians on common problems, with the objective of improving understanding between the two peoples.

Several syndicated radio programs also were being produced. Montoya, at Albuquerque, produced some of these. Bruce Baird, a Chippewa-Oneida Indian, was producing "The Indian Hour" regularly at KOST at Vermillion, South Dakota, and syndicating it to several stations in the Dakotas and Iowa. Sammy White's syndicated radio programs included three weekly half-hour shows for the Oklahoma News Network called "Indians for Indians." These involved mostly Indian music and culture.

In another Dakota effort, a series of twenty-three taped programs was produced by KDSU, the North Dakota State University station at Fargo. The half-hour tapes, made available to stations of the state, interpreted Indian heritage and discussed social problems relating to Indians. The series, entitled "From Eagles to Crows," was based on interviews with more than 150 Indians. Its focus was primarily on Indians and Indian issues of North Dakota.

Beginning in early 1977 a regional news network, the Navajo North Radio Network, was sending tapes or telephone transmissions of fifteen-minute daily news and feature programs to subscribing stations throughout Arizona and New Mexico. The "Navajo Nation Report" also was being offered for television.

Producing radio and television tapes was only one segment of the work of the Navajo Film and Media Commission, begun in 1960 as a watchdog agency to oversee the work of establishment film companies in an effort to prevent media exploitation of Navajos. The commission was expanded in 1974 to regulate all matters regarding "filming, photography, recordings and interviews of Navajo people for the development of films, books, news releases, pamphlets, brochures, documentaries, broadcasts, and other forms of written or pictorial descriptions of the Navajo Nation, its environmental surroundings, and its people."[20] The intent was to counteract the proliferating stereotypes and false pictures of Navajos and Indians in general as portrayed in the establishment media. At its communications center in Window Rock, Arizona, the commission also has served as a media training ground for young Navajos. Filmmaking has been one outgrowth of this activity. Several other Indian groups likewise have gone into film production. Recognizing the power of the film medium, Indian filmmakers—along with such Indian actors as Will Sampson and Raymond Tracey—have turned to film as a way of counteracting the Hollywood stereotypes of Indians.

One successful Indian film group is Circle Films, centered in Albuquerque, New Mexico. Since its inception in the early 1970s, it has produced more than a dozen educational films dealing with various tribes and telling their stories from an Indian point of view. Another educational-film group active in the field is Shenandoah Film Productions. This Indian-owned company, headquartered in Arcata, California, was started in 1968. In addition to 16mm films, productions of the company have included slide-tape programs, sound filmstrips, and sound recordings. Other film groups have sprung up. The Yakima Nation Media Services, for instance, has produced several films, including "The Price We Paid," a portrayal of the construction of Washington State's Grand Coulee Dam and the poverty it brought to Indians. The Annual American Indian Film Festival, begun in 1976, recognizes the work of Indian filmmakers and actors and serves as a kind of antidote to the stereotypical Hollywood approach to American Indians.

Another sort of logical media progression, this one in the form of satellite communications, was making inroads into Indian communities. In 1978 the First Americans Commission for Telecommunications was formed to work out the details of establishing an audio-video linkup that would connect Indian centers at a dozen different locations from Alaska to Washington, D.C. The project grew out of two satellite demonstration projects that had been run earlier that year with NASA and RCA satellites. Indians at several scattered locations—four in the first experiment, six in the second—spent four days in wide-ranging discussion with each other and with BIA officers in Washington. The project coordinator was Jerry Elliott, of NASA and the American Indian Science and Engineering Society. Elliott proposed a two-year service based on the success of the demonstration projects.[21]

Along with their involvement in individual radio, television and satellite programs and projects, Indians were also recognizing the need to form larger groups to work cooperatively. One of these was the Native American Public Broadcasting consortium. The group, in operation since 1977, set out to be a clearing house for Indian programming on public-broadcasting stations. A film-videotape library was developed, along with a distribution network for getting them into station owners' hands. Gradually the consortium expanded its role, serving tribal communication needs and becoming a consultant to tribes working on developing their own radio stations. It also moved into the training and employment of Indians in the media, a vital but often neglected link in the chain of Indian media involvement. Building a bank of national programs and making plans for a national Indian network were other activities the consortium was beginning.[22]

CHAPTER ELEVEN

The Movement Toward
Media Associations

The development of associations for Indian press and broadcast enterprises is a logical step on the path toward effective communications. As the boundaries of tribal, intertribal, and pan-Indian affairs became less and less distinct, the needs of Indians for information increasingly interrelated. Tribes and urban Indian communities have realized that they cannot afford the luxury of isolation. That knowledge hit home especially hard among Indians during the decade of the 1970s. The era became one of backlash against Indians, with new and powerful threats to their very survival coming from many sides. In such a climate the need for greater intertribal awareness became imperative.

In recognition of these needs, many national and regional associations of Indian journalists have been formed, complete with news services for disseminating information on a wide scale.

Although a logical outgrowth of Indian needs, these associations could not simply be willed into existence. Their problems have been as many and varied as the problems of the Indian press itself—financial, organizational, and professional. They have shared the same struggles for survival that mark the life (and, frequently, the death) of Indian newspapers and broadcasting operations.

Media-association development also parallels the development of many an Indian media operation. The drive, the vision, and the hopes for success are counterbalanced by low budgets and long hours, along with the inevitable infighting that stems from trying to represent diverse views and philosophies.

By far the most ambitious such organization was the American Indian Press Association (AIPA) which was active from 1970 to 1975. The story of the origins, growth, and eventual decline of this group is both instructive and dramatic. That story will form the material of the bulk of this chapter, which then will be concluded with a survey of other media-association activities during recent years.

That the AIPA and other associations have arisen within the past ten years is evidence of the strength of the contemporary American Indian press. It must be acknowledged, however, that these are not the first press groupings in the history of American Indian journalism. Ninety years earlier, during the late 1880s, Indian editors in Oklahoma Territory formed the first Indian editors' association.[1] Although it was short-lived, the association set a precedent. It took nearly a century for its pioneering efforts to be repeated.

From its inception in 1970 the AIPA set broad national goals for itself. It was to be the basis for a communications network for American Indians. AIPA's function, as stated by its founders, was to improve communications among Indian people and between Indians and non-Indians. Although the AIPA sought to accomplish these missions in various ways, the primary vehicle of the group was a news service for channeling important national Indian news to local and regional Indian newspapers.

The rise of AIPA was meteoric, its effect lasting. If on the one hand the organization reflected the resurgence in Native American publications, on the other it was itself the spark that ignited many more journalistic efforts in Indian country. Charles Trimble, an Oglala Sioux, is generally given credit for being the one most responsible for bringing AIPA from idea to active organization. He was also largely responsible for the rapid rise and expansion of the association during its first two years, when he served as executive director.

Trimble had worked for several years with an organization called American Indian Development (AID), which was active in promoting Indian educational projects and offering fund-raising help to Indian organizations. In 1969, Trimble (then vice-president of AID), took over editorship of *Indian Times*, a Denver newspaper. His work with that paper, along with growing association with other Indian editors and study of Indian newspapers as part of his graduate work in journalism, deepened his belief in the needs of tribes and organizations for communications services. "Another concern, widespread among Indian communicators," he wrote subsequently, is the lack of proper interpretation of events and priorities in Indian affairs on the part of the mass media. All too often, the mass media will give extensive coverage to sensational and relatively unimportant events in Indian affairs while completely ignoring . . . more significant needs and events.[2]

Trimble persuaded AID to seek funding for a national Indian journalist conference to explore these issues. Funding for a conference to improve communication among Indian people proved hard to find, however, as eventually did funding to keep AIPA going, according to Trimble.[3] In time the Federal Office of Education said that limited funds would be available for a conference. Buoyed by that hope, AID set up a planning meeting. It was held in Spokane, Washington, in July, 1970. That meeting, however, quickly moved beyond a conference agenda-setting affair to become the organizational meeting at which the groundwork for AIPA was laid.

Ten editors of Indian newspapers, representing many tribes and many parts of the country, were in attendance. Trimble later summarized the points discussed during the two-day conference.[4] They deserve attention here because of their importance to the press association that was to be formed.

Delegates agreed that the need for Indian newspapers was great and that it was growing stronger, because American Indians needed clear information to help them regain their land rights and other legal rights, some of which were under attack. The so-called moccasin telegraph—the word-of-mouth transmission of information—no longer was adequate (if ever it had been). "The moccasin telegraph is only as reliable as its non-Indian counterpart—the rumor mill," wrote Trimble.[5] Furthermore, because of the Indians' unique and uneasy relationship with the federal government, the many federal programs that were couched in mostly legalistic language could be interpreted in more understandable terms by a news service for Indians. This was especially true of programs espousing Indian self-determination. As Trimble put the case: "It seems absurd that self-determination can be expounded without provisions for the improvement of communications to inform and guide the people in such a massive venture."[6]

Another issue discussed was that of the financial dependency of Indian newspapers and its effect on editorial freedom. Because of low advertising and subscription revenues, most Native American papers were dependent on tribal government, the federal government, and church-related or other organizations for support. That raised the touchy problem of displeasing funding sources by espousing unpopular causes, the delegates pointed out. The best remedy, they agreed, was for the papers to gain as much Indian readership support as possible. Subscriptions and subsequent advertising revenue would allow some independence. To gain that support, however, the papers needed to carry more features that would enhance their appeal—a function that ongoing training programs and a national news service could aid.

A related problem discussed was the widespread misinterpretation of Indian affairs by the mass media. In part, that was seen as stemming from the inability of the media to determine valid sources of information about Indians. The conferees did, however, commend the mass media for what they called "their efforts in intercultural understanding."[7]

After their discussion of these and other problems, the participants listed the functions that a press organization could fill. Among them were instruction to help improve the editorial and technical quality of Indian newspapers, interpretation of legal and technical information affecting Indian people, information exchanges among Indian newspapers, funding assistance, talent searches to find and help train Indian youth for journalism careers, dissemination of entertainment and informational items to papers, and establishment of sources of expertise in Indian affairs for use by the mass media and general public.[8] Many of these aims were eventually written into the bylaws of what would come to be known as the American Indian Press Association.

The conferees devised a regional setup by which the United States was divided into eight sections, with a team appointed for each area to do further research on the structure of the organization and to gain grass-roots support for it. A questionnaire also was sent to tribal newspaper editors to sound out their reaction to establishing a press association. In a speech he gave later in 1970 at the annual convention of the National Congress of American Indians in Anchorage, Alaska, Trimble offered a rationale for establishing the American Indian Press Association: "Indian power means different things to different people. We're going under the assumption—we're betting—that the essence of Indian power is a truly informed Indian public."[9]

The founding group met again in September, 1970, in Durango, Colorado.[10] The participants reported on the results of their research into the acceptance throughout Indian country of the idea of a press association. At this meeting Trimble was named executive director. After the meeting Trimble headed for Washington, D.C., to seek funding. By November a $24,000 development grant earlier promised to AID came through, giving the organization some running room.

In late November the founders again got together, this time at the offices of the American Indian Historical Society in San Francisco, to map their strategy. Because of the momentum gained by the association through increasing public exposure, it decided to speed the development of the news service and to begin scheduling editor workshops and conferences. Trimble's executive directorship was made official, and James Jefferson, editor of the *Southern Ute Drum*, was named president of the association. For the time being, their office would remain in Denver. The board also voted to adopt the name Indian Press Association, reasoning that the single term would cover Canadian Indians and metis as well as American Indian. The change was short-lived, because within a couple of months Trimble was advised that an organization called the Indian Press Association already existed—headquartered in New Delhi, India, but with representatives in the United States.

In early January, 1971, the first editors' conference took place in Denver, bringing together editors of twenty selected newspapers for a one-day session that included an official press conference with the United States commissioner of Indian affairs. Trimble spent part of January in Washington again, looking for funding. In early February, a meeting of five board members took place in Washington. This group acted on a broad range of matters, including the AIPA budget, constitution and bylaws, funding plans, and additional funding and proposals. A full board meeting took place on February 27 and 28 in Denver, by which time the organization was running under full steam. And on March 9, AIPA was incorporated as a nonprofit organization in Colorado. The constitution and bylaws were reviewed in detail and unanimously adopted. Jefferson's election as president was formalized.

By the time AIPA was incorporated, Trimble was working hard to secure funding to expand the operation and move it to Washington, D.C. The move was seen as necessary to get AIPA to where the action was, both financial and legislative. To be effective, both the organization and its news service would have to be headquartered there. AIPA was offered space in the offices of the National Congress of American Indians, but funding for the move was still in the air. In the meantime Trimble got in touch with Richard La Course, a Yakima-Umatilla who was writing for the *Seattle Post-Intelligencer*, about operating the news service.

Within a month, Trimble had made the move, had brought on La Course, and had written the board that he felt that, to keep up the impetus of the past few months, "the executive director has got to take more initiative and make decisions to cause our programs to get rolling." [11] At the same time he was aware of the organization's tenuous financial base. He mentioned this to the board in a comment not unlike one that most editors of Indian newspapers could make:

> I admit that we are taking quite a chance in the actions I've taken. Our funding will not hold out for the remainder of the fiscal year if we do not get the grant or contract. . . . I'm sure you all understand, however, that my salary is on the line also. If we do not get the additional funds, and if we deplete our existing funds, I am well aware that I cannot be paid either. [12]

His wife, Ana, had been working as an unpaid volunteer for several months. By the end of June his funding fears were realized. "The American Indian Press Association is broke," he wrote to board members. "This is not to say that the association is finished, but we have some rough times ahead if we are to stay in existence. Our financial crisis stems from a number of problems, the most important of which is my naïveté in thinking money would be relatively easy to come by." [13] He was sharply critical of the BIA, which had long assured him that money would be available, only to back out at the end. "I have learned a valuable, if bitter, lesson," he wrote.[14] Trimble also told a researcher early in 1972 that the BIA's reluctance to fund the association stemmed from the bureau's realization that the AIPA was not going to play a public relations function for the bureau.[15] Indeed, AIPA press releases were frequently critical of the BIA.

In mid-1971 also came the first inkling of impending problems with getting a tax-exempt status for organization. Philanthropic foundations told Trimble they could offer support only if AIPA contributions were tax-exempt. But he had learned, he wrote, that the news service might be considered a business rather than an educational or humanitarian effort. His report also contained a bright note on the news service, which Trimble called a complete success. News from Washington was going out in weekly packets to member newspapers, "and our stories are being used." La Course, with help from Thomas Edwards, a *Cincinnati Post and Times Star* reporter who had signed on for a couple of months, was covering the Capitol for Indian editors throughout the country with news and frequently hard-hitting investigative reports. The process was working, whether the Internal Revenue Service called it business or education.

Because of the success of the news service and the volume of stories being picked up by Indian newspapers, Trimble was able to report to the board by the end of October that "AIPA is already recognized as somewhat of an institution by all federal agencies and on the Hill. It is considered quite a powerful tool for Indian causes."[16] Ironically, it was that power that sent AIPA into the economic buzz saw. Trimble reported on his attempt to get funding from the Economic Development Administration. His poignant comment was:

> I approached the EDA (Ray Tanner) and presented our plans and they were extremely interested. They suggested that we ask for much more money and offered to rush the proposal through and give it their full support. After some delay, I was told that they could not seriously consider our proposal if we were going to continue to say bad things about the government and the administration. I have been told by some people in Washington that, when the government is afraid of you, that is some measure of success of the news service. That didn't help our financial situation, but we cannot promise any government agency that we'll be nice Indians if they'll give us money.[17]

Their federal (and foundation) funding avenues virtually blocked, Trimble and La Course sought financial help from various church organizations. They were moderately successful. AIPA also contracted with NCAI to produce some publications for that organization. And a media-relations service also was developed during 1971. Under Rose Robinson, this was a contract service that had AIPA doing the press-relations work for Indian programs and conferences throughout the country. This arrangement also facilitated thorough coverage of these programs by the news service. Funding problems prevented AIPA from having more than one board meeting in 1971. In 1972 the first board meeting took place in Washington on January 19–20. La Course reported on the progress of the news service. He spoke at length about how he organized coverage of the news, including news not only from Washington but from Indian country itself. He spoke also of his work in developing contacts in the federal bureaucracy and of new areas of investigative reporting that the service was opening.

Despite the success of the news service, another problem was dogging AIPA. Trimble brought it to the attention of board members at the January, 1972, meeting. Subscriptions from Indian newspapers were not coming in as fast as many of the founders had hoped. Trimble had not yet mounted much of a subscription drive because he had not been able to guarantee that AIPA would stay in operation. A subscription campaign was begun, but after more than a month the drive had brought in only five more member papers. By the end of July the total had climbed to fifty-five members. The annual membership cost to Indian papers was $40. The directors had hoped to generate as much as $19,000 through subscriptions. But by mid-1972 only slightly more than $2,000 had been raised. They also expected up to $36,000 from church funding, but realized only $6,000 in the first half of 1972. Interestingly, $5,000 of that was in the form of a grant from the Episcopal chuch for use in the legal work of applying for a tax-exempt status from the IRS.

Despite its limited funding AIPA continued to expand during 1972. Regional conferences with newspaper editors and staffs were held in May and June in Sacramento, Albuquerque, and Minneapolis. The news service opened a summer internship program that brought young Indian journalists to Washington, D.C., giving them valuable training and providing the service with a manpower boost in the process. The groundwork was laid for expanding membership in the electronic media.

For one project Trimble and La Course went to Pine Ridge, South Dakota, to give technical assistance to the *Oglala Nation News*, a biweekly. The paper was started in the wake of disruptions over the death of Raymond Yellow Thunder. Trimble and La Course also took a trip to Canada that year to study a sophisticated Indian communications setup in Alberta.

The year's second board meeting took place on August 4 in Denver. Trimble expressed concern that only those activities directly related to AIPA's primary goal of getting the news to Indian people should be accepted for discussion. The directors also considered the need for a policy defining the extent to which AIPA should support editors on their own political and professional issues. *Akwesasne Notes*, for instance, had looked to AIPA for support in a fight of its own with the IRS. Another issue the board tackled was how to broaden its network of news dissemination. Trimble suggested beginning a national publication to supplement the news releases that were being sent out. La Course suggested making of it a paper whose articles could be clipped and reprinted in the members' publications. The publication also could include tips on technical and editorial aspects of journalism. He also suggested that AIPA look into the possibility of renting the BIA cable to send its stories via wire.

Plans were laid for the first annual AIPA convention, which was set for November 16–18 in Denver. Directors decided to institute an award for journalistic achievement, to be presented at the convention. They named it the Marie Potts Award for Excellence in Indian Journalism. Marie Potts, a Maidu who was by then more than seventy years old, had published the *Smoke Signal* in Sacramento for thirty years. One of the founding members of AIPA, she was considered the dean of Indian journalists.

The convention brought together about seventy-five Indian journalists for three days of business meetings, speeches, panel discussions and workshops. A highlight of the convention was a speech on "The Indian World Today" by Vine Deloria, Jr., a Sioux author-lawyer who has written on a wide range of Indian-rights issues. The Marie Potts Award for 1972, carrying a five-hundred-dollar prize, went to *Akwesasne Notes*.

A month before the convention, however, an event had occurred that would have profound effects on AIPA's future. The National Council of American Indians elected Trimble its executive director. He accepted the position. Rose Robinson was appointed acting executive director of the association after Trimble's departure. She took a leave of absence from her job as editor of the BIA *Indian Board* to take the directorship. A board meeting was held in Washington, D.C., on January 18–19, 1973, at which Robinson was formally elected director. After that, she resigned from government service to devote full time to AIPA. At the meeting Robinson reported that the struggle to obtain a tax-exempt status continued. One alternative approach that might work would be to set up a separate arm of AIPA to receive tax-deductible contributions, she said.

In 1973 the first of what was to be an annual *American Indian Media Directory* appeared. It was a comprehensive listing of Indian newspapers, newsletters, magazines, radio, television, and film, as well as theater, printing services, and selected publications dealing entirely or in part with Indians and Indian affairs. Indian college and high school publications also were listed. The directory, which carried the designation "1974 Edition" (although released in 1973) was the result of two years of compiling work headed by La Course.

Another significant accomplishment of AIPA in 1973 was the publication of *Medium Rare*, a monthly newsletter for members. It contained information on subjects ranging from journalism to public affairs. Especially noteworthy was the AIPA policy statement on advocacy journalism and Indian crises, stated in the March issue that year. The policy was prepared by Robinson and was printed, according to the newsletter, in answer to frequent questions about the association's position on such volatile Indian issues as the Wounded Knee takeover. The statement read, in part:

> The AIPA, as a matter of journalistic policy, does not take sides on political issues, particularly when those issues are on the local tribal or intertribal level. Our policy of *political* non-involvement in local or

tribal politics should assure that no political adversaries will benefit from their association with AIPA, and that none should be harmed.

Our policy of *journalistic* involvement, however, is total: to provide to our readership . . . balanced, complete and accurate reportage of all sides of disputes and situations of conflict . . . ideological bias on the part of a working Indian reporter, we believe, will hinder rather than aid in meeting the information needs of a broad Indian readership in the full perspective which troubling conflict situations deserve. Our sole purpose for existence is to improve the channels—and the content—of communication among Indian people and to provide news of events that vitally affect Indian lives.[18]

At the second 1973 board meeting, held on July 20 in Marquette, Michigan, plans were drawn up for the second annual AIPA convention. Board members decided it would take place on October 26–27 in Tulsa, Oklahoma. In what was fast becoming an activist era for Native Americans, the theme of the convention was an exploration of the relationship between the media and the so-called Indian Movement. The keynote speaker was Frye Gaillard, editor of the *Race Relations Reporter*, Nashville, Tennessee. Also scheduled were workshops in advertising, photojournalism, and Indian radio. In a comment in *Medium Rare* urging attendance at the convention, Robinson stated:

The world of the Indian press is fermenting and developing now, and it's very exciting. I see a professionalism emerging.

To my mind, the Indian journalism field is the most exciting field in Indian affairs today because we're right in the middle of everything that's going on. And now Indians . . . are beginning to write their own contemporary Indian history.[19]

At a board meeting immediately afterward, Robinson was reappointed executive director for another year. Tom Cook, associate editor of *Akwesasne Notes*, was elected AIPA president. And, continuing its practice of acknowledging excellence in journalism, the association presented the Marie Potts Journalism Award to Alaska's *Tundra Times* and its editor, Howard Rock.

Difficult times lay ahead for the organization in 1974. For economic as well as personal and sociological reasons, the momentum that the organization had attained in its first few years was not sustained. The situation regarding board meetings in 1974 is perhaps instructive. Robinson explained:

> While we called four board meetings in 1974, none were official business meetings because we could not achieve a quorum. Lack of funds to pay for board member travel and per diem was the major cause. Those who were able to attend had their expenses paid by their respective employers.[20]

On the AIPA agenda in 1974 was a plan to produce a history of Native American journalism. It was to have been written by La Course, but it did not appear. During the year, La Course himself left Washington for Albuquerque. From there he continued to operate what then was called the Southwest News Bureau. He kept the title of AIPA news director. The Washington bureau of the news service also continued to operate for much of the year, now under Susan Shown Harjo, a Cheyenne-Creek. *Medium Rare* was still published.

The main event of 1974 was the third annual AIPA convention, by then referred to as a "communications conference."[21] The national conference took place in Santa Fe, New Mexico, on November 7 and 8. The conference theme was "The Indian Image," and La Course was the keynote speaker. He discussed stereotypes of Indians by non-Indians, as well as stereotypes of Indians by other Indians and the hampering effect of the stereotypes in the attempt to present an accurate picture of people and events. La Course wrote about white stereotypes of Indians:

> The white community has the collective jitters about Indians in general. The old stereotype of the Indian wrapped in a blanket, dragging a spear in the dust, has been replaced by that of a young, long-haired man wearing an upside-down flag and carrying a weapon. This is the image conveyed by national TV and the wire services.[22]

He cited, as examples of Indian stereotypes of other Indians, the image of reservation Indians versus urban Indians, mixed bloods versus full bloods, militants versus conservatives, East versus West. La Course said that such stereotypes are caused by a lack of information and can be changed by accurate news coverage, which is the role of the Indian press. About one hundred people attended the conference. In her director's report to the conference, Robinson said that AIPA membership had grown to 225. She told the conferees that AIPA had devoted most of its energies in 1974 to keeping its news service active. Expansion into other activities had been difficult because of funding problems. Even the basic operations had exceeded income, she said, and the organization would run about $12,000 short of expenditures unless immediate funding could be found.[23]

In a message to the conference, BIA Commissioner Morris Thompson attested to the significance of AIPA, which he called "a respected vital part of the Indian scene." He said that when he visited reservations he was now being asked informed questions on Indian policy by tribal members who had read of the issues in the Indian press.[24] In official action at the 1974 conference, AIPA opened its membership to electronic media. Three Indian producers of television shows and one producer of a radio show were elected to the board of directors, expanding the board to fourteen members.

The conferees also voted to explore the creation of an American Indian Press Foundation to receive tax-exempt donations and grants and to distribute them to Indian media development projects. They also voted to request that President Gerald Ford ask Congress for a five-million-dollar annual appropriation for the development of American Indian media systems patterned after a new Canadian Native Communications Policy. The third annual Marie Potts achievement award went to *Wassaja* and its editor, Rupert Costo. According to the nominating sheet, the award was presented for *Wassaja*'s exposé of a California front organization that was collecting advertising money supposedly in the name of Indian newspapers. The newspapers apparently never saw it. Also during the convention, Robinson submitted a letter of resignation as director, effective at the end of the following January. Harriett Skye, editor of the *United Tribes News*, was elected president for 1975.

A board meeting was held on February 2 and 3, 1975, in Denver. Although the names of six applicants for the executive director's position were announced, the board voted to ask Robinson to stay on the job until the end of April. A search for her replacement would continue. After presentations to the board by BIA staff members Tom Oxendine and Lynn Engles on working affiliations between AIPA and BIA, Robinson was authorized by the board to obtain a five-thousand-dollar loan to explore such an affiliation. Susan Shown Harjo was named AIPA news director.

In early April, Robinson sent a memo to board members that constituted her final report as director. It painted a grim, almost hopeless picture of AIPA's financial status.[25] She said she had advanced her departure date to April 14, primarily because there was enough money left to pay only one salary. She said that she thought the remaining money should go to Susan Harjo. She recommended that the board discontinue the southwest bureau, which had been operating for six months. News-release packets from Washington, D.C., had been slowed to twice a month. In the report, Robinson announced that Laura Waterman Wittstock, a Seneca, had agreed to take over as interim acting executive director until a permanent director could be found. Trimble, still with the National Congress, had agreed to pay her way to Washington from Minneapolis, where she was directing a project of compiling media meterials on, by, and for Indians for the National Indian Education Association.[26]

Robinson returned to the BIA, where she worked in the office of public information. Using BIA facilities, she helped the AIPA board set up two conference telephone calls in 1975, one on May 21, and the other on August 29. The calls replaced the board meetings. Transcripts show that a great many subjects were discussed in each conference call, but the specter of a flat-broke organization hung over all the discussions. Several proposals—such as setting up regional news bureaus to be funded by other sources—were advanced, but none moved beyond the proposal stage. Between funding and subsequent personnel problems, the association seemed to be dissolving even while the conference calls were in progress.

Finally, no avenues were left. A tax-exempt status was impossible to attain, and IRS demands for tax payments became incessant. Wittstock stayed in Washington, D.C., until October. "Things got really bad and we operated as a nonprofit news service," she said later.[27] She then closed shop and went back to Minneapolis, where she returned to her job at the Indian Education Association. For all practical purposes the AIPA as a vital, functioning organization was dead.

Although hopes for its revival were kept alive for several years after its demise, most people close to the organization gradually acknowledged that it was not to be. The IRS problem alone would block any revival efforts, they agreed.

The formation and successful tenure of a press association, however, gave other Indian groups the impetus and model they needed for development of associations and press-media groups. Thus in the second half of the decade widespread activity was taking place, most of it on a regional rather than national basis.

One of the strongest among such groups took shape in 1978: the Northwest Indian News Association. The group initially claimed a membership of about twenty-five Indian media organizations in Oregon, Washington, Idaho, and Montana. Along with a professional association of editors, it used its own news service, created along the lines of a UPI operation and combining mail and telephone service for the dissemination of news items of interest to members. The service utilized a news clearinghouse and delivery system that had been set up a year or so earlier by the *Sho-Ban News*, Fort Hall, Idaho. It was supported by subscriber fees. Plans were laid to move the news-service headquarters to Portland in 1979. The first president of the NWIPA was Mark Trahant, also the editor of the *Sho-Ban News*.[28]

At least two other regional groups were organized in the wake of AIPA's five-year effort. Migizi was a group of Minneapolis and other Minnesota Indian communications people who worked mostly with the electronic media. The Southwest Indian Media Collective started in Albuquerque in 1977 under the auspices of the National Indian Youth Council. The latter attracted about twenty-six subscribers from among Indian media groups in Arizona and New Mexico.[29]

Newspaper business managers also were getting together. The Indian Newspaper Publishers Association, a cooperative venture under which papers set uniform advertising rates and lobbied as a bloc for ad sales, got underway in 1977. In its early days the association involved newspapers in the five northwestern states and had hopes of expanding nationally. The president was Robert Johnson of the Small Tribes of Western Washington in Sumner. A private, profit-making news service in Washington, D.C., had been in operation since the early 1970s: NEWS Photo News was supplying national and Indian country photographs for Indian newspapers and television programs.

The service was run by George Ortez, a Mescalero Apache. Another continuing professional activity was a series of BIA media conferences being conducted throughout the country. Some of these were in the form of regional meetings; others were telephone conference programs bringing together editors and others at scattered locations.

Several groups, organized for the purpose of giving Indian people the training necessary to qualify them for media-related jobs, also were in business. One of the more ambitious of these was initiated in southern California by Jerry Thompson, a Cherokee who operated his own advertising agency. Beginning in 1977, Thompson set about finding Indians who were interested in media work. He established several training programs, the first of them in graphic arts. The service was expanded to Albuquerque and to Dallas in 1978. It was a self-funded enterprise.[30] A year earlier Thompson had set four goals for his training service: to serve as a communication liaison between Indians and the mass media; to be a training ground for Indians in journalism and the communication arts generally; to establish an exchange of information among reservation, rural, and urban American Indians; and to encourage the development of individually or tribally owned communications businesses.[31]

Other communications groups, including the Seattle-based Indians into Communications, the Navajo Film and Media Commission, and the Native American Public Broadcasting Consortium also were providing training services. By the end of 1978, Charles Trimble, the man who began the renaissance in professional associations in 1970, was again talking about the need for a national Indian newspaper, a long-held dream of his. Trimble's news organization would be divided into perhaps six regional operations. News and advertising could be national, with local or regional inserts as necessary. Trimble stepped down as executive director of NCAI in late 1978 to direct a comprehensive Washington-based lobbying effort for Indians under the name United Effort Trust, which was designed to counteract the anti-Indian legislation sharpening in the United States during the late 1970s.[32]

CHAPTER TWELVE

Conclusion

As American Indian journalism moves beyond its first 150 years, many voices are rising from it, struggling to be heard among the ever-increasing national and worldwide cries that compete for our attention. The relative strength of Indian media today is both a testimony to the unconquered will of Indian peoples and a signal that they shall be heeded in this noisy world.

This book is a testimony to the current vitality of Indian journalism; it is a spin-off of the widespread activity in communications throughout Indian country.

Intending to offer a historical context, we have tried to stay within the confines of 150 years of Indian communications. Given the strong contemporary movement in communications involving Native Americans, however, the study has of necessity gone beyond its own limits.

Although predictions are always risky, anyone close to Indian media today gets the feeling that it is a young giant just awakening. The hopeful signs of such a stirring are evident in the numbers of media projects just now reaching the proposal stage. A word of caution, however, is in order here: to some extent, recent activity may reflect the quantity of federal grants and other available aid as much as it reflects a renaissance in Indian journalism. In the past few years government support has been widely available, especially for training and short-term employment.

What is still missing from the Indian media scene is a sense of stability. Newspapers, newsletters, house organs, and radio or TV programming start and stop, wax and wane, their existence always dependent on the vagaries of staffing or funding. And, as de facto tribal house organs, many publications necessarily risk incurring the wrath of tribal officials when they take an independent—or even investigative—stand on public issues. There also exists the perennial danger that Indian journalists will relinquish their jobs for "bigger and better" positions in Indian affairs.

Thus, stable communications enterprises—and their primary advantage, quality workmanship—remain largely the hope of the future, not a current reality. The need for communication among Indians does, however, remain. That need has spurred much of the recent activity and has compelled Indians to rise to difficult challenges.

No one, particularly Indians themselves, thinks that the problems of the next few years will be easily solved. At this point, major tribes are undergoing many internal struggles over leadership, resource management, and other questions that are creating upheaval and discord for Indians. As for external obstacles, the picture is not much brighter. Many people, Indians and non-Indians alike, see a growing climate of hostility in this country that bodes ill for the always uneasy peace that prevails between Indians and white America. Nor can one separate these internal and external difficulties from the difficulty of trying to communicate them to one's readers or listeners.

Nonetheless, if their history, which now includes more than 150 years, has manifested anything about Indian journalists, it has shown that the odds for survival are with them, despite incredible obstacles. Viewed in that long light, the challenges of the coming years, although strong, are likely to be met and surmounted.

Appendices

Indian Press Freedom Guarantees

No Indian tribe in exercising powers of self-government shall make or enforce any law prohibiting the free exercise of religion or abridging the freedom of speech, or of the press, or the right of the people peaceably to assemble and/or petition for a redress of grievances.

25 U.S.C. 1302

The Constitution of the United States says that neither the federal nor state governments shall make any law "abridging the freedom of speech, or of the press; or the right of the people peaceably to assemble, and to petition the government for a redress of grievances." The Indian Bill of Rights (of 1968) contains identical protections.

All persons have the right to believe as they wish and to express their opinions openly and freely. The right to influence others through discussions and speeches and in print is a basic freedom. The right to hold, express, teach, and advocate ideas also includes the right to join peacefully with others for the same purpose. Freedom of the press protects not only newspapers, magazines, and books, but it also protects all other forms of printed matter as well as movies, radio, and television. All citizens have the right to criticize any government official, no matter how important. A person is entitled to support peaceful changes in the administration and form of government. This freedom is essential to self-government. In order that people be able to govern themselves, they must be able to listen to the ideas of others and also express their own opinions freely.

The freedom of speech and press are not limited to governmental matters but allow discussion of all issues, nor are these freedoms limited to opinions that are popular or that others consider to be true or acceptable. Their primary purpose is to protect beliefs that are unpopular, including those which can cause strong disagreement and dispute. The U.S. Supreme Court has stated: "A function of free speech under our system of government is to invite dispute. It may indeed best serve its high purpose when it induces a condition of unrest, creates dissatisfaction with conditions as they are, or even stirs people to anger."

. . . Freedoms of expression are not absolute. Reasonable limitations may be placed on the exercise of speech, press, protest, and assembly. Obscenity, libel, and slander are not constitutionally protected. Criminal conduct is not protected merely because it involves speech. A person does not have the right to use speech to cause violence or persuade others to do so. Free speech does not allow persons to force their beliefs on others. Use of streets and other public places can be subject to reasonable limitations so that those using them do not interrupt traffic, make excessive noise, or in other ways interfere with rights of others. But official restrictions on speech and the press must be limited to what is necessary to protect the public welfare.

The inclusion of free speech, press, and assembly in the Indian Bill of Rights has caused many tribal spokesmen to complain that these principles are not part of traditional Indian culture and should not be applied to Indian society. They have argued that tribes are not ordinary governments, but are close-knit, family-like groups, and that the exercise of free speech in this atmosphere would lead to the disruption of discipline and the breakdown of tribal life.

Congress concluded, however, that tribal Indians should be entitled to the same freedoms of expression as other American citizens. Although the courts will, hopefully, demonstrate respect for Indian heritage while applying these freedoms, they will not tolerate acts by tribal governments which completely ban freedoms of expression. A tribal council, for instance, cannot prohibit members from distributing a newspaper on the reservation merely because it is critical of the tribal government. Nor can it prevent members from assembling peacefully in order to express their ideas and listen to the opinions of others.

from *American Indian Civil Rights Handbook*,
issued by the U.S. Commission on Civil Rights.

An Address to the Whites

Delivered in the First Presbyterian Church, May 26, 1826 by Elias
Boudinot, A Cherokee Indian

To those who are unacquainted with the manners, habits, and improvements of the Aborigines of this country, the term *Indian* is preg-
nant with ideas the most repelling and degrading. But such impressions,
originating as they frequently do, from infant prejudices, although they
hold too true when applied to some, do great injustice to many of this race of
beings.

Some there are, perhaps even in this enlightened assembly, who at the
bare sight of an Indian, or at the mention of the name, would throw back
their imaginations to ancient times, to the ravages of savage warfare, to the
yells pronounced over the mangled bodies of women and children, thus
creating an opinion, inapplicable and highly injurious to those for whose
temporal interest and eternal welfare, I come to plead.

What is an Indian? Is he not formed of the same materials with your-
self? For "of one blood God created all the nations that dwell on the face of
the earth." Though it be true that he is ignorant, that he is a heathen, that
he is a savage; yet he is no more than all others have been under similar
circumstances. Eighteen centuries ago what were the inhabitants of Great
Britain?

You here behold an *Indian*, my kindred are *Indians*, and my fathers
sleeping in the wilderness grave—they too were *Indians*. But I am not as my
fathers were—broader means and nobler influences have fallen upon me. Yet
I was not born as thousands are, in a stately dome and amid the congratula-
tions of the great, for on a little hill, in a lonely cabin, overspread by the
forest oak, I first drew my breath; and in a language unknown to learned and
polished nations, I learnt to lisp my fond mother's name. In after days, I
have had greater advantages than most of my race; and I now stand before
you delegated by my native country to seek her interest, to labour for her
respectability, and by my public efforts to assist in raising her to an equal
standing with other nations of the earth.

The time has arrived when speculations and conjectures as to the prac-
ticability of civilizing the Indians must forever cease. A period is fast ap-

proaching when the stale remark—"Do what you will, an Indian will still be an Indian," must be placed no more in speech. With whatever plausibility this popular objection may have heretofore been made, every candid mind must now be sensible that it can no longer be uttered, except by those who are uninformed with respect to us, who are strongly prejudiced against us, or who are filled with vindictive feelings towards us; for the present history of the Indians, particularly of that nation to which I belong, most incontrovertibly establishes the fallacy of this remark. I am aware of the difficulties which have ever existed to Indian civilizations. I do not deny the almost insurmountable obstacles which we ourselves have thrown in the way of this improvement, nor do I say that difficulties no longer remain; but facts will permit me to declare that there are none which may not easily be overcome, by strong and continued exertions. It needs not abstract reasoning to prove this position. It needs not the display of language to prove to the minds of good men, that Indians are susceptible of attainments necessary to the formation of polished society. It needs not the power of argument on the nature of man, to silence forever the remark that "it is the purpose of the Almighty that the Indians should be exterminated." It needs only that the world should know what we have done in the last few years, to foresee what yet we may do with the assistance of our white brethren, and that of the common Parent of us all.

It is not necessary to present to you a detailed account of the various aboriginal tribes, who have been known to you only on the pages of history, and there but obscurely known. They have gone; and to revert back to their days, would be only to disturb their oblivious sleep; to darken these walls with deeds at which humanity must shudder; to place before your eyes the scenes of Muskingum Sahta-goo and the plains of Mexico, to call up the crimes of the bloody Cortes and his infernal host; and to describe the animosity and vengeance which have overthrown, and hurried into the shades of death those numerous tribes. But here let me say, that however guilty these unhappy nations may have been, yet many and unreasonable were the wrongs they suffered, many the hardships they endured, and many their wandering through the trackless wilderness. Yet, notwithstanding the obloquy with which the early historians of the colonies have overshadowed the character of the ignorant and unfortunate natives, some bright gleams will occasionally break through, that throw a melancholy lustre on their memories. . . . Facts are occasionally to be met with in their rude annals, which, though recorded with all the colouring of prejudice and bigotry, yet speak for themselves, and will be dwelt upon with applause and sympathy when prejudice shall have passed away.

Nor is it my purpose to enter largely into the consideration of the remnants, of those who have fled with time and are no more—They stand as monuments of the Indian's fate. And should they ever become extinct, they must move off the earth, as did their fathers.

My design is to offer a few disconnected facts relative to the present improved state, and to the ultimate prospects of that particular tribe called Cherokees to which I belong.

The Cherokee Nation lies within the chartered limits of the states of Georgia, Tennessee, and Alabama. Its extent as defined by treaties is about 200 miles in length from East to West, and about 120 in breadth. This country which is supposed to contain about 10,000,000 of acres exhibits great varieties of surface, the most part being hilly and mountaneous, affording soil of no value. The vallies, however, are well watered and afford excellent land, in many parts particularly on the large streams, that of the first quality. The climate is temperate and healthy, indeed I would not be guilty of exaggeration were I to say, that the advantages which this country possesses to render it salubrious, are many and superior. Those lofty and barren mountains, defying the labour and ingenuity of man, and supposed by some as placed there only to exhibit omnipotence, contribute to the healthiness and beauty of the surrounding plains, and give to us that free air and pure water which distinguish our country. These advantages, calculated to make the inhabitants healthy, vigorous, and intelligent, cannot fail to cause this country to become interesting. And there can be no doubt that the Cherokee Nation, however obscure and trifling it may now appear, will finally become, if not under its present occupants, one of the Garden spots of America. And here, let me be indulged in the fond wish, that she may thus become under those who now possess her; and ever be fostered, regulated and protected by the generous government of the United States.

The population of the Cherokee Nation increased from the year 1810 to that of 1824, 2000 exclusive of those who emigrated in 1818 and 19 to the west of the Mississippi—of those who reside on the Arkansas the number is supposed to be about 5000.

The rise of these people in their movement towards civilization, may be traced as far back as the relinquishment of their towns; when game became incompetent to their support, by reason of the surrounding white population. They then betook themselves to the woods, commenced the opening of small clearings, and the raising of stock; still however following the chase. Game has since become so scarce that little dependence for subsistence can be placed upon it. They have gradually and I could almost say universally forsaken their ancient employment. In fact, there is not a single family in the nation, that can be said to subsist on the slender support which the wilderness would afford. The love and practice of hunting are not now carried to a higher degree, than among all frontier people whether white or red. It cannot be doubted, however, that there are many who have commenced a life of agricultural labour from mere necessity, and if they could, would gladly resume their former course of living. But these are individual failings and ought to be passed over.

On the other hand it cannot be doubted that the nation is improving, rapidly improving in all those particulars which must finally constitute the inhabitants an industrious and intelligent people.

It is a matter of surprise to me, and must be to all those who are properly acquainted with the condition of the Aborigines of this country, that the Cherokees have advanced so far and so rapidly in civilization. But there are yet powerful obstacles, both within and without, to be surmounted in the march of improvement. The prejudices in regard to them in the general community are strong and lasting. The evil effects of their intercourse with their immediate white neighbours, who differ from them chiefly in name, are easily to be seen, and it is evident that from this intercourse proceed those demoralizing practices which in order to surmount, peculiar and unremitting efforts are necessary. In defiance, however, of these obstacles the Cherokees have improved and are still rapidly improving. To give you a further view of their condition, I will here repeat some of the articles of the two statistical tables taken at different periods.

In 1810 There were 19,500 cattle; 6,100 horses; 19,600 swine; 1,037 sleep; 467 looms; 1,600 spinning wheels; 30 waggons; 500 ploughs; 3 sawmills; 13 grist-mills &c. At this time there are 22,000 cattle; 7,600 Horses; 46,000 swine, 2,500 sheep; 762 looms; 1,488 spinning wheels; 172 waggons; 2,943 ploughs; 10 saw-mills; 31 grist-mills; 62 Blacksmith-shops; 8 cotton machines; 18 schools; 18 ferries; and a number of public roads. In one district there were, last winter, upwards of 0000 [*sic*] volumes of good books; and 11 different periodical papers both religious and political, which were taken and read. On the public roads there are many decent Inns, and few houses for convenience, &c., would disgrace any country. Most of the schools are under the care and tuition of Christian missionaries, of different denominations, who have been of great service to the nation, by inculcating moral and religious principles into the minds of the rising generation. In many places the word of God is regularly preached and explained, both by missionaries and natives; and there are numbers who have publicly professed their belief and interest in the merits of the great saviour of the world. It is worthy of remark, that in no ignorant country have the missionaries undergone less trouble and difficulty, in spreading a knowledge of the Bible, than in this. Here, they have been welcomed and encouraged by the proper authorities of the nation, their persons have been protected, and in very few instances have some individual vagabonds threatened violence to them. Indeed it may be said with truth, that among no heathen people has the faithful minister of God experienced greater success, greater reward for his labour, than in this. He is surrounded by attentive hearers, the words which flow from his lips are not spent in vain. The Cherokees have had no established religion of their own, and perhaps to this circumstance we may attribute, in part, the facilities with which missionaries have pursued their ends. They cannot be called idolators; for they never worshipped Images. They believe in a Supreme Being, the Creator of all, the God of the white, the red, and the black man. They also believed in the existence of an evil spirit who resided, as they thought, in the setting sun, the future place of all who in their life time had done iniquitously. Their prayers were addressed alone to the Supreme Being, and which if written would fill a large volume, and display much sincerity, beauty, and sublimity. When the ancient customs of the Cherokees were in their full force, no warrior thought himself secure, unless he had addressed his guardian angel; no hunter could hope for success, unless before the rising sun he had asked the assistance of his God, and on his return at eve he had offered his sacrifice to him.

There are three things of late occurance, which must certainly place the Cherokee Nation in a fair light, and act as a powerful argument in favor of Indian improvement.

First. The invention of letters.

Second. The translation of the New Testament into Cherokee

And third. The organization of a Government

The Cherokee mode of writing lately invented by George Guest, who could not read any language nor speak any other than his own, consists of eighty-six characters, principally syllabic, the combinations of which form all the words of the language. Their terms may be greatly simplified, yet they answer all the purposes of writing, and already many natives use them.

The translation of the New Testament, together with Guest's [Sequoyah's] mode of writing, has swept away that barrier which has long existed, and opened a spacious channel for the instruction of adult Cherokees. Persons of all ages and classes may now read the precepts of the Almighty in their own language. Before it is long, there will scarcely be an individual in the nation who can say, "I know not God neither understand I what thou sayest," for all shall know him from the greatest to the least. The aged warrior over whom has rolled three score and ten years of savage life, will grace the temple of God with his hoary head; and the little child yet on the breast of its pious mother shall learn to lisp its Maker's name.

The shrill sound of the Savage yell shall die away as the roaring of far distant thunder; and Heaven wrought music will gladden the affrighted wilderness. "The solitary places will be glad for them, and the desert shall rejoice and blossom as a rose." Already do we see the morning star, forerunner of approaching dawn, rising over the tops of those deep forests in which for ages have echoed the warrior's whoop. But has not God said it, and will he not do it? The Almighty decrees his purposes, and man cannot with all his ingenuity and device countervail them. They are more fixed in their course than the rolling sun—more durable than the everlasting mountains.

The Government, though defective in many respects, is well suited to the condition of the inhabitants. As they rise in information and refinement, changes in it must follow, until they arrive at that state of advancement, when I trust they will be admitted into all the privileges of the American family.

The Cherokee Nation is divided into eight districts, in each of which are established courts of justice, where all disputed cases are decided by a Jury, under the direction of a circuit Judge, who has jurisdiction over two districts. Sheriffs and other publice officers are appointed to execute the decisions of the courts, collect debts, and arrest thieves and other criminals. Appeals may be taken to the Superior Court, held annually at the seat of Government. The Legislative authority is vested in a General Court, which consists of the National Committee and Council. The National Committee consists of thirteen members, who are generally men of sound sense and fine talents. The National Council consists of thirty-two members, beside the speaker, who act as the representatives of the people. Every bill passing these two bodies, becomes the law of the land. Clerks are appointed to do the writings, and record the proceedings of the Council. The executive power is vested in two principal chiefs, who hold their office during good behaviour, and sanction all the decisions of the legislative council. Many of the laws display some degree of civilization, and establish the respectability of the nation.

Polygamy is abolished. Female chastity and honor are protected by law. The Sabbath is respected by the Council during session. Mechanics are encouraged by law. The practice of putting aged persons to death for witchcraft is abolished and murder has now become a governmental crime.

From what I have said, you will form but a faint opinion of the true state and prospect of the Cherokees. You will, however, be convinced of three important truths.

First, that the means which have been employed for the christianization and civilization of this tribe, have been greatly blessed. Second, that the increase of these means will meet with final success. Third, that it has now become necessary, that efficient and more than ordinary means should be employed.

Sensible of this last point, and wishing to do something for themselves, the Cherokees has thought it advisable that there should be established, a Printing Press and a Seminary of respectable character; and for these purposes your aid and patronage are now solicited. They wish the types, as expressed in their resolution, to be composed of English letters and Cherokee characters. Those characters have now become extensively used in the nation; their religious songs are written in them; there is an astonishing eagerness in people of all classes and ages to acquire a knowledge of them; and the New Testament has been translated into their language. All this impresses on them the immediate necessity of procuring types. The most informed and judicious of our nation, believe that such a press would go further to remove ignorance, and her offspring superstition and prejudice, than all other means. The adult part of the nation will probably grovel on in ignorance and die in ignorance, without any fair trial upon them, unless the proposed means are carried into effect. The simplicity of this method of writing, and the eagerness to obtain a knowledge of it, are evinced by the astonishing rapidity with which it is acquired, and by the numbers who do so. It is about two years since its introduction, and already there are a great many who read it. In the neighbourhood in which I live, I do not recollect a male Cherokee, between the ages of fifteen and twenty five, who is ignorant of this mode of writing. But in connexion with those for Cherokee characters, it is necessary to have types for English letters. There are many who already speak and read the English language, and can appreciate the advantages which would result from the publication of their laws and transaction in a well-conducted newspaper. Such a paper, comprising a summary of religious and political events, &c. on the one hand; and on the other, exhibiting the feelings, disposition, improvements, and prospects of the Indians; their traditions, their true character, as it once was and as it now is; the ways and means most likely to throw the mantle of civilization over all tribes; and such other matter as will tend to diffuse proper and correct impressions in regard to their condition—such a paper could not fail to create much interest in the American community, favourable to the aborigines, and to have a powerful influence on the advancement of the Indians themselves. How can the patriot or the philanthropist devise efficient means, without full and correct information as to the subjects of his labour. And I am inclined to think, after all that has been said of the aborigines, after all that has been written in narratives, professedly to elucidate the leading traits of their character, that the public knows little of that character. To obtain a correct and complete knowledge of these people, there must exist a vehicle of Indian intelligence, altogether different from those which have heretofore been employed. Will not a paper published in an Indian country, under proper and judicious regulations, have the desired effect? I do not say that Indians will produced learned and elaborate dissertations in explanation and vindication of their own character; but they may exhibit specimens of their intellectual efforts, of their eloquence, of their moral, civil and physical advancement, which will do quite as much to remove prejudice and to give profitable information.

The Cherokees wish to establish their Seminary, upon a footing which will insure to it all the advantages, that belong to such institutions in the states. Need I spend one moment in arguments, in favour of such an institution; need I speak one word of the utility, of the necessity, of an institution of learning; need I do more than simply to ask the patronage of benevolent hearts, to obtain that patronage.

When before did a nation of Indians step forward and ask for the means of civilization? The Cherokee authorities have adopted the measures already stated, with a sincere desire to make their nation an intelligent and a virtuous people, and with a full hope that those who have already pointed out to them the road of happiness, will now assist them to pursue it. With that assistance, what are the prospects of the Cherokees? Are they not indeed glorious, compared to that deep darkness in which the nobler qualities of their souls have slept. Yes, methinks I can view my native country, rising from the ashes of her degradation, wearing her purified and beautiful garments, and taking her seat with the nations of the earth. I can behold her sons bursting the fetters of ignorance and unshackling her from the vices of heathenism. She is at this instant, risen like the first morning sun, which grows brighter and brighter, until it reaches its fulness of glory.

She will become not a great, but a faithful ally of the United States. In times of peace she will plead the common liberties of America. In times of war her intrepid sons will sacrifice their lives in your defence. And because she will be useful to you in coming time, she asks you to assist her in her present struggles. She asks not for greatness; she seeks not wealth; she pleads only for assistance to become respectable as a nation, to enlighten and ennoble her sons, and to ornament her daughters with modesty and virtue. She pleads for this assistance, too, because on her destiny hangs that of many nations. If she complete her civilization—then may we hope that all our nations will—then, indeed, may true patriots be encouraged in their efforts to make this world of the West, one continuous abode of enlightened, free, and happy people.

But if the Cherokee Nation fail in her struggle, if she die away, then all hopes are blasted, and falls the fabric of Indian civilization. Their fathers were born in darkness, and have fled in darkness; without your assistance so will their sons. You see, however, where the probability rests. Is there a soul whose narrowness will not permit the exercise of charity on such an occasion? Where is he that can withhold his mite from an object so noble? Who can prefer a little of his silver and gold, to the welfare of nations of his fellow beings? Human wealth perishes with our delay, but that wealth gained in charity still remains on earth, to enrich our names, when we are gone, and will be remembered in Heaven, when the miser and his coffers have mouldered together in their kindred earth. The works of a generous mind sweeten the cup of affliction; they enlighten the dreary way to the cold tomb; they blunt the sting of death, and smooth his passage to the unknown world. When all the kingdoms of this earth shall die away and their beauty and power shall perish, his name shall live and shine as a twinkling star; those for whose benefit he done his deeds of charity shall call him blessed, and they shall add honor to his immortal head.

There are, with regard to the Cherokees and other tribes, two alternatives; they must either become civilized and happy, or sharing the fate of many kindred nations, become extinct. If the General Government continue its protection, and the American people assist them in their humble efforts, they will, they must rise. Yes, under such protection, and with such assistance, the Indian must rise like the Phoenix, after having wallowed for ages in ignorance and barbarity. But should this Government withdraw its care, and the American people their aid, then, to use the words of a writer, "they will go the way that so many tribes have gone before them; for the hordes that still linger about the shores of Huron, and the tributary streams of the Mississippi, will share the fate of those tribes that once lorded it along the proud banks of the Hudson; of that gigantic race that are said to have existed on the borders of the Susquehanna; of those various nations that flourished about the Potomac and the Phappahannoc, and that peopled the forests of the vast valley of Shenandoah. They will vanish like a vapour from the face of the earth, their very history will be lost in forgetfulness, and the places that now know them will know them no more."

There is, in Indian history, something very melancholy, and which seems to establish a mournful precedent for the future events of the few sons of the forest, now scattered over this vast continent. We have seen every where the poor aborigines melt away before the white population. I merely speak of the fact, without at all referring to the cause. We have seen, I say, one family after another, nation after nation, pass away; until only a few solitary creatures are left to tell the sad story of extinction.

Shall this precedent be followed? I ask you, shall red men live, or shall they be swept from the earth? With you and this public at large, the decision chiefly rests. Must they perish? Must they all, like the unfortunate Creeks (victims of the unchristian policy of certain persons), go down in sorrow to their grave?

They hang upon your mercy as to a garment. Will you push them from you, or will you save them? Let humanity answer.

American Indian Media—A Directory

NEWSPAPERS AND MAGAZINES

Alaska

AHTNA Kanas, Drawer G, Copper Center, AK   99753
Aleutian Current, 725 Christensen Dr., Anchorage, AK   99501
Arctic Reporter, P.O. Box 253, Barrow, AK   99723
Bering Straits Native Corp. Newsletter, P.O. Box 3396, Anchorage, AK 99501
Bristol Bay Native Corp. Newsletter, P.O. Box 220, Anchorage, AK   99510
Calista—Voice of the People, 516 Denali St., Anchorage, AK   99501
Caribou News, Box 726, Kotzebue, AK   99752
CIRA and CINA Newletter, P.O. Drawer 4-N, Anchorage, AK   99509
Chugach Natives, Inc. Newsletter, 903 W. Northern Lights Blvd., Suite 201, Anchorage, AK   99503
Doyon, Ltd. Newsletter 201 1st Ave., Fairbanks, AK   99701
Hi-Lites of Native Business, P.O. Box 10–223, Anchorage, AK   99511
NANA Newsletter, 4796 Hardy Dr., Anchorage, AK   99503
NEEK (News of the Native Community), P.O. Box 4360, Mt. Edgecumbe, AK   99835
New River Times, 950 Cowles St., Fairbanks, AK   99701
Point Hope News, Native Village of Point Hope, Point Hope, AK   99766
Sealaska Shareholder, One Sealaska Plaza, Suite 400, Juneau, AK   99801
Tlingit and Haida Tribal News, One Sealaska Plaza, Suite 200, Juneau, AK 99801
Uqualug-Aanich, 313 E St., Anchorage, AK   99501
Tundra Times, 639 I St., Anchorage, AK   99501
The Voice of Brotherhood, 423 Seward St., Juneau, AK   99801

Arizona

Apache Drumbeat, Bylas, AZ   85330
Au-Authm, Office of Management and Program Development, Rt. 1, Box 215, Scottsdale, AZ   85256

Canyon Shadows, General Delivery, Supai, AZ   86435

Contemporary Indian Affairs, Navajo Community College Press, Many Farms, AZ   86503

DNA in Action, Window Rock, AZ   86515

Fort Apache Scout, Box 898, Whiteriver, AZ   85941

Fort McDowell Newsletter, Route 1, Box 700, Scottsdale, AZ   85256

Fort Yuma Newsletter, Box 890, Yuma, AZ   85356

Ganado Today, Ganado Mission, Ganado, AZ   86505

The Ganado Story, College of Ganado, Ganado, AZ   86505

Gum-U "How Are You?", Box 168, Supai, AZ   86425

Hopi Action News, The Winslow Mail, Winslow, AZ   86047

Hopi Crier, Hopi Day School, Oraibi, AZ   86039

ICAP Newsletter, Arizona State University, Tempe, AZ   85281

Indian Highways, Cook Christian Training School, 708 S. Lindon Lane, Tempe, AZ   85281

Indian Programs, University of Arizona, Tucson, AZ   85721

Journal of American Indian Education, Arizona State University, Tempe, AZ   85281

Navajo Area Newsletter, Box 629, Window Rock, AZ   86515

Navajo Times, Box 867, Window Rock, AZ   86515

Oneo Newsletter, Box 589, Ft. Defiance, AZ   86504

The Padre's Trail, St. Michaels, AZ   86511

Papago Bulletin, Box 364, Sells, AZ   85364

Papago Runner, The Papago Tribe of Arizona, Box 837, Sells, AZ   85634

Pima Maricopa Echo, Gila River Indian Community, Box 338, Sacaton, AZ   85247

Qua-Toqtii, Box 226, New Oraibi, AZ   86039

Quechan News, Box 1169, Yuma, AZ   85364

Redskin, Phoenix Indian High School, Phoenix, AZ   85012

River Tribes Review, Colorado River Agency, Parker, AZ   85344

Rough Rock News, Dine' Biolta' Baahani, Rough Rock Demonstration School, Rough Rock, AZ   86503

Sandpainter, Box 791, Chinle, AZ   86503

Sleeping Red Giant, Community Services, Sacaton, AZ   85247

Smoke Signals, Colorado River Tribes Adult Education, Route 1, Box 23-B, Parker, AZ   85344

Sun Tracks: An American Indian Literary Magazine, Department of English, University of Arizona, Tucson, AZ   85720

Sundevil Roundup, Rough Rock Community High School, Star Route 1, Rough Rock, AZ   86503

The Thunderer, American Indian Bible Institute, Inc., 10020 North 15th
    Ave., Phoenix, AZ   85021
Tumbleweed Connection, The College of Ganado, Ganado, AZ   86505
Wi Gegaba, Box 9, Supai, AZ   86435
Yaqui Bulletin, 4730 W. Calle Tetakusin, Tucson, AZ   85710
Yoida Nava, Arizona Western College, Yuma, AZ   85364

California

American Indian, 225 Valencia, San Francisco, CA   94103
American Indian Bar Association, 319 MacArthur Blvd., Oakland, CA 94610
American Indian Culture and Research Journal, American Indian Studies Cen-
    ter, University of California, Campbell Hall, Rm 3220, Los Angeles,
    CA   90024
Bear Facts, 3415 Dwinelle Hall, N.A.S. Student Services, University of Cal-
    ifornia, Berkeley, CA   94720
California Newsdrum, 225 Valencia St., San Francisco, CA   94103
Chemehuevi Newsletter, 2804 West Avenue 31, Los Angeles, CA   90065
Coyote, Powhatan Press, Route 1 Box 2170, Davis, CA   95616
Cherokee Examiner, Box 687, South Pasadena, CA
Drumbeat, P.O. Box 715, San Mateo, CA   94401
Early American, Newsletter of California Indian Education Assoc., P.O. Box
    4095, Modesto, CA   95350
Humming Arrows, Native American Cultural Center, Box 2325, Stanford,
    CA   94305
Indian Archives, Antelope Indian Circle, Box 790, Susanville, CA   96130
The Indian Crusader, 4009 S. Halldale Ave., Los Angeles, CA   90062
Indian Historian, 1451 Masonic Ave., San Francisco, CA   94117
Indians Illustrated, 3028 W. Beverly Blvd., Los Angeles, CA   90057
Indian Life, Christian Hope Indian Eskimo Fellowship, P.O. Box 2600,
    Orange, CA   92669
Indian Newsletter, Box 40, Pala, CA   92059
Indian Voice, Box 2033, Santa Clara, CA   95051
Indigena, News from Indian American, Box 4073, Berkeley, CA   94704
Lassen-Modoc Newsletter, Box 266, Susanville, CA   96130
Namequa Speaks, Native American Woman's Action Council, 4339 Califor-
    nia Street, San Francisco, CA   94118
Native American Students Bulletin, Office of Native American Students, Uni-
    versity of California, Riverside, CA   92507
Newsletter, Concern for Indians, Box 5167, San Francisco, CA   94101

Newsletter, Indian Center of San Diego, 1523 Fifth Ave., San Diego, CA 92101

The Smoke Signal, Federated Indians of California, 2727 Santa Clara Way, Sacramento, CA 95817

Smoke Signals, Box 2477, Santa Clara, CA 95051

Speaking Leaves, Box 2000, Vacaville, CA 95688

Take Ten, 1623 5th Ave., San Diego, CA 92101

Talking Leaf, 1127 W. Washington Blvd., Los Angeles, CA 90015

Teepee Talk, Box 501, Porterville, CA 93258

Tehipite Topics, Box 5396, Fresno, CA 93755

Tribal Spokesman, 2969 Fulton Ave., Sacramento, CA 95821

Tribe of Five Feathers News, Box W, Lompoc, CA 93436

Tsen-Akamak, Route 1, Box 2170, Davis, CA 95616

The Uida Reporter, 1541 Wilshire Blvd., Suite 307, Los Angeles, CA 90017

Wassaja, 1451 Masonic Ave., San Francisco, CA 94117

Winter Count, 367 W. Spezier Ave., Burbank, CA 91502

Colorado

Coalition of Indian Controlled School Boards, 811 Lincoln, Suite 4, Denver, CO 80203

Denver Native Americans United, 2210 E. 16th Ave., Denver, CO 80206

Echo, Towaoc Community Newspaper, Ute Mountain Ute Agency, Towaoc, CO 81334

Indian Times, Box 4131, Santa Fe Station, Denver, CO 80204

Indian Travel Newsletter, Westland Bank Bldg. Suite 550, 10403 W. Colfax Ave., Lakewood, CO 80215

National Indian Health Board, 1020 15th St., Room 4E, Denver, CO 80202

Native American Rights Fund, 1506 Broadway, Boulder, CO 80302

Rising Up, Indian Awareness Group, Box 1000, Englewood, CO 80110

Southern Ute Drum, Tribal Affairs Bldg., Ignacio, CO 81137

USS News, Box 18285 Capitol Hill Station, Denver, CO 80218

District of Columbia

Access, Office of Minority Business Enterprise, Department of Commerce, Washington, D.C. 20230

American Indian Journal, Institute for the Development of Indian Law, 927 15th St. N.W., Suite 200, Washington, D.C. 20005

American Indian National Bank Newsletter, 1701 Pennsylvania Ave. N.W., Washington, D.C.   20006

AIO Alert, Americans for Indian Opportunity, 1822 Jefferson Place N.W., Washington, D.C.   20003

American Indian Society of Washington Newsletter, 519 5th St. S.E., Washington, D.C.   20003

Cena News, 733 15th St. N.W., Washington, D.C.   20006

Highlights, National Tribal Chairman's Association, Suite 207, 1701 Pennsylvania Ave. N.W., Washington, D.C.   20006

Indian Courts Newsletter, National American Indian Court Judges Association, 1000 Connecticut Ave. N.W., Washington, D.C.   20036

Indian Law Reporter, American Indian Lawyers Training Program, Inc., 1000 Wisconsin Ave. N.W., Washington, D.C.   20007

Indian Manpower Bulletin, Room 400, 1741 Rhode Island Ave. N.W., Washington, D.C.   20210

Indian Record, Department of the Interior, Bureau of Indian Affairs, 1951 Constitution Ave. N.W., Washington, D.C.   20245

Legislative Review, Institute for Development of Indian Law, 927 15th St. N.W., Washington, D.C.   20006

Native American, Office of Public Information, 200 Independence Ave. S.W., Washington, D.C.   20201

NCAI Sentinel Bulletin, National Congress of American Indians, Suite 700, 1430 K St., Washington, D.C.   20005

NCIO News, 726 Jackson Pl. N.W., Washington, D.C.   20036

News, U.S. Senator Warren G. Magnuson, 127 Senate Office Building, Washington, D.C.   20510

Source Directories, Indian Arts & Crafts Board, U.S. Department of the Interior, 18th and C Sts. N.W., Washington, D.C.   20240

UIPA News, United Indian Planners Association, 800 18th St. N.W., Suite 500, Washington, D.C.   20006

Florida

Alligator Times, Seminole Tribe CAP, 6073 Stirling Rd., Hollywood, FL 33024

Feathered Shaft, United Southeastern Tribes, 1970 Main St., Sarasota, FL 33577

Georgia

Cherokee Nation, 1276 North Ave. N.E., Atlanta, GA   30307

Hawaii

The Native Hawaiian, Alu Like Native Hawaiian Program, 1316 Kaumalii St., Honolulu, HI   96817

Idaho

Coeur D'Alene Council Fires, Coeur d'Alene Tribal Office, Route 1, Plummer, ID   83851
From Where the Sun Now Stands, Nez Perce Tribe of Idaho, Box 246, Lapwai, ID   83541
Indian Progress, 1095 Division St., Noblesville, ID   46060
NAS-NW Newsletter, University of Idaho, Moscow, ID   83843
Nee-Me-Poo Tum Tyne, Lapwai, ID   84540
New Breed News, North American Indian League, Box 7309, Boise, ID   83707
Sho-Ban News, Box 306, Ft. Hall, ID   83201

Illinois

The Indian Christian, 221 Kellogg Place, Wheaton, IL   60187
Meeting Ground, Newberry Library, 60 W. Walton St., Chicago, IL   60610
Nahow, Native American Program, University of Illinois Circle Campus, Box 4348, Chicago, IL   60680
Native American Publication, 2853 N. Elston Ave., Chicago, IL   60618
Redletter, 4546 N. Hermitage, Chicago, IL   60640

Indiana

Indian Progress, 300 Nixon St., Lot 50, Noblesville, IN   46060

Iowa

City Smoke Signals, 405 W. 7th St., Sioux City, IA   51103
The Iowa Indian, Sioux City Public Library, 6th and Jackson Sts., Sioux City, IA   51105

Kansas

Indian Leader, Haskell Indian Junior College, Lawrence, KS   66044
Mid-America All Indian Center Newsletter, 1650 E. Central   Wichita, KS   67214

N.A.L.C., 1014 Armstrong, Kansas City, KS   66044
Nish Nau Bah Newsletter, Indian Center of Topeka, Inc., 407 W. Lyman Rd.,
    Topeka, KS   66044
Nish-Na-Ba, American Indian Culture Group, Box 2, Lansing, KS   66043

Louisiana

Whispering Wind Magazine, 8009 Wales St., New Orleans, LA   70126

Maine

The Aroostook Indian, Box 223, Houlton, ME   04730
Indian School Bulletin, T.R.I.B.E., Inc., Bar Harbor, ME   04609
Maine Indian Newsletter, Pine Street, Freeport, ME   04032
Mawiw-Kilun, Indian Township, Princeton, ME   04668
Wabanaki Alliance, 95 Main St., Orono, ME   04473

Maryland

American Indian Study Center Newsletter, 211 S. Broadway, Baltimore, MD
    21231
Evening Sun, Calvert and Center St., Baltimore, MD   21200

Massachusetts

The Circle, Boston Indian Council, Inc., 105 S. Huntington Ave., Jamaica
    Plain, MA   02130
Mittark, Wampanog Indians, Mashpee, MA   02649
Newsletter, Boston Indian Council, 150 Tremont St., Boston, MA   02111

Michigan

Great Lakes Voice, Box 305, St. Ignace, MI   49781
Indian Talk, 457 Briarwood S.E., Grand Rapids, MI   49506
The Michigan Indian, Baker Olin Building West Room 313, 3423 N. Logan
    St., Lansing, MI   48926
Native Sun, Detroit Indian Center, N.A.I.A. of Detroit, Inc., 360 John Rd.,
    Detroit, MI   48226
Nishnawbe News, The Organization of North American Indian Students,
    University Center, Northern Michigan University, Marquette, MI
    49855

Tribal Trails, 911 Franklin Street, Petoskey, MI   49770

W.A.N.T. Newsletter, Women of American Native Tribes, 103 E. Liberty, Room 200, Ann Arbor, MI   48108

Wasso-Gee-Wad-Nee Council, Marquette Branch Prison, Box 779, Marquette, MI   49855

Minnesota

AIM News, 1337 E. Franklin Ave., Minneapolis, MN   55404

Anishinabe News, Box 55, Stillwater, MN   55082

De-Bah-Ji-Mon, Box 308, Leach Lake Reservation, Cass Lake, MN   56633

Focus Newsletter, Capitol Square Building, St. Paul, MN   55101

Indian Education, National Indian Education Assn., 3036 University Ave. S.E., #3, Minneapolis, MN   55414

Indian Voice, American Indian Folklore Group, Box 55, Stillwater, MN   55082

Native Heritage, Minnesota Indian Youth News, 1905 Third Ave. S., Minneapolis, MN   55404

Nett Lake News, Nett Lake, MN   55772

Ni-Mah-Mi-Kwa-Zoo-Min, Minnesota Chippewa Tribe, Box 217, Cass Lake, MN   56633

Newsletter, American Indian Association, Department of American Indian Studies, University of Minnesota, 1314 Social Science Building, West Bank Campus, Minneapolis, MN   55455

Newsletter, Indian Community Center, American Indian Fellowship Assn., 101 N. First Ave. E., Duluth, MN   55802

No-Dah-Mo-Win (The News), Bois Forte Reservation, Nett Lake, MN 55722

Oshkabewis, Indian Studies Program, Bemidji State University, Bemidji, MN   56601

Red Lake Reservation Neighborhood Centers Newsletter, Red Lake, MN   56671

The Seventh Fire, American Indian Movement, 261 E. 8th St., St. Paul, MN   55101

Smoke Signals, St. Paul Indian Center, 475 Cedar St., St. Paul, MN   55102

Spirit of the People, The National Newsletter of Native American Solidarity Committee, Box 3426, St. Paul, MN   55165

White Earth Reservation, Box 274, White Earth, MN   56591

Mississippi

Choctaw Community News, MBCI Tribal Building, Route 7, Box 21, Philadelphia, MS   39350

Missouri

Heart of America Indian Center Newsletter, 3220 Independence Ave., Kansas City, MO   64124

Montana

Ah-Chi-Mo-Win, Rocky Boy Reservation, Chippewa-Cree Tribe, Box Elder, MT   59521

The Arrow, St. Labre's Indian School, Ashland, MT   59003

Birney Arrow, Box 552, Busby, MT   59016

Blackfeet Cap News, Browning, MT   59417

Browning Sentinel, Box 340, Browning, MT   59417

Buffalo Grass Newsletter, Missoula Indian Center, 508 Toole, Missoula, MT 59801

Camp Crier, Ft. Belknap Agency, Box 8, Harlem, MT   59526

Char-Koosta, Confederated Salish and Kootenai Tribes, Dixon, MT   59831

Free Press, Box 1730, Havre, MT   59501

Glacier Reporter, Box R, Browning, MT   59417

Helena Indian Alliance, Box 2532, Great Falls, MT   59401

Hi-Line Indian Alliance Newsletter, Box 2213, Havre, MT   59501

Ho Tanka, Brockton High School, Brockton, MT   59213

The Hunter Newsletter, North American Indian League, Box 7, Deer Lodge, MT   59722

Hunter Quarterly, North American Indian League, Box 7, Deer Lodge, MT 59722

Indian Signs, Blackfeet Tribal Business Council, Browning, MT   59417

Ko:Tta':Hilik, Crow Agency, MT   59022

Medicine Bundle, Opportunities, Inc., 510 1st N., Great Falls, MT   59401

The Morning Star People, St. Labre Indian School, Ashland, MT   59004

National Association of Blackfeet Indians News Bulletin, Box 340, Browning, MT   59417

Rocky Boy News, Rocky Boy Route, Box Elder, MT   59521

Tsisististas Press, Northern Cheyenne Tribe, Lame Deer, MT   59043

Wontanin Wowapi, Box 493, Poplar, MT   59255

Nebraska

Indian Progress, Committee of Friends, 1403 21st St., Central City, NB 68826

Native American, Indian Center Industry Assoc., 2224 Leavenworth St., Omaha, NB   68102

Nebraska Trails, Indian Center, 902 O St., Lincoln, NB   68508
Winnebago Indian News, Winnebago Tribal Council, Winnebago, NB 68071

Nevada

The Desert Breeze, Box 256, Nixon, NV   89424
Elko Community News, Nevada Intertribal Council, Elko, NV   89801
Many Smokes, Box 5895, Reno, NV   89503
The Native Nevadan, 650 South Rock Blvd., Reno, NV   89502
Newsletter, Pyramid Lake Indian Reservation, Nixon, NV   89424
Valley Roundup, Box 38, Owyhee, NV   89832
WRPT Newsletter, Walker River Indian Reservation, Box 190, Schurz, NV
   89427
Warpath, Stewart Indian School, Stewart, NV   89437

New Jersey

Pow Wow Trails, Box 258, South Plainfield, NJ   07080

New Mexico

American Indian Law Newsletter, American Indian Law Students Association,
   University of New Mexico School of Law, 1117 Stanford Dr. N.E.,
   Albuquerque, NM   87106
Americans Before Columbus, National Indian Youth Council, 201 Hermosa
   N.E., Albuquerque, NM   87106
The Apache Scout, Mescalero Apache Tribe, Mescalero, NM   88340
Black Mesa Fact Sheet, Central Clearinghouse, 107 Cienega St., Santa Fe,
   NM   87501
Broncos Monthly News, Sanostee Rural Station, Shiprock, NM   87420
Capital News, Santo Domingo, NM   87052
Cochiti Lake Sun, Box 70, Cochiti, NM   87041
The Concerned Indian, Amerind, Inc., Box 482, Albuquerque, NM   87103
Drumbeat, Institute of American Indian Arts, Cerrillos Road, Santa Fe,
   NM   87501
Eight Northern Pueblos News, Route 1, Box 71, Santa Fe, NM   87528
Four Directions, Kiva Club, 1812 Las Lomas N.E., Albuquerque, NM 87131
Indian Education Resources Center Bulletin, 123 4th St. S.W., Box 1788, Albu-
   querque, NM   87103

Indian Extension News, New Mexico State University, Las Cruces, NM 88001

Indian Forerunner, Eight Northern Pueblos, P.O. Box 927, San Juan Pueblo, NM 87566

Indian Voice, Southwest Indian Polytechnical Institute, Box 1045, Albuquerque, NM 87114

Jicarilla Chieftain, Box 147, Dulce, NM 87528

Keresan, P.O. Box 3151, Laguna, NM 87026

Messenger, San Fidel, NM 87049

National Indian Council on Aging, Inc., Box 2088, Albuquerque, NM 87103

Navajo Assistance, Box 96, Gallup, NM 87301

Newborn, Institute of American Indian Arts, Cerrillos Road, Santa Fe, NM 87501

Nineteen Pueblos News, Box 6067, Albuquerque, NM 87107

Northern Pueblos Agency News Digest, Northern Pueblos Agency, Box 580, Santa Fe, NM 87501

The Red Times, Box 46, New Laguna, NM 87038

The Singing Sands, Ramah Navajo High School, Ramah, NM 87321

Southern Pueblos Agency Bulletin, 1000 Indian School Road N.W., Albuquerque, NM 87103

Southwestern Association on Indian Affairs, Box 1964, Santa Fe, NM 87501

Thunderbird, Albuquerque Indian School, 1000 Indian School Road N.W., Albuquerque, NM 87103

Tsa'Aszi', Pine Hill, CPO Box 12, Pine Hill, NM 87321

Warriors, CPO Box 12, Pine Hill, NM 87321

Zuni Carrier, Zuni Pueblo, Zuni, NM 87327

Zuni Legal Aid Newsletter, Zuni Legal Aid and Defender Society, Box 368, Zuni, NM 87327

Zuni Tribal Newsletter, Zuni Tribal Office, Box 339, Zuni, NM 87327

New York

AICH Newsletter, American Indian Community House, 10 E. 38th St., New York, NY 10016

Akwesasne Notes, Mohawk Nation, via Rooseveltown, NY 13683

American Indian Horizon, Box 18, Church Street Station, New York, NY 10008

American Indian News, 5 Tudor City Place, New York, NY 10017

American Indian Women Newsletter, 20-53 19th St., Astoria, Queens, NY 11102

Clan Destiny, Seneca Indian Historical Society, Irving, NY   14081
Ethnohistory, American Society for Ethnohistory, Amherst, NY   14226
Indian Affairs, Association on American Indian Affairs, 432 Park Avenue S.,
    New York, NY   10016
Indian Family Defense, Association of American Indian Affairs, 432 Park Avenue South, New York, NY   10016
Indian Natural Resources, Association of American Indian Affairs, 432 Park
    Avenue South, New York, NY   10016
Kinzua Planning Newsletter, Seneca Nation of Indians, Box 231, Salamanca,
    NY   14779
O He Yoh Noh, Box 231 Haley Building, Salamanca, NY   14779
Pow-wow Trails, 72 Kingdom Ave., Staten Island, NY   10312
Si Wong Geh, Cattaraugus Indian Reservation Community Newspaper, Box
    93, Irving, NY   14081
Tonawanda Indian News, Bloomingdale Road, Akron, NY   14001
War Drums Newsletter, American Indian Cultural Workshop, 144-09 161st
    St., Jamaica, NY   11434

North Carolina

The Carolina Indian Voice, Box 1075, Pembroke, NC   28372
Cherokee Boys Club Newsletter, Box 507, Cherokee, NC   29719
Cherokee One Feather, Box 501, Cherokee, NC   28719
The Cherokee Times, Box 105, Cherokee, NC   28719
Qualla Reservation News, Cherokee Agency, Cherokee, NC   28719

North Dakota

The Action News, Box 607, New Town, ND   58763
Arrow News, Mandaree High School, Mandaree, ND   58737
Bells of Saint Ann, St. Ann's Indian Mission, Belcourt, ND   58316
Dakota Student, University of North Dakota, Box 8177, University Station,
    Grand Forks, ND   58201
Dakota Sun, Standing Rock Community College, Box 483, Fort Yates,
    ND   58538
E'Yanpaha, Devil's Lake Sioux Tribe, Public Information Office, Fort Totten, ND   58335
Northern Light, St. Michael's Mission School, St. Michael, ND   58370
Sentinel, White Shield School, Roseglen, ND   58775

Standing Rock Eyapaha, Box 483, Fort Yates, ND   58538
Three Tribes Herald, New Town, ND   58770
Turtle Mountain Echo, Box 432, Belcourt, ND   58316
United Tribes News, 3315 S. Airport Rd., Bismarck, ND   58501
Wahpeton Highlights, Wahpeton Indian School, Wahpeton, ND   58075
Weekly Bulletin, Wahpeton School, Wahpeton, ND   58075

Ohio

Calumet, Four Points Intertribal Council, Box 283, Bellbrook, OH   45305
Cleveland Crier, 2600 Church Avenue N.W., Cleveland, OH   44113

Oklahoma

American Indian Baptist Voice, Okmulgee, OK   74447
American Indian Crafts and Culture, Box 3538, Tulsa, OK   74152
American Indian Law Review, College of Law, University of Oklahoma, 300
    E. Timberdell, Norman, OK   73019
Association of American Indian Physicians' Newsletter, 6801 S. Western, Suite
    206, Oklahoma City, OK   73139
Bishinik, Drawer 1201, Durant, OK   74701
The Buckskin, Eufaula, OK   74432
Camp Crier, 1214 N. Hudson, Oklahoma City, OK   73103
Cavo Transporter, Box 34, Concho, OK   73022
Cherokee Advocate, Box 948, Tahlequah, OK   74464
Cheyenne-Arapaho Bulletin, Box 38, Concho, OK   73022
The Chickasaw Times, 1525 Melrose Dr., Norman, OK   73069
Creek Nation Times, Creek Nation of Oklahoma, Box 1114, Okmulgee, OK
    74447
Five Tribes Journal, Box AF, Muskogee, OK   74401
Indian America Quarterly, Box 52009, Tulsa, OK   74152
Indian Education Record of Oklahoma, Tulsa Indian Youth Council, Inc., 716
    South Troost, Tulsa, OK   74114
Indian Journal, Indian Journal Printing Company, Eufaula, OK   74432
Indian School Journal, Chilocco Indian School, Chilocco, OK   74635
Indian Visions, 1707 N. Broadway, Room 108, Oklahoma City, OK   73103
Muskogee Nation News, Box 1114, Okmulgee, OK   74447
OIO Newsletter, Oklahomans for Indian Opportunity, 555 Constitution, Nor-
    man, OK   73069 (see text)

Osage Nation News, Box 1346, Pawhuska, OK   74056
Seminole Campfire, Route 1, Box 229-E, Seminole, OK   74868
Smoke Dreams, Riverside High School, Anadarko, OK   73005
Smoke Signals, Bacone College, Muskogee, OK   74401
Talking Leaves, Skiatook, OK   74070
Tulsa Indian News, Indian Emphasis Program, 1240 E. 5th Pl., Tulsa, OK
    74120

Oregon

Bear Tracks, 2576 South East 157th, Portland, OR   97236
Chemawa American, Chemawa Indian School, Salem, OR   97303
Confederated Umatilla Journal, Box 638, Pendleton, OR   97801
Hemchucks Hemulga, Organization of Forgotten Americans, 3954 S. 6th,
    Klamath Falls, OR   97601
Indian Time, 528 Cottage St. N.E., Old Garfield School, Suite 400, Salem,
    OR   97310
Lakota Oyata-Ki, Oregon State Penitentiary, 2605 State St., Salem, OR
    97310
Mak Luks Hemcunga (Indian Talk), c/o OFA, Box 1257, Klamath Falls, OR
    97601
Many Smokes, Box 1961, Klamath Falls, OR   97601
Newsletter, Indian Study Center of Oregon, Box 92, Monmouth, OR 97361
Northwest Portland Area Indian Health Board, 1501 Standard Plaza, 1100 SW
    Sixth Ave., Portland, OR   97204
Pacific Northwest Indian Program, Northwest Regional Educational Lab, 710
    SW 2nd, Portland, OR   97204
Rainbow People, Box 164, John Day, OR   97845
Spilyay Tymoo, Box 735, Warm Springs, OR   97761
Tomahawk, Box 428, Warm Springs, OR   99761

Pennsylvania

Indian Truth, Indian Rights Association, 1505 Race St., Philadelphia, PA
    19102
The Peacemaker, 1663 Bristol Pike, Cornwells Heights, PA   19020
Pan-American Indian Newsletter, League of Nations, 1139 Lehman Place,
    Johnston, PA   15902

South Dakota

Blue Cloud Quarterly, Blue Cloud Abbey, Marvin, SD   57251
Crazy Horse News, Box 1788, Rapid City, SD   57701
Dakota Wowapipahi, Box 157, Marty, SD   57361
The Drumbeat, Crow Creek Reservation High School, Stephan, SD   57346
Eagle Butte News, Eagle Butte, SD   57629
Great Plains Observer, 218 S. Egan, Madison, SD   57042
The Indian, American Indian Leadership Council, Route 3, Box 9, Rapid
    City, SD   57701
Indian Life, Box 84, Rapid City, SD   57701
Keyapi, Fort Thompson, SD   57339
Lakota Eyapaha, Oglala Sioux Community College, Pine Ridge, SD 57770
Letan Wankatakiya, University of South Dakota, Vermillion, SD   57069
The Little Bronzed Angel, St. Paul's Indian Mission, Marty, SD   57361
Little Sioux, Rosebud Educational Society, St. Francis, SD   57572
Luchip/Nilb Spearhead, Lutheran Social Services, 600 W. 12th St., Sioux
    Falls, SD   57104
News Bulletin, Cheyenne River Agency, Eagle Butte, SD   57625
Oglala Nation News, Box 320, Pine Ridge, SD   47770
Paha Sapa Wahosi, South Dakota State College, Spearfish, SD   57783
PILC-Pierre Indian Learning Center, Star Route 3, Pierre, SD   57501
Red Cloud Country, Red Cloud Indian School, Pine Ridge, SD   57770
Rosebud Sioux Herald Eyapaha, Box 65, Rosebud, SD   57570
The Scout, Episcopal Church, Lower Brule, SD   57548
Shannon County News, Pine Ridge, SD   57770
Sioux Journal, Eagle Butte, SD   57625
Sinte Gleska College News, Library/Media Center, Sinte Gleska College, Mis-
    sion, SD   57555
Sioux Messenger, Yankton Sioux Tribe, Route 3, Wagner, SD   57380
Sioux San Sun, PHS Indian Hospital, Rapid City, SD   57701
Sisseton Agency News, Sisseton Agency, Sisseton, SD   57262
Sota-Eya-Ye-Yapi, Sisseton-Wahpeton Sioux Tribes of Lake Traverse Reserva-
    tion, Sisseton, SD   57262
The Spirit, Flandreau Indian School, Flandreau, SD   57028
Talk About Learning, Pine Ridge Reservation, Pine Ridge, SD   57770
Todd County Tribune and Eyapaha, Mission, SD   57555
United Sioux Tribes News, Star Route 3, Pierre, SD   57501
War Cry, Fort Thompson, SD   57339
Woyakapi, St. Francis Mission, St. Francis, SD   57572

Tennessee

Chahta Anumpa, The Choctaw Times, Box 12392, Nashville, TN   37212
Uset Help Newsletter, 1101 Kermit Drive, Suite 100, Nashville, TN   37217

Texas

Talking Leaves, American Indian Center, 722 N. Beacon St., Dallas, TX
    75223
Raven Speaks, 3061 Cridello, Dallas, TX   75220

Utah

Eagle Views, Intermountain Indian School, Brigham City, UT   84302
The Eagle's Eye, Tribe of Many Feathers, 360A Brimhall Bldg., Indian Edu-
    cation Department, Brigham Young University, Provo, UT   84602
Indian Affairs, Brigham Young University, Provo, UT   84601
Indian Liahona, 115 E. So. Temple St., Salt Lake City, UT   84111
Newsletter, St. Christopher's Mission, Episcopal Church, Bluff, UT   84512
Utah Indian Journal, Division of Indian Affairs, University of Utah, Salt Lake
    City, UT   84112
Utah Navajo "Baa Hane," Utah Navajo Development Council, Blanding,
    UT   84511
Ute Bulletin, Box 129, Ft. Duchesne, UT   84026

Washington

A.I.E. Newspaper, East 905 Third Ave., Spokane, WA   99202
Alaska Native Times, 1515 Dexter Ave. N., Seattle, WA   98109
American Indian Club Newsletter, Box 7, Gonzaga University, Spokane, WA
    99202
Anica News Highlights, 1306 Second Ave., Seattle, WA   98101
Chinook, 215 Viking Union, Western Washington State College, Belling-
    ham, WA   98225
Columbia River Indian News, Box 5, Cooks, WA   98605
Confederated Indian Tribes, Washington State Penitentiary, Box 520, Walla
    Walla, WA   99362
Dsuq' Wub' Siatsub, The Suquamish News, The Suquamish Tribe, Box 556,
    Suquamish, WA   98392
Epitaph (The Reservation), 228 South 2nd St., Yakima, WA   98901

Directory of American Indian Print and Broadcast Media

Four Winds, Box 520, Walla Walla, WA 99362

Independent American, Star Route, Coulee Dam, WA 99116

Indian Cultural Education Newsletter, 3602 West Government Way, Seattle, WA 98199

Indian Voice, Small Tribes of Western Washington, Box 578, Sumner, WA 98390

Kee-Yoka, Community Action Program, LaConner, WA 98257

Klah'Che'Min, Squaxin Tribal Center, Route 1, Box 257, Shelton, WA 98584

Klallam Newsletter, Port Gamble-Klallam Nation Tribal Council, Box 28, Kingston, WA 98346

Lummi Indian News, Box 309, Marietta, WA 98268

Makah Dakah, Box 547, Neah Bay, WA 98357

Makah Viewers, Box 115, Neah Bay, WA 98357

Many Smokes, Box 9167, Spokane, WA 99209

Native Northwest, 802 E. 1st St., Toppenish, WA 98948

NCSIT Newsletter, National Coalition to Support Indian Treaties, 814 NE 40th St., Seattle, WA 98105

Northwest Indian Fisheries Commission Newsletter, 2625 Parkmont Lane, Building C, Olympia, WA 98502

Northwest Indian News, Seattle Indian Center, Box 4322, Pioneer Square Station, Seattle, WA 98104

Northwest Indian Times, Gonzaga University, Spokane, WA 99202

Northwest Passage, Quinault Tribal Affairs, Box 1118, Bellingham, WA 98225

Nugguam, Quinault Tribal Affairs, Box 1118, Taholah, WA 98587

Our Heritage, Box 451, Nespelem, WA 99155

Quileute Newsletter, Quileute Tribal CAP, LaPush, WA 98350

Rawhide Press, Box 393, Wellpinit, WA 99040

The Renegade, Box 719, Survival of American Indians Association, Tacoma, WA 98401

Renegade, Frank's Landing, Nisqually, WA 98501

See Yahtsub, Marysville, WA 98270

Smoke Talk, Box 500, Steilacoom, WA 98388

The Squaw's Message, Sisterhood of American Indians, Box 17, Gig Harbor, WA 98335

Squol-Quol, A Magazine of the Pacific Northwest, Lummi Tribal Office, Marietta, WA 98268

Tacoma Indian News, 519 E. 28th, Tacoma, WA 98421

Tribal Tribune, Box 150, Nespelem, WA 99155

Voice of Prison, Box 520, Walla Walla, WA   99362
The Washington Newspaper, 3838 Stone Way North, Seattle, WA   98103
Washington State Reformatory, Box 77, Monroe, WA   98272
Wenatchee Indian Spokesman, Box 125, Peshastin, WA   99847
Yakima Drum Beat, Box 31, Toppenish, WA   98948
Yakima Nation Review, Box 386, Toppenish, WA   98948

Wisconsin

Anishnabe News, Native American Student Movement, University of Wisconsin-Milwaukee, Box 67, Milwaukee, WI   53201
Bayfield School Communicator, Urban-Rural School Development Program, Joint District 1, Bayfield, WI   54814
Great Lakes Agency News, Great Lakes Indian Agency, Ashland, WI   54806
Menominee County and Town News, Keshena, WI   54135
Menominee Tribal News, Menominee Restoration Office, Box 397, Keshena, WI   54135
Milwaukee Indian News, 3701 W. Lisbon, Milwaukee, WI   53208
Moccasin Trails, Lakeland Union High School, Lac du Flambeau, WI 54538
Native American Council, University of Wisconsin-River Falls, 204 Hagestad Student Center, River Falls, WI   54022
Quin A'Month A', c/o Stockbridge Historical Library Museum, Route 1, Box 300, Bowler, WI   54416
Red Cliff Tribal News, Box 529, Bayfield, WI   54814
The Voice, Laona, WI   54511
We-Sa-Mi-Dong, Route 2, Hayward, WI   54843
Wisconsin Inter-Tribal News, Box 4, Odanah, WI   54861

Wyoming

American Indian News, Office of Native American Program, Box 217, Ft. Washakie, WY   82514
Arapahoe Agency Courier, Arapahoe Agency, WY   82510
Smoke Signals, All American Indian Days, Box 451, Sheridan, WY   82301
Wind River Journal, Box 217, Fort Washakie, WY   82514
The Wind River Rendezvous, St. Stephens Indian Mission, St. Stephens, WY   82524

RADIO AND TELEVISION

Alaska

KBRW, Box 149, Barrow, AK   99723
KCAM, Box 125, Glennallen, AK   99588
KIAK, Box 2828, Fairbanks, AK   99701
KICY, Box 820, Nome, AK   99762
KIFW-TV, Box 299, Sitka, AK   99835
KJNP, Box 0, North Pole, AK   99705
KNOM, Box 988, Nome, AK   99762
KOTZ, Box 78, Kotzebue, AK   99752
KTOO-FM, 224 4th St., Juneau, AK   99801
KUAC-AM, University of Alaska, Fairbanks, AK   99701
KVOK, Box 53, Kodiak, AK   99615
KYUK, Box 468, Bethel, AK   99559

Arizona

KCLS, Box 640, Flagstaff, AZ   86001
KDJI, Box 430, Holbrook, AZ   86025
KHAC, Navajo Bible School, Window Rock, AZ   86515
KIKO, Box 1543, Globe, AZ   85501
KINO, Drawer K, Winslow, AZ   86047
KOAI-TV, Box 1843, Flagstaff, AZ   86001
KPGE, Box CC, Page, AZ   86040
KTKT, Box 5585, Tucson, AZ   85703
KVSL, Box 940, Show Low, AZ   85901

California

KCVR, Box 600, Lodi, CA   95240
KEWQ, Box KEWQ, Paradise, CA   95969
KGER, Box 7126, Long Beach, CA   90807
KLAC, 5746 Sunset Blvd., Los Angeles, CA   90028
KMET, 5746 Sunset Blvd., Los Angeles, CA   90028
KPCS, 1570 E. Colorado, Pasadena, CA   91106
KPFA, 2207 Shattuck Ave., Berkeley, CA   94704
KPOO, Box 11008, San Francisco, CA   94101
KRDU, 597 N. Alta Ave., Dinuba, CA   93618

Colorado

KIUP, Box 641, Durango, CO   81301
KSUT, Southern Ute Tribe, Community Center Building, Ignacio, CO
   81137
KVFC, Box 740, Cortez, CO   81321

Idaho

KSIH, Idaho State University, Pocatello, ID   83201
KWIK, Box 2005, Pocatello, ID   83201

Iowa

KWSL, Box 1230, Sioux City, IA   51102

Massachusetts

WRYT, 312 Stuart St., Boston, MA   02116

Michigan

WDET, 5035 Woodward Ave., Wayne State University, Detroit, MI 48202

Minnesota

KAXE, Box 474, Grand Rapids, MN   55744
KQRS, 917 N. Lilac Dr., Minneapolis, MN   55422
KUOM, University of Minnesota, Minneapolis, MN   55455
WDIO-TV, 10 Observation Rd., Duluth, MN   55811
WTCN-TV, 441 Boone Ave. N., Minneapolis, MN   55427

Montana

KHDN, Box 389, Hardin, MT   59034
KLTZ, Box 671, Glasgow, MT   59230
KOJM, Box K, Havre, MT   59501
KOYN, Box 956, Billings, MT   59101
KPAX-TV, Box 3500, Butte, MT   59701
KRTV-TV, Box 1331, Great Falls, MT   59403

KTVQ-TV, Box 2557, Billings, MT   59103
KVCK, Box 668, Wolf Point, MT   59201
KXLF-TV, Box 3500, Butte, MT   59701

Nebraska

KCSR, Box 913, Chadron, NB   69337
KVSH, 126 W. Third St., Valentine, NB   69201

Nevada

KVLV, 1155 Gummow Dr., Fallon, NV   89406

New Mexico

KANW, Box 25704, Albuquerque, NM   87125
KENN, Box K, Farmington, NM   87401
KGAK, 401 E. Coal Ave., Gallup, NM   87301
KKIT, Box 737, Taos, NM   87571
KNME-TV, 1130 University Blvd., Albuquerque, NM   87106
KOAT-TV, Box 4156, Albuquerque, NM   87106
KRZE, Box 1529, Farmington, NM   87401
KTDB, Box 18, Ramah, NM   87321
KUNM, Campus & Grant Blvd., University of New Mexico, Albuquerque,
      NM   87131
KWYK, 1515 W. Main, Farmington, NM   87401
KYVA, 306 S. First St., Drawer K, Gallup, NM   87301

New York

WBAI, 359 E. 62nd St., New York, NY   10021
WPOW, 305 E. 40th St., Staten Island, NY   10016
WYRD, 3000 Erie Blvd. E., Syracuse, NY   13224

North Dakota

KBMR, Box 1233, Bismarck, ND   58501
KEYA, Box 190, Belcourt, ND   58316
KFYR-TV, Box 1738, Bismarck, ND   58501
KNDR, Box 1836, Bismarck, ND   58501

Oklahoma

KBEL, Box 400, Idabel, OK   75455
KEOK, Box 497, Tahlequah, OK   74464
KIHN, Box 430, Hugo, OK   74743
KKMA, Box 66, Pryor, OK   74361
KOCO-TV, Box 32325, Oklahoma City, OK   73132
KOLS, Box 66, Pryor, OK   74361
KRPT, Box 969, Anadarko, OK   73005
KTLQ, Box 497, Tahlequah, OK   74464
WNAD, University of Oklahoma, Box 640, Norman, OK   73069

Oregon

KOAC-TV, Oregon State University, Corvallis, OR   97331
KPTV-TV, 735 S.W. 20th Pl., Portland, OR   97205

Pennsylvania

WVCH, Third and Avenue of the States, Philadelphia, PA   19013

South Dakota

KCCR, Box 309, Pierre, SD   57501
KELO-TV, Phillips at 13th, Sioux Falls, SD   57102
KESD, South Dakota State University, Brookings, SD   57006
KEVW-TV, Box 677, Rapid City, SD   57701
KGFX, Box 1197, Pierre, SD   57501
KINI, St. Francis, SD   57572
KOBH, Box 611, Hot Springs, SD   57747
KOLY, Box 1300, Mobridge, SD   57601
KOTA, Box 1760, Rapid City, SD   57709
KOTA-TV, Box 1760, Rapid City, SD   57701
KQHU, Box 794, Yankton, SD   57078
KTOQ, Box 962, Rapid City, SD   57701
KWYR, Box 491, Winner, SD   57580
WNAX, North 3rd & Mulberry, Yankton, SD   57078

Utah

KCDR, Southern Utah State College, Cedar City, UT   84720
KRGO, 5065 W. 2100 St., Salt Lake City, UT   84120

KVEL, Box 307, Vernal, UT   84078
KUTA, Box 790, Blanding, UT   84511

Virginia

WFAX, 161-B Hillwood Ave., Tower Square, Falls Church, VA   22046

Washington

KAOS, No. 305, Evergreen State College, Olympia, WA   98505
KENE, Box 350, Toppenish, WA   98948
KGMI, Box 943, Bellingham, WA   98225
KOMW, Box 151, Omak, WA   98841
KRAB, 1406 Harvard Ave., Seattle, WA   98122
KRNB, Makah Radio, P.O. Box 283, Neah Bay, WA   98357
KTOY, 1101 S. Yakima Ave., Tacoma, WA   98405

Wyoming

KOVE, Box 430, Lander, WY   82520

Notes

CHAPTER ONE

1. Elmo Scott Watson, "The Indian Wars and the Press, 1866–67," *Journalism Quarterly* 17 (1940): 302.
2. William Blankenburg, "The Role of the Press in an Indian Massacre," *Journalism Quarterly* 45 (1968): 64.
3. Ibid., p. 65.
4. Ibid., p. 61.
5. Ibid., p. 70.
6. *Bismarck Tribune*, extra edition, July 6, 1876, reprinted in *Wassaja*, August, 1975.
7. Ibid.
8. Elmo Scott Watson, "The Last Indian War, 1890–91: A Study of Newspaper Jingoism," *Journalism Quarterly* 20 (1943): 205.
9. Ibid., p. 208.
10. Douglas C. Jones, "Teresa Dean: Lady Correspondent Among the Sioux Indians," *Journalism Quarterly* 49 (1972): 656–62.
11. *Chicago Herald*, January 20, 1891, in Jones, "Teresa Dean," p. 658.
12. Jones, "Teresa Dean," p. 659.
13. Ibid., p. 662.
14. Terri Schultz, "Bamboozle Me Not at Wounded Knee," *Harper's*, June, 1973, p. 56.
15. Publisher's Introduction to *Voices from Wounded Knee*, p. 1.
16. Ibid.
17. Ibid., p. 136.
18. Neil Hickey, "Our Media Blitz Is Here to Stay," *TV Guide*, December 22, 1973, p. 22.
19. Ibid., p. 22–23.
20. "An Empty Black Pit," *Akwesasne Notes*, Early Autumn, 1973, p. 4. Almost every issue of *Akwesasne Notes*, *Wassaja*, and other publications carried further developments in the mineral-rights struggle.
21. "Yavapais' Historic Struggle to Keep Fort McDowell," *Wassaja*,

October, 1976, p. 10; "Pima Hopes Dashed," *Indian Affairs*, no. 92 (July–November, 1976), p. 2.

22. Estelle Fuchs and Robert J. Havighurst, *To Live on This Earth*.

23. *Wassaja*, January, 1973.

24. *Voices from Wounded Knee*, p. 261; "SD Reservation Ambush: 2 FBI Agents 'Executed,'" *Akwesasne Notes*, Early Winter, 1975, pp. 5–9.

25. *Voices from Wounded Knee*, p. 260.

26. Rick Brown, "The High Cost of Gresham," *Once a Year* 79 (1975): 6–8.

27. Ada Deer, head (at the time of the takeover) of the Menominee Restoration Committee, who opposed the action, in conversation with the authors.

28. Richard La Course, "'Backlash': Indian Media and the 'State of Siege,'" *Red Current*, Spring, 1978, p. 4.

29. Because of possible repercussions, the source remains unnamed. But it was thought appropriate to include this quote because it so effectively mirrors sentiments heard from many quarters.

30. Rupert Costo, ed., *Textbooks and the American Indian*.

31. Philip French, in "The Indian in the Western Movie," *Art in America* 60 (1972): 32–39, begins to study this problem, as does Franklin Ducheneaux in "The American Indian Today: Beyond the Stereotypes," *Today's Education* 62 (May, 1973): 22–23. One is reminded also of Chief Bromden, an Indian character in Ken Kesey's *One Flew over the Cuckoo's Nest*.

32. Anna Lee Stensland, *Literature by and About the American Indian: An Annotated Bibliography*, p. 3.

33. Rita Keshena, "The Role of American Indians in Motion Pictures," *American Indian Culture and Research Journal* 1 (1974): 26.

34. Richard La Course, "Image of the Indian," *Air Time*, January, 1975, p. 6.

35. Edward R. Murrow, in an address to the RTNDA convention, Chicago, Ill., October 15, 1958, quoted in Harry J. Skornia, *Television and Society* (New York: McGraw-Hill, 1965), pp. 228–29.

36. *Report of the National Advisory Commission on Civil Disorders* (New York: Bantam Books, 1968), p. 372.

37. Ibid., p. 383.

38. Ibid., p. 384.

Notes

CHAPTER TWO

1. Carolyn Foreman, *Oklahoma Imprints, 1835–1907: A History of Printing in Oklahoma Before Statehood.*
2. Ibid., p. xxi.
3. *Indian Progress*, October 22, 1875.
4. *College Paper*, Stillwater, Oklahoma, March 4, 1903.
5. Foreman, *Oklahoma Imprints*, p. 130.
6. Ibid., p. 132.
7. Ibid., pp. xix–xxii.
8. Ibid., p. xix.
9. *Indian Journal*, August 25, 1887.
10. See Traveller Bird, *Tell Them They Lie: The Sequoyah Myth*, and Thomas E. Sanders and Walter W. Peek, *Literature of the American Indian*, p. 8. Sequoyah's English last name was spelled differently by many authors: Gist, Guess, and Guest appear frequently.
11. George E. Foster, *Sequoyah: The American Cadmus and Modern Moses*, p. 100.
12. Grant Foreman, *Sequoyah*, pp. 88–97.
13. John B. Davis, "The Life Work of Sequoyah," *Chronicles of Oklahoma* 8 (1930): 161.
14. Ralph Henry Gabriel, *Elias Boudinot: Cherokee and His America*, p. 104.
15. Ibid., p. 28–29.
16. "Sequoyah: The Inventor of the Cherokee Alphabet," *Indian Journal*, August 2, 1877. The name appears under various spellings.
17. Foreman, *Sequoyah*, p. 69.
18. James Mooney, *Myths of the Cherokee*, pp. 110–11.
19. *Cherokee Phoenix*, April 24, 1828.
20. Cullen Joe Holland, "The Cherokee Indian Newspapers 1828–1906: The Tribal Voice of a People in Transition" (Ph.D. diss., University of Minnesota, 1956), pp. 27–28.
21. Elias Boudinot, *An Address to the Whites: Delivered in the First Presbyterian Church on the 26th of May, 1826*, pp. 12–13. Boudinot's name is spelled Boudinott in earlier work; he apparently simplified the ending early in his career.
22. Foreman, *Sequoyah*, p. 13.
23. Reprinted in *Indian Chieftain*, June 17, 1886, p. 3.
24. Samuel Carter, III, *Cherokee Sunset: A Nation Betrayed*, p. 77.
25. *Cherokee Phoenix*, May 14, 1828.

26. Foreman, *Sequoyah*, p. 31.

27. George E. Foster, "Journalism Among the Cherokee Indians," *Magazine of American History*, July–December, 1877, p. 66.

28. *Cherokee Phoenix*, April 3, 1828. "The most nearly complete file of this newspaper in existence is one of the most prized possessions of the British Museum in London," quoted in G. Foreman, *The Five Civilized Tribes: A Brief History*, p. 33.

29. Compare Foreman, *Oklahoma Imprints*, p. xvi.

30. *Cherokee Phoenix*, August 18, 1829.

31. Ibid., May 29, 1830, and August 19, 1831.

32. Ibid., July 11, 1831.

33. Ibid., February 12, 1831.

34. Ibid., August 11, 1832; Carter, *Cherokee Sunset*, pp. 138ff.

35. Foreman, *The Five Civilized Tribes*, p. 293.

36. *Cherokee Phoenix*, August 24, 1833.

37. Ibid., May 31, 1834.

38. Foreman, *Sequoyah*, pp. 15–16. In fitting recognition of the paper's importance, the *Cherokee Phoenix* office has recently been rebuilt on the restored capitol site in Georgia.

39. Grace Ernestine Ray, *Early Oklahoma Newspapers: History and Description of Publications from Earliest Beginnings to 1889*, p. 17.

40. Frederick Webb Hodge, ed., *Handbook of American Indians North of Mexico*, p. 232.

41. Foreman, *Five Civilized Tribes: A Brief History*, p. 28.

42. "The Gilcrease Cherokee Advocate Press," Thomas Gilcrease Institute of American History and Art, Gilcrease Historical Leaflet no. 4.

43. George E. Foster, "Journalism Among the Cherokee Indians," pp. 65–70.

44. Foreman, *Oklahoma Imprints*, p. 78.

45. *Cherokee Advocate*, April 2, 1846.

46. *Cherokee Messenger*, September, 1858. In some religious rivalry typical of the times, the Baptists ignored the prodigious amounts of translated religious materials prepared by Elias Boudinot and Samuel Worcester.

47. Ibid.

48. T. L. Ballenger, "Early College Journalism," *New Cherokee Advocate*, May 30, 1950.

49. *Wreath of Rose Buds*, February 11, 1857.

50. *Godey's Lady's Book*, January, 1857, p. 82.

51. *Choctaw Intelligencer*, June 20, 1850.

52. Henry Rowe Schoolcraft, *The Indian Tribes of the United States:*

Their History, Antiquities, Customs, Religion, Arts, Language, Traditions, Oral Legends, and Myths, ed. Francis S. Drake, pp. 542–546.

53. Foreman, *Oklahoma Imprints*, p. 131.

CHAPTER THREE

1. *American Newspaper Directory*, 1871.

2. Carolyn Foreman, *Oklahoma Imprints, 1836–1907: A History of Printing in Oklahoma Before Statehood*, p. 80.

3. *Cherokee Advocate*, March 1, 1876.

4. Foreman, *Oklahoma Imprints*, p. 28.

5. Ibid., September 14, 1872.

6. Oliver Knight, *Following the Indian Wars: The Story of the Newspaper Correspondents Among the Indian Campaigns*.

7. Angie Debo, *The Rise and Fall of the Choctaw Republic*, pp. 226; *Oklahoma Star*, February 27, 1874.

8. *Star-Vindicator*, March 17, 1877.

9. Ibid., January 5, 1876.

10. Ibid., 1877.

11. Foreman, *Oklahoma Imprints*, p. 164–65.

12. Grace Ernestine Ray, *Early Oklahoma Newspapers: History and Description of Publications from Earliest Beginnings to 1889*, p. 64.

13. *Caddo Free Press*, August 8, 1878.

14. Debo, *Choctaw Republic*, p. 226.

15. *Choctaw News*, October 11, 1878.

16. Debo, *Choctaw Republic*, p. 192.

17. Ibid., p. 227.

18. *Indian Citizen*, May 11, 1889, and March 28, 1891.

19. Debo, *Choctaw Republic*, pp. 226–27.

20. *American Newspaper Directory*, p. 987.

21. Ibid.

22. *Cheyenne Transporter*, August 25, 1880.

23. *Indian Progress*, October 22, 1875.

24. Ibid.

25. Ibid.

26. Foreman, *Oklahoma Imprints*, p. 190.

27. *Indian Journal*, December 7, 1876.

28. Foreman, *Oklahoma Imprints*, p. 191.
29. *Indian Journal*, July 4, 1902.
30. Foreman, *Oklahoma Imprints*, p. 226.
31. Frederick Webb Hodge, ed., *Handbook of American Indians North of Mexico*, p. 233.
32. Foreman, *Oklahoma Imprints*, p. 94.
33. *Indian Journal*, August 11, 1887.
34. *Indian Chieftain Supplement*, March 18, 1897.
35. Foreman, *Oklahoma Imprints*, p. 93.
36. Ibid.
37. Ray, Carolyn Foreman, and Hodge omit mention of the *Sentinel*, and it is missing from collections in libraries and historical society collections examined by the authors.
38. Foreman, *Oklahoma Imprints*, p. 90.
39. Ibid., p. 85; Foreman says that it began in 1886 at Vinita, O.T.
40. Ibid., p. 76.
41. Ibid., p. 85–87.
42. *Cherokee Advocate*, April 25, 1896.
43. Ibid., September 14, 1901.
44. *The Gilcrease Cherokee Advocate Press*, Gilcrease Historical Leaflet no. 4, 1963, Thomas Gilcrease Institute of History and Art, Tulsa, Okla.
45. U.S., Department of the Interior, Bureau of Indian Affairs, *Report of the Commissioner of Indian Affairs*, 45th Cong., 2d sess., 1877.
46. Foreman, *Oklahoma Imprints*, pp. 84–85.
47. Alfred L. Bush and Robert S. Fraser, *American Indian Periodicals in the Princeton University Library: A Preliminary List*, p. 80.
48. *Narragansett Dawn*, October, 1936.
49. *NCAI Bulletin Newsletter*, October, 1947.
50. *New Cherokee Advocate*, May 3, 1950.

CHAPTER FOUR

1. Angie Debo, *The Rise and Fall of the Choctaw Republic*, p. 192.
2. Althea Bass, *Cherokee Messenger*, pp. 302–303.
3. Frederick Webb Hodge, ed., *Handbook of American Indians North of Mexico*, Smithsonian Institution, Bureau of American Ethnology Bulletin 30, p. 232.
4. *Union List of Serials in Libraries of the United States and Canada*, 3d ed., 2:1256.

5. Hodge, *Handbook*, p. 232.

6. *Frontier Scout*, July 13, 1865.

7. *Dictionary Catalog of the Edward E. Ayer Collection of Americana and American Indians in the Newberry Library*, p. 315.

8. Carolyn Foreman, *Oklahoma Imprints, 1835–1907: A History of Printing in Oklahoma Before Statehood*, p. 245.

9. Grace Ernestine Ray, *Early Oklahoma Newspapers: History and Description of Publications from Earliest Beginnings to 1889*, pp. 74–78.

10. *Indian Record*, June 1886, and March, 1887.

11. Hodge, *Handbook*, p. 233.

12. Alfred L. Bush and Robert S. Fraser, *American Indian Periodicals in the Princeton University Library: A Preliminary List*, p. 17.

13. From correspondence with current staff.

14. Bush and Fraser, *Periodicals*, p. 16.

15. From personal correspondence with editor.

16. Ray, *Early Oklahoma Newspapers*, p. 29.

17. Hodge, *Handbook*, p. 229.

18. Debo, *Choctaw Republic*, p. 237.

19. Foreman, *Oklahoma Imprints*, p. 236.

20. William E. Connelly, *History of the Newspapers and Magazines Published in Kansas*, pp. 180–81.

21. From authors' correspondence with editor.

22. Foreman, *Oklahoma Imprints*, p. 236.

23. Ibid.

24. Bush and Fraser, *Periodicals*, p. 17.

25. Hodge, *Handbook*, p. 233.

26. Bush and Fraser, *Periodicals*, p. 18.

27. *The Ganado Story*, n.d. (Spring, 1976?).

28. Bush and Fraser, *Periodicals*, pp. 56, 71, 75.

29. From authors' interview with editors Carole Wright and Manuel Pino, Albuquerque, N.M., July, 1977.

30. *Project MEDIA*, March, 1977.

31. *Navaho Education Newsletter*, May, 1977.

32. From authors' correspondence with editor, August, 1977.

33. Ibid.

CHAPTER FIVE

1. Jeannette Henry, interview with authors, August, 1978.
2. "Open Letter to All Members of the American Indian Press . . . ," *Medium Rare*, September–December, 1974, p. 4.
3. This point was emphasized by a black reporter for the *Milwaukee Journal*. Describing his method of coping with the biases in the white-majority press, he wrote, "Objectivity in journalism is the way one comes to terms and makes peace with a world one does not like but will not oppose" (Sharon Murphy, *Other Voices: Black, Chicano, and American Indian Press*, pp. 43–44).
4. "Indians in the Media Seminar," address, Bemidji, Minnesota, April 12, 1977.
5. D'Arcy McNickle, *Native American Tribalism: Indian Survivals and Renewals*, p. 169.
6. Beverly Geary, in an unpublished plea for support for an Indian newspaper on the Northern Cheyenne Reservation, Lame Deer, Montana.
7. Ibid.
8. Richard La Course, "Indians and the Media: A Panel Discussion," *Civil Rights Digest*, Fall, 1973, p. 44.
9. Tanna Beebe at The Communications Seminar, Billings, Mont., June 29, 1977.
10. As reported in *Sho-Ban News*, May 18, 1977.
11. *United Tribes News*, April 29, 1976, p. 2.
12. Untitled comments in *Air Time* 1 (January, 1975): 3.
13. Geary, unpublished comments.
14. Ibid.
15. 25 U.S.C. 1302 (see Appendix 1 for the complete statement of this section and for further commentary taken from Michael R. Smith, *American Indian Civil Rights Handbook*, p. 16–18, U.S. Commission on Civil Rights, 1972.

CHAPTER SIX

1. *Wassaja*, January, 1973.
2. Ibid.
3. Ibid., June, 1976.
4. Ibid., June, 1976.
5. Ibid.
6. Ibid.

7. Ibid., January, 1976.

8. "About AIPA's Santa Fe Confab," *Medium Rare* 12 (September–December, 1974): 3.

9. Rupert Costo, ed., *Textbooks and the American Indian*.

10. *Wassaja*, January, 1976.

11. Rupert Costo, in comments to the authors, August, 1978.

12. *Wassaja*, June, 1973.

13. Rupert Costo, from transcripts of extemporaneous remarks made during question-and-answer period with students at the University of Oregon School of Journalism, February 22, 1977, through Eric Maloney.

14. *Wassaja*, June, 1973.

15. Jeannette Henry, in comments to the authors, August, 1978.

16. Ibid. It should be pointed out that *Wassaja*, audited twice in three years, received a letter from the IRS after both audits reaffirming its tax-exempt status without criticism.

17. "We Never Intended to Start a Newspaper: A History of *Akwesasne Notes*," *Akwesasne Notes*, Early Summer, 1976, pp. 6–8. Much of the information for this section was taken from interviews with the *Notes* staff in the summer of 1976, supported heavily by information contained in "We Never Intended to Start a Newspaper."

18. This was the origin of White Roots of Peace, a traveling communications group that was a part of the *Notes* staff.

19. "We Never Intended," *Akwesasne Notes*, Early Summer, 1976, pp. 6–7. See also Don A. Christensen, "The American Indian Press Association: Its History, Activities, and Organization" (Master's thesis, Michigan State University, 1974), pp. 13–58.

20. "We Never Intended," *Akwesasne Notes*, Early Summer, 1976, pp. 6–7.

21. Ibid.

22. Ibid., p. 6; the article offers the following comment: "It was at this time that Watergate broke out in the news. Whether it is a coincidence or not, *Notes'* official non-undercover harassment ceased on any kind of coordinated level."

23. From information supplied by *Notes* staff members, July, 1976.

24. "A New Way to Help Notes," *Akwesasne Notes*, Autumn, 1978.

25. "Voices from the Earth," *Akwesasne Notes*, Autumn, 1978.

26. "We Never Intended," *Akwesasne Notes*, Early Summer, 1976.

CHAPTER SEVEN

1. *Dine' Baa-Hani*, June 5, 1972.
2. *Qua Toqti* editor Lawrence Hamanam in an interview at Oraibi, Arizona, July, 1977.
3. Alfred L. Bush and Robert S. Fraser, *American Indian Periodicals in the Princeton University Library: A Preliminary List*, p. 26.
4. *Ni-Mah-Mi-Kwa-Zoo-Min* editor Betty Blue in interview, July, 1975. The title change came in 1978 when tribal linguists pointed to the need for the reflexive *Mah*.
5. Ibid.
6. Ibid.
7. *Ni-Mi-Kwa-Zoo-Min*, December, 1975, p. 2.
8. Ibid.
9. Ibid.
10. *Jicarilla Chieftain*, July 18, 1977, p. 2.
11. Mary F. Baca Polanco, in interview at Dulce, New Mexico, July, 1977.
12. Clark David Gardner, principal chief, Choctaw Nation, in response to questionnaire, July, 1977.
13. Verna Bunn, editor of *Makah Viewers*, response to questionnaire, July, 1977.
14. *Rawhide Press* editor Barbara Reutlinger, response to questionnaire, July, 1977.
15. Editor, *Menominee Tribal News*, response to questionnaire, July, 1977.
16. Grace Miller, response to questionnaire, July, 1977.
17. *Char-Koosta* editor Lonnie Desimonis, response to questionnaire, June, 1977.
18. The activist publication *Americans Before Columbus*, discussed earlier under agency publications, was, according to its editors, partly a response to this feeling.
19. *Spilyay Tymoo* editor Sid Miller, correspondence with authors, July 12, 1976.
20. *Indian Voice*, August, 1976.

CHAPTER EIGHT

1. Lael Morgan, *History of the* Tundra Times, p. 3.
2. Ibid.
3. Ibid.
4. *Voice of Brotherhood*, November, 1963.
5. *Caribou News*, May 24, 1977.
6. Pamela Herman, in response to survey questionnaire, August, 1977.
7. W. Bruce Van Brocklin, letter to the authors, March, 1975.
8. Ellis R. ("Jack") Haikey, in response to survey questionnaire, August, 1976.
9. *Talking Leaf*, April, 1977.
10. Linda K. St. Cyr, in response to survey questionnaire, August, 1977.
11. Unsigned response to survey questionnaire, August, 1977.
12. Ray Murdock, interview with the authors, April, 1977.
13. Ibid.
14. Connie Nordine, editorial assistant, in a telephone interview, December, 1978.

CHAPTER NINE

1. *Indian Historian*, vol. 9, no. 2 (Spring, 1976), inside back cover.
2. "Letters," *Indian America*, vol. 9, no. 1 (Spring, 1975).
3. *Many Smokes*, Spring, 1977.
4. Authors' correspondence with *Tsa Aszi* editors, 1978.
5. Ibid.; from authors' correspondence with *Clan Destiny* editors, 1978.
6. Questionnaire response by *Sun Tracks* staff, 1976.
7. *Indian Law Reporter* 2 (December, 1976).
8. *The American Indian Journal* was formed by the merger of the *Legislative Review* and *Educational Journal* in October, 1975.
9. Questionnaire response by staff, July, 1977.
10. National Tribal Chairmen's Association (NTCA), *Highlights*, May, 1977.
11. *Indian Family Defense*, April, 1977, pp. 1–6.
12. NTCA, *Highlights*, May, 1977, p. 1.
13. *Wassaja*, August–September, 1978, p. 22.

14. *Indian Education*, March, 1977, p. 2.
15. Editor James Chase, in correspondence with authors, July, 1976.
16. *Lakota Oyate-Ki*, Winter, 1976.
17. *Indian American Folklore Group Newsletter*, May 6, 1977.

CHAPTER TEN

1. Tim Giago, in telephone interview, November, 1978.
2. See, for instance, Wilbur Schramm, *Mass Media and National Development*, and Daniel Lerner, *The Passing of Traditional Society*.
3. Stephen E. Rada, "Ramah Navajo Radio and Cultural Preservation," *Journal of Broadcasting* 22 (Summer, 1978): 361–71.
4. Ibid., p. 370.
5. Richard La Course, in a speech delivered at Association for Education in Journalism Convention, Seattle, Wash., August, 1978.
6. Jerry Elliott, in telephone interview, November, 1978.
7. Bonnie Schomp, "Administrative Law: Current Progress of Native American Broadcasting—Status of Indian Ownership," *American Indian Law Review* 4 (Summer, 1976): 98.
8. In his convention speech in Seattle, Wash., in August, 1978, and in other public addresses, La Course spoke of the decreasing time lags between white society's development of new communications media and Indian society's utilization of them. Thus, Indians adapted print to their use two hundred years after its development. The lag with radio was about twenty years, with television ten years, and with satellites eight years.
9. From response to survey questionnaires, November, 1977.
10. Ibid.
11. A parallel phenomenon has developed in white society, where growing numbers of television personalities run, often successfully, for public office.
12. Kathryn Jensen, manager of KUAC, Fairbanks, Alaska, in response to survey questionnaire, November, 1977.
13. Gilbert Leivas, in telephone interview, December, 1978.
14. The station's function as community newspaper is underscored by literary statistics in a report prepared by the Navajo Employment Commission. The report ("Navajo Manpower") includes a wealth of information on literacy rates. Perhaps most striking is the statistic that more than 50 percent of Navajo women do not speak English, much less read it.

15. Curtus Schultz, station manager, in response to survey questionnaire and follow-up interviews at the station.
16. Tom Busch, response to questionnaire.
17. Ibid.
18. Ibid.
19. Gover's Navajo programming formula was so successful that he applied to the FCC for an FM license. If the license was approved, he planned to move KWYK to FM, change the AM call letters to KNDN, and make the station's programming totally Navajo. The FM station was to be an automated, English-language adult-rock format. At this writing the application was still pending.
20. Virgil Wyaco, executive director of the Navajo Film and Media Commission, in a resolution to the Navajo Tribal Council, 1974.
21. Jerry Elliott in telephone interview, December, 1978.
22. Frank Blythe, executive director, Native American Public Broadcasting Consortium, in telephone interview, November, 1978.

CHAPTER 11

1. Carolyn Foreman, *Oklahoma Imprints, 1835–1907: A History of Printing in Oklahoma Before Statehood,* pp. xxi–xxii.
2. Charles E. Trimble, "A Report on a Planning Meeting for an American Indian Journalist Conference and an American Indian News Service Organization," November, 1970, p. 1. (This report was prepared by Trimble, and mimeographed copies were sent to those who had attended the meeting.)
3. Trimble, in an interview with the author, August, 1976.
4. Trimble, "A Report," pp. 3–8.
5. Ibid., p. 4.
6. Ibid., p. 5.
7. Ibid., p. 6.
8. Ibid., p. 7.
9. Charles E. Trimble, "The American Indian Press Association" (speech to delegates at National Congress of American Indians annual convention, Anchorage, Alaska, October 22, 1970).
10. The information on this and subsequent AIPA meetings comes from minutes and other official documents of the association.
11. Trimble, "Report to the President and Board Members of the

American Indian Press Association, April 12, 1971," p. 1. (Copies of these and other meeting summaries were distributed to board members.)

12. Ibid., p. 3.

13. Trimble, "Report to the President and Board Members of the American Indian Press Association, June 30, 1971," p. 1.

14. Ibid.

15. Don A. Christensen, "The American Indian Press Association: Its History, Activities and Organization" (Master's thesis, Michigan State University, 1974), pp. 27–28. Christensen also cites and discusses some of the internal problems of the BIA during the Nixon era, a time when the bureau's effectiveness was greatly inhibited.

16. Trimble, "Report to the President and Board Members of the American Indian Press Association, October 30, 1971," p. 1.

17. Ibid.

18. *Medium Rare*, vol. 1, no. 2 (March, 1973), p. 2.

19. Ibid., vol. 1, no. 5 (August–September, 1973), p. 2.

20. Rose Robinson, in a letter to the authors, August, 1976.

21. Robinson said that she had learned that outside funding was more of a likelihood for a conference than for a convention.

22. *Medium Rare*, vol. 2, no. 6 (September–December, 1974), p. 2.

23. Ibid.

24. Ibid., p. 3.

25. Robinson, "Report to the President and Board Members of the American Indian Press Association, April, 1975."

26. Ibid.

27. Laura Wittstock, in an interview with the authors, June, 1976.

28. Mark Trahant, in a telephone interview, December, 1978.

29. In late 1980, the Alaska Native Media Association was formed.

30. Jerry Thompson, in a telephone interview, November, 1978.

31. "AICC: Training Ground in 'Satellite Age,'" *Red Current*, vol. 1, no. 1 (Spring, 1978), p. 16.

32. Charles Trimble, in a telephone interview, December, 1978.

Bibliography

BOOKS

Andrews, Ralph W. *Indian Leaders Who Helped Shape America*. Seattle: Superior Publishing Co., 1971.

Barrows, William. *The Indian Side of the Indian Question*. Boston: Lothrop, 1888.

Bass, Althea Leach. *Cherokee Messenger: A Life of Samuel Austin Worcester*. Norman: University of Oklahoma Press, 1936.

Bird, Traveller. *Tell Them They Lie: The Sequoyah Myth*. Los Angeles, Westernlore Publishers, 1976.

Boudinot, Elias, a Cherokee Indian. *An Address to the Whites, Delivered in the First Presbyterian Church on the 26th of May, 1826*. Philadelphia: Printed by William F. Geddes, 1826.

Brown, Dee. *Bury My Heart at Wounded Knee*. New York: Bantam Books, 1971.

Carter, Samuel, III. *Cherokee Sunset: A Nation Betrayed*. New York: Doubleday, 1976.

Coblenty, Caterin (Cato). *Sequoyah*. 1946. Reprint. New York: David McKay, 1962.

Commission on the Rights, Liberties and Responsibilities of the American Indian. *The Indian: America's Unfinished Business*. Norman: University of Oklahoma, 1966.

Connelly, William E. *History of the Newspapers and Magazines Published in Kansas from the Organization of the Kansas Territory, 1854, to January, 1916, Together with Brief Statistical Information of Counties, Cities and Towns of the State*. Topeka: Kansas State Printing Plant, W. R. Smith, State Printer, 1916.

Costo, Rupert, ed. *Textbooks and the American Indian*. San Francisco: Indian Historical Press, 1970.

Debo, Angie. *The Rise and Fall of the Choctaw Republic*. Norman: University of Oklahoma Press, 1934.

Foreman, Carolyn Thomas. *Oklahoma Imprints, 1835–1907: A History of*

Printing in Oklahoma Before Statehood. Norman: University of Oklahoma Press, 1936.

Foreman, Grant. *Sequoyah.* Norman: University of Oklahoma Press, 1934.

Foster, George E. *Se-quo-yah.* Tahlequah, Cherokee Nation: H. B. Stone, 1885.

Foster, George E. *Sequoyah: The American Cadmus and Modern Moses.* Philadelphia: Indian Rights Association, 1885.

Friar, Ralph, and Friar, Natasha. *The Only Good Indian: The Hollywood Gospel.* New York: Drama Book Specialists, 1972.

Fuchs, Estelle and Havighurst, Robert J. *To Live on This Earth.* Garden City, New York: Anchor Press, 1973.

Gabriel, Ralph Henry. *Elias Boudinot: Cherokee and His America.* Norman: University of Oklahoma Press, 1941.

Gibson, Arrell Morgan. *The Chickasaws.* Norman: University of Oklahoma Press, 1972.

Hamilton, Charles. *Cry of the Thunderbird: The American Indian's Own Story.* Norman: University of Oklahoma Press, 1972.

Hargrett, Lester. *Oklahoma Imprints, 1835–1890.* New York: R. R. Bowker Co., 1951.

————, comp. *The Gilcrease-Hargrett Catalogue of Imprints.* Norman: University of Oklahoma Press, 1972.

Karolevitz, Robert. *Newspapering in the Old West.* Seattle: Superior Publishing Co., 1966.

Kilpatrick, Jack Frederick, and Kilpatrick, Anna Gritts, eds. *New Echota Letters: Contributions of Samuel A. Worcester to the Cherokee Phoenix.* Dallas: Southern Methodist University Press, 1968.

————. *The Shadow of Sequoyah: Social Documents of the Cherokees, 1826–1964.* Norman: University of Oklahoma Press, 1965.

Knight, Oliver. *Following the Indian Wars: The Story of Newspaper Correspondents Among Indian Campaigns.* Norman: University of Oklahoma Press, 1960.

LaPointe, Frank (Rosebud). *The Sioux Today.* New York: Crowell-Collier Press, 1972.

Lerner, Daniel. *The Passing of Traditional Society.* Glencoe, Ill.: Free Press, 1958.

McNickle, D'Arcy. *Native American Tribalism: Indian Survivals and Renewals.* New York: Oxford University Press, 1973.

Mooney, James. *Myths of the Cherokee.* 1900. Reprint. New York: Johnson Reprint Corp., 1970.

Moquion, Wayne, and Van Doren, Charles. *Great Documents in American Indian History*. New York: Praeger, 1973.

Murphy, Sharon. *Other Voices: Black, Chicano, and American Indian Press*. Dayton, Ohio: Pflaum/Standard, 1974.

Prucha, Francis Paul. *The Indian in American History*. New York: Holt, Rinehart and Winston, 1971.

Ray, Grace E. *Early Oklahoma Newspapers*. Norman: University of Oklahoma Press, 1928.

Sanders, Thomas E. (Napawanock-Cherokee), and Peek, Walter W. (Metacomtet-Marragonsett-Wapanowig). *Literature of the American Indian*. Beverly Hills, Calif.: Glencoe Press, 1973.

Schramm, Wilbur. *Mass Media and National Development*. Stanford, Calif.: Stanford University Press, 1964.

Smith, Michael R. *American Indians Civil Rights Handbook*. Washington, D.C.: Commission on Civil Rights, 1972.

Thomas, Isaiah. *The History of Printing in America with a Bibliography of Printers and an Account of Newspapers*. American Antiquarian Society, Transactions and Collections, vols. 5 and 6. Albany, New York, 1874.

U.S. Senate. Committee on Labor and Public Welfare. *Indian Education: A National Tragedy, a National Challenge*. Washington, D.C.: Government Printing Office, 1969.

Vogel, Virgil J. *This Country Was Ours: A Documentary History of American Indians*. New York: Harper and Row, 1972.

Voices from Wounded Knee. Roosevelttown, N.Y.: Akwesasne Notes Press, 1974.

Watson, Elmo Scott. *A History of Newspaper Syndicates in the United States 1865–1935*. Chicago, 1936.

Schoolcraft, Henry Rowe. *The Indian Tribes of the United States: Their Histories, Antiquities, Customs, Religion, Arts, Language, Traditions, Oral Legends, and Myths*. Edited by Francis S. Drake. Philadelphia: J. B. Lippincott, 1884.

ARTICLES

"American History: A Native American View." *Library Journal* 96 (February 15, 1971): 678–80.

Blankenburg, William. "The Role of the Press in an Indian Massacre, 1871." *Journalism Quarterly* 45 (Spring, 1968): 61–70.

Broderick, Dorothy. "Hi, Ho, Silver and All That." *Library Journal*, September, 1971, pp. 2852–53.

Davis, John D. "The Life and Work of Sequoyah." *Chronicles of Oklahoma* 8 (1930): 149–80.

Deloria, Vine, Jr. "The Most Important Indian." *Race Relations Reporter* 5 (November, 1974): 26–28.

Duchineaux, Franklin. "The American Indian Today: Beyond Stereotypes." *Today's Education* 65 (May, 1973): 22–24.

Ellis, Richard N. "The Apache Chronicle." *New Mexico Historical Review* 47 (July, 1972): 257–83.

Foster, George E. "Journalism among the Cherokee Indians." *Magazine of American History*, July–December, 1887, pp. 65–70.

French, Phillip. "The Indian in the Western Movie." *Art in America* 60 (July–August, 1972): 32–39.

Halliburton, R., Jr. "Black Slavery among Cherokees." *American History Illustrated* 9 (October, 1976): 13–19.

Hill, Ann. "Wounded Knee: Refusing to Be Invisible." *Freedomways*, vol. 13, no. 4, pp. 324–40.

Keshena, Rita. "The Role of American Indians in Motion Pictures." *American Indian Culture and Research Journal*, vol. 1, no. 2 (1974).

Josephy, Alvin M., Jr. "The Custer Myth." *Life*, July 2, 1971, pp. 48–60.

La Course, Richard. "A Different Kind of Indian Occupation." *Race Relations Reporter* 5 (July, 1974): 35–40.

Loftus, Desmond. "Communication in the North." *North* 17 (July–August, 1970): 14–19.

Malone, Henry T. "The Cherokee Phoenix: Supreme Expression of Cherokee Nationalism." *Georgia Historical Quarterly* 34 (September, 1950): 163–88.

McMurtrie, Douglas C. "The Shawnee Sun: The First Indian Language Periodical Published in the United States." *Kansas Historical Quarterly* (November, 1933): 339–42.

Messenbaugh, Laura M. "Newspaper Collections of the Oklahoma Historical Society." *Chronicles of Oklahoma* 30 (1942): 403–404.

Nichols, Roger L. "Printers' Ink and Red Skins: Western Newspapermen and the Indians." *Kansas Quarterly* 3 (Fall, 1971): 82–88.

"A Report from Pine Ridge, Conditions on Oglala Sioux Reservation." *Civil Rights Digest*, Summer, 1975, pp. 28–38.

Riley, Sam G. "The Cherokee Phoenix: The Short, Unhappy Life of the First American Indian Newspaper." *Journalism Quarterly* 53 (Winter, 1976): 666–71.

Bibliography

Schultz, Terry. "Bamboozle Me Not at Wounded Knee." *Harper's Magazine*, June, 1973, pp. 46–56.
Smith, Desmond. "Wounded Knee: The Media Coup d'État." *Nation*, June 25, 1973, pp. 806–809.
Smithsonian Institution Folklife Festival. "Indians and the Media: A Panel Discussion." *Civil Rights Digest* (Fall, 1973): 41–45.
Troy, Anne. "The Indian in Adolescent Novels." *Indian Historian* (Winter, 1975): 34–35.
Turcheneske. "The Arizona Press and Geronimo's Surrender." *Journal of Arizona History*, Summer, 1973, pp. 133–48.
Wilkerson, Gerald. "Colonialism Through the Media." *Indian Historian*, Summer, 1974, pp. 29–32.
———. "Contemporary Indian Media Papers—I: Colonialism Through the Media—Creation of CEE-TRUGH." *Medium Rare*, vol. 2, no. 2 (February, 1974).
Watson, Elmo Scott. "The Indian Wars and the Press, 1866–67." *Journalism Quarterly* 17 (December, 1940): 301–12.
———. "The Last Indian War, 1890–91: A Study of Newspaper Jingoism." *Journalism Quarterly* 20 (September, 1943): 205–24.
Weisman, Joel D. "About That 'Ambush' at Wounded Knee." *Columbia Journalism Review*, September–October, 1976, pp. 28–31.
Witt, Shirley Hill. "The Brave Hearted Women: The Struggle at Wounded Knee." *Civil Rights Digest*, Summer, 1976, pp. 39–45.

BIBLIOGRAPHIES, DIRECTORIES, AND COLLECTIONS

American Newspaper Directory. New York: George P. Rowell and Co., 1876–1910.
Bush, Alfred L., and Fraser, Robert S. *American Indian Periodicals in the Princeton University Library: A Preliminary List*. Princeton: Princeton University Library, 1970.
Cherokee Advocate. September 26, 1844–September 28, 1853, and April 26, 1870–March 3, 1906 (all but sixteen issues in the Library of Congress holdings).
Cherokee Phoenix. February 21, 1828–May 31, 1834 (all but three issues on microfilm in the Library of Congress).
Chicago. Newberry Library. *Dictionary Catalog of the Edward E. Ayer Collection*. Boston: G. K. Hall, 1961.
Compiled Laws of the Cherokee Nation. Published by authority of the National

Council, Tahlequah, I.T., Advocate Printing Co., 1881. Reprint. Wilmington, Del.: Scholarly Resources, 1973.

Connelly, William E. *History of Kansas Newspapers: A History of Newspapers and Magazines Published in Kansas from the Organization of the Kansas Territory, 1854, to January 1, 1916.* Topeka: Kansas State Printing Plant, 1916.

Dockstader, Frederick J. *The American Indian in Graduate Studies: A Bibliography of Theses and Dissertations.* 2d ed. New York: Museum of the American Indian, Heye Foundations, 1973.

Hirshfelder, Arlene. "Bibliography of Sources and Materials for Teaching About American Indians." *Social Education*, May, 1972, pp. 488–500.

Hodge, Frederick Webb, ed. *Handbook of American Indians North of Mexico.* Smithsonian Institution, Bureau of American Ethnology Bulletin 30, part 2. Washington, D.C.: Government Printing Office, 1910.

Josephy, Alvin M., Jr. *The Indian Heritage of America.* New York: Alfred A. Knopf, 1968.

Marquis, Arnold. *A Guide to America's Indians: Ceremonials, Reservations, and Museums.* Norman: University of Oklahoma Press, 1974.

Morgan, Lael. *History of the* Tundra Times. Fairbanks, Alaska: Eskimo, Indian, Aleut Printing Co., 1972.

National Indian Directory. Washington, D.C.: National Congress of American Indians, 1975.

Native American Materials in the University of Idaho Library and Center of Native American Development. Moscow, Idaho: University of Idaho Library, 1972.

Perkins, David, and Tanis, Norman, comps. *Native Americans of North America: A Bibliography Based on Collections in the Libraries of California State University, Northridge.* Metuchen, N.J.: Scarecrow Press, 1975.

Reynolds, Edwin C. *The Seminoles.* Norman: University of Oklahoma Press, 1957.

Stensland, Anna Lee. *Literature by and About the American Indian: An Annotated Bibliography.* Urbana, Ill.: National Council of Teachers of English, 1973.

Tulsa, Okla. Thomas Gilcrease Institute of History and Art. The Gilcrease Cherokee Advocate Press. Gilcrease Historical Leaflet no. 4, 1963.

Union List of Serials in Libraries of the United States and Canada. 3d ed. 5 vols. New York: H. W. Wilson Co., 1965.

U.S. Library of Congress. *Newspapers on Microfilm.* 6th ed. Compiled by

George A. Schwegman, Jr. Washington, D.C.: Government Printing Office.

THESES AND DISSERTATIONS

Beckett, Ola Lorraine. "The Cherokee Phoenix and Its Efforts in the Education of the Cherokees." Master's thesis, University of Oklahoma, 1934.

Blizzard, William Leland. "The Frontier Press of Colorado in the Ute Indian Uprising of 1879: A Case Study in Public Opinion." Master's thesis, University of Kansas, 1935.

Brizee, Robert L. "The Stereotype of the Indian in the New Mexico Press." Master's thesis, University of New Mexico, 1954.

Crelly, Frances Lois. "What a Newspaper Reveals About a Tri-Ethnic Community." Master's thesis, University of Colorado, 1935.

Debo, Angie Elbertha. "History of the Choctaw Nation from the End of the Civil War to the Close of the Tribal Period." Ph.D. dissertation, University of Oklahoma, 1933 [extensive bibliography, pp. 416–424].

Green, Rayna Diane. "The Only Good Indian: The Images of Indians in American Vernacular Culture." Ph.D. dissertation, University of Indiana, 1973 [extensive bibliography, pp. 415–445].

Gribskov, Margaret Elise T. H. "A Critical Analysis of Textbook Accounts of the Role of Indians in American History." Ph.D. dissertation, University of Oregon, 1973.

Halpin, William John. "The Sioux Indian War of 1876 as Reported in the *New York Herald.*" Master's thesis, Queens College, City University of New York, 1970.

Holland, Cullen Joe. "The Cherokee Indian Newspapers, 1828–1906: The Tribal Voice of a People in Transition." Ph.D. dissertation, University of Minnesota, 1956.

Kennedy, Lawrence Michael. "The Colorado Press and the Red Man: Local Opinion About Indian Affairs, 1859–1870." Master's thesis, University of Denver, 1967.

Luebke, Barbara Francine. "Profiles of the Navajo Times and Dine' BAAHANI: A Preliminary Examination of Two Navajo Newspapers." Master's thesis, University of Oregon, 1972.

Olson, Rolf H. "The Nez Percé, the Montana Press, and the War of 1877." Master's thesis, University of Montana, 1964.

Richmond, Gordon Donald. "A Study of Minnesota Newspaper Coverage of the Sioux Uprising from August 20 to October 3, 1862." Master's thesis, University of Minnesota, 1962.

Scullin, Michael. "Ethnicity and the Local Press in an Indian/White Community." Master's thesis, University of Illinois, 1969.

Timmons, David R. "Elements of Prejudice Toward Negroes and Indians As Found in Daily Newspapers of Seminole County, Oklahoma, 1950–1959." Master's thesis, University of Oklahoma, 1970.

Index

Index

Index

Red Alert: 125
Red Cliff Tribal News: 103
Red Cloud: 6
Red Current: 126
Red Man and Helper: 62
Red Times: 68
Red Warrior (Tuskahoman): 53
"Red-White TV Dialog": 142
Redletter: 116
Regional associations: 145
Religion and journalism: 16, 25, 43, 56
Removal: 26, 28–29, 32, 33, 35
Reservations: 28
Robert F. Kennedy Memorial Foundation
   Journalism Award Citation: 90
Robertson, Rev. S. W.: 59
Robinson, Rose: 152, 155–58
Rock, Howard: 110, 155
Ross, John: 24, 29–31, 33
Ross, William P.: 33–34, 47–48, 50
Rough Rock News: 67
Rowell, George P.: 39

Saint Louis Globe-Democrat: 49
Sampson, Will: 13, 143
Sanford, Anise: 63
Saxon and Miles: 34
School News: 62
Schoolcraft's Indian Tribes: 37
Seattle Post-Intelligencer: 150
Self-Determination Act (Title 638): 108
Seminole: 17, 47
Sentinel: 52
Seneca Indian Historical Society: 122
Sequoyah (George Guess): 21–22, 26–27,
   34–35, 47, 51
Sequoyah Memorial: 36, 61
Shawnee Sioux language: 32
Shawnee Sun (Siwinowe Kesibwi): 32, 56
Shenandoah Film Productions: 143
Sho-ban News: 104, 159
Si Wong Geh: 98
Signals: 52
Silverheels, Jay: 13
Sina Sapa Wacekiye Taeyanpaha: 58
Sioux: 13
Sioux Messenger: 100
Sisseton Courier: 100

Sitting Bull: 5
Siwinowe Kesibwi: see Shawnee Sun
Skye, Harriett: 71, 142, 157
Smiser, Butler S.: 45
Smithsonian Institution: 52
Smoke Signals (Parker, Arizona): 55, 93
Smoke Signals (Sacramento, California): 54,
   103, 104, 153
Smoke Signals (Sheridan, Wyoming): 55
Smoke Signals (Staten Island, New York): 55
Smoke Signals (Washington): 101
Society of American Indians (SIA): 53, 60
Sota Eya Ye Yapi: 100
Southern Advocate: 32
Southern Ute Drum: 93, 149
Southwest Indian Media Collective: 159
Southwest News Bureau: 156, 158
Special publications: 20
Spilyay Tymoo: 108
Spirit of the People: 66
Standing Rock Eyapaha: 54
Standing Rock Star: 107
Standley, J. S.: 45
Star-Vindicator: 42–43
State Library Commission of Iowa: 116
Stereotyping: 3, 13, 15, 156
Stone, B. H.: 40, 49
Stone, I. W.: 44
Suicide: 9
Sun Tracks: 122

Tacoma Indian News: 118
Tahlequah: 27, 31, 36
Tahlequah Arrow: 50, 63
Tahlequah Courier: 49–50
Tahlequah Sentinel: 49–50
Tahlequah Telephone: 40, 49
Take Ten: 116
Talking Leaf: 53–54, 115
Tappan and Dennet: 34
Taylor, Frank: 34
Teacher Corps: 97
Television: 131, 154
Terry, Gen. Alfred: 47
Textbooks and the American Indian: 12
Thomas Gilcrease Institute of American His-
   tory and Art: 52
Thompson, Jerry: 160

Index

Thompson, Morris: 157
Thompson, Neely: 44
Time: 8
Tishomingo City: 38
Title 638 (Self-Determination Act): 108
Tomahawk: 40
Tonekei (Sammy White): 142
Town Crier: 65
Townsend, Samuel: 62
Tracey, Raymond: 13, 143
Trahant, Mark: 159
Trail of Tears: 30, 32
Treaties: 30, 32, 34, 50
Tribal government: 34
Tribal Spokesman: 113
Tribal subsidy: 17
Tribal Tribune: 54, 109
"Tribal Voices from the Land": 142
Trilingual: 17
Trimble, Charles: 146–47, 149–53, 158,
    160
Tsa'Aszi: 122
TSISTSISTAS Press: 77, 96
Tuberculosis: 9
Tulsa Human Services Agency: 118
Tulsa Indian News: 118
Tulsa Indian Youth Council: 128
Tumbleweed Connection: 64
Tundra Times: 110–11, 155
Turtle Mountain Echo: 99
Tuskahoman: see Red Warrior
Twin City Topics: 45

Unemployment: 9
United Effort Trust: 160
United Press International: 8, 92, 159
United States Border Patrol: 86
United States Code: 77
U.S. government: 32, 17, 50, 51, 54; De-
    partment of the Interior: 73; Office of Ed-
    ucation: 147; Office of Economic
    Opportunity: 118; Office of Native Ameri-
    can Programs: 113, 116; Subcommittee on
    Indian Affairs: 9; *see also* Bureau of Indian
    Affairs *and* Internal Revenue Service
United Tribes Educational Technical Center:
    107
United Tribes News: 71, 75, 107, 142, 157

United Tribes Newsletter: 100
Utah Division of Indian Affairs: 114
Utah Indian Journal: 114
Utah Native American Consortium:
    114
Ute Bulletin: 101
Utility companies: 9

Vidette: 48
Vindicator: 41–42, 46
The Voice of Brotherhood: 111–12
Voices from the Earth (White Roots of
    Peace): 89
Voices from Wounded Knee: 90

Wabanak Alliance: 115
Wahpetan Highlights: 65
Washington Post: 8–9
Wassaja: 10, 12, 53, 80–86, 90, 95, 120,
    157
Watie, Stand: 31
Weewish Tree: 120
Weekly Arizonan: 3
Western Cherokees: 31
Whispering Wind Magazine: 121
White, Kate: 63
White, Sammy: *see* Tonekei
White Cloud Journal: 126
White Earth Reservation Newsletter: 95
White Roots of Peace: *see* Voices from the
    Earth
Wig-I-Wam: 117
Williamson, John P.: 57
Wind River Boarding School: 62
Wind River Industrial School: 62
Wind River Progress: 62
Winnebago Indian News: 118
Wisconsin Inter-Tribal News: 119
Wittstock, Laura Waterman: 158
Woloch Pi: 122
Woopedah: 64
Worcester, Samuel: 23–26, 29, 31
Word Carrier (Iapi Oaye): 57
World Council of Churches Special Fund to
    Combat Racism: 90
Wotanin Wowapi: 106
Wounded Knee, (1870s): 6, 7, 41; (1973):
    7–11, 87, 90, 154; (1975): 10

229

Index